Anne E. Graham came into the possesion of the infamous 'Ripper Diary' when it was given to her by her father. He later claimed that it had been in the family because his own father was the illegitimate son of Florence Maybrick, meaning that Florence was Anne's great-grandmother.

An interest in her own family and a desire to get to the bottom of the diary's origins subsequently led Anne to work with Paul Feldman's research team on his book *Jack the Ripper: The Final Chapter*. She is at present reading for a degree in Liverpool, where she lives with her daughter.

Carol Emmas also helped to research Paul Feldman's book and shares a particular interest in Florence's life. Also at Liverpool's John Moores University, studying history, Carol lives in the north-west of England with her partner and daughter.

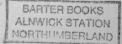

THE LAST VICTIM

*The extraordinary life of
Florence Maybrick,
the wife of Jack the Ripper*

Anne E. Graham and Carol Emmas

HEADLINE

First published in 1999
by HEADLINE BOOK PUBLISHING

First published in paperback in 1999
by HEADLINE BOOK PUBLISHING

10 9 8 7 6 5 4 3 2 1

ISBN 0 7472 6206 3

Typeset by
Letterpart Limited, Reigate, Surrey

Printed and bound in Great Britain by
Mackays of Chatham PLC, Chatham, Kent

HEADLINE BOOK PUBLISHING
A division of the Hodder Headline Group
338 Euston Road
London NW1 3BH

www.headline.co.uk
www.hodderheadline.com

This book is dedicated to

Caroline, Peter and Adele
and to the memories of
William Graham and Robert Johnson

Also to Paul Feldman,
without whose energy and encouragement
this book may not have been written

ACKNOWLEDGEMENTS

We would like to thank the following people for their invaluable help and cooperation in producing this book:

Carol Cain of the Mobile Press Register; Paul Begg; Jane Conway-Gordon; Paul Daniels, editor of *Ripperologist* for his comments on the Jack the Ripper chapter; Nicola Danson; Adele and Amelia Emmas; Sally Emvy; Stewart Evans; Melvin Fairclough; Paul Feldman and family; Martin and Karen Fido; Caroline Graham; Mary Graham; Alan and Sydna Grimes and family; Catherine Harrison; John Harrison; Shirley Harrison; Martin Howells; Pauline Irving; Albert, Valerie and Tracy Johnson; Janette Mahoney; Peter Marot; Doreen Montgomery; Peggy Murphy; Martine Rooney; Stephen Ryder; Keith Skinner; Richard and Molly Whittington-Egan; Trevor and Alice Williams.

We would also like to thank the following bodies for their assistance:

The Trevor L. Christie collection held at the American Heritage Center, Wyoming; Richmond Chancery Court, Richmond, Virginia; Liverpool Central Library Public Records Office; Spellow Lane Library, Liverpool; the Public Records Office, Kew; the British Library; John Moores University Library.

FOREWORD

by Keith Skinner

The alleged 'Diary of Jack the Ripper' has always been shrouded in controversy, ever since it first came into the public domain back in 1992. Many words have already been written on the subject and I will not dwell on the detailed arguments over its authenticity and status. However, for those not already familiar with the Diary and its contents, it may be useful to start with a general introduction to the subject and an explanation of Anne Graham's own part in the story. For the following paragraphs, I am very grateful to my associates, Martin Fido and Paul Begg, for generously allowing me to plagiarise the entry for the 'Maybrick Journal' from our current edition of *The Jack The Ripper A–Z* (1996).

For ease of identification, I have referred to this intriguing document throughout as 'the Diary', which, of course, is a misnomer. It is very much a personal journey of thoughts and feelings, handwritten into a Victorian guardbook, commonly used for sticking in photographs and scraps, and for writing in commonplaces, words of wisdom, poetry, comments from visitors etc. Traces of gum and card support this physical analysis. The first 64 pages have been removed. The extant writing consists of 63 pages and there are 17 blank pages at the end of the book. The writing, signed 'Jack the Ripper', purports to be a record of the Ripper's activities from about April 1888 to May 1889. Internal evidence proves beyond doubt that the author is or is intended to be James Maybrick, a Liverpool cotton broker who died in suspicious circumstances in May 1889.

The Diary first came to light in March 1992 when a Mr Michael Barrett (who was, at the time, Anne Graham's husband) approached a London literary agency, claiming that he had been given the Diary in Liverpool in May 1991 by a friend named Tony Devereux (now deceased), who had told him nothing beyond assurances that it was genuine. Barrett identified the supposed author of the Diary as Maybrick, and soon writer Shirley Harrison and her research associate, Sally Evemy, were commissioned to undertake preliminary research with a view to writing a book.

In June 1992, Robert Smith secured publication rights for Smith Gryphon Ltd, and Paul Feldman, in December 1992, bought the video rights to the book with an option on the film rights. Ink and paper tests were commissioned, with conflicting results. Ripper authorities noted factual problems in the internal content and very early on the argument became polarised; genuine document versus modern hoax. Rival factions emerged, generating much hostility and bitterness, the repercussions of which are still being felt to this day.

On 27 June 1994, the *Liverpool Daily Post* reported Mike Barrett's claim to have forged the Diary using a scrapbook bought from an auctioneers and ink from the Bluecoat Art Shop. He claimed to have only days to live, and said he'd 'worked on the Diary for five years' (i.e. since 1987). The following day the confession was withdrawn by his solicitors who said he 'was not in full control of his faculties when he made that statement, which was totally inaccurate and without foundation'. Although Barrett could not name the ink, the art shop suggested to journalist Harold Brough that it was most likely a manuscript ink manufactured by Diamine.

The following month, Anne, Mr Barrett's recently estranged wife (they would later divorce and she would revert to her maiden name of Graham), told Paul Feldman that she had seen the Diary and its contents in 1968, though she was not more than mildly curious, being only a teenager. She had taken possession of it in the late 1980s. Her father, Mr Billy Graham (now deceased), confirmed her story, saying the Diary had been left to him by his grandmother shortly before WWII and he had first been aware of it when he came home on leave in 1943, finally receiving it when his father died in 1950.

Anne Graham stated that Mike had aspirations to be a writer so she placed the Diary in his possession as inspiration for a work of fiction. Concerned that he might pester her terminally ill father, she took it 'on the spur of the moment' to Tony Devereux, asking him to give it to Mike without acknowledging its source.

On 30 October 1995, Alec Voller, head chemist at Diamine, saw the Diary for the first time, and declared the ink was not Diamine's. He observed irregular fading and bronzing, both indicators of age, saying, 'The general appearance is characteristic of documents I have seen which are 90+ years old and it is certainly not out of the realms of possibility that it dates back to 1889. Certainly [the ink] did not go on the paper within recent years.' Against this opinion, however, should be set the observation that it is apparently relatively easy to create an ink which will give the impression of being old.

Thus the ink tests are contradictory and inconclusive. The authenticated formal handwriting of James Maybrick does not match the Diary. The inclusion of obscure information about Maybrick has led to the tentative suggestion that somebody close to the Maybrick family wrote the Diary, with the rider that it might represent a family or local tradition associating him with the Ripper.

Two years on (1998), the controversy continues to rage. The argument has now spread to the Internet where the Diary has its own discussion board. Strange and desperate theories are pitched into the debate by strange and desperate people. In September 1998, the Diary was featured at the Fifth International Investigative Psychology Conference at the University of Liverpool. The theme was 'New Directions in Offender Profiling', and the focus was the psychopathology of the Diary and its place in the study of serial killers.

And right at the heart of this acrimonious dispute is Anne Graham who, with her co-author, Carol Emmas, has produced this new study of the Maybrick mystery. Both authors have utilised and responsibly evaluated the wealth of new information excavated by Paul Feldman's robust and tenacious investigation into the Diary's provenance and his genuine quest for truth. Valid questions are raised about James Maybrick's famous younger brother, Michael, the professional musician whose presence at Battlecrease House in 1889 struck such a discordant note. These are questions which have not been artificially manufactured or induced. They existed then as they do now.

As a member of Paul Feldman's research team, I first met Anne Graham in Liverpool in August 1994 and was introduced to Carol Emmas a few months later in Peterborough at a 'Maybrick Family Get-Together', organised by Paul. There was an oral tradition in Anne's family loosely connecting her step-great-grandmother to one of the Maybrick servants at Battlecrease House in Aigburth, where the Maybrick tragedy unfolded. Anne and Carol helped Paul to explore this fascinating link and I noticed Anne becoming increasingly more interested in Florence Maybrick. Thus I introduced Anne and Carol to the seven boxes, containing approximately 425 Home Office files relating to Florence Maybrick's case, preserved at the Public Record Office in Kew, West London. Whilst Carol concentrated on the research in Liverpool, Anne and I spent many hours carefully sifting and studying these documents and, through the generosity of Paul Feldman, we were able to photocopy a sizeable quantity of the material. In June 1995, Anne catalogued the contents of each box and her meticulous summary listing has been give to the Public Record Office, where it serves as a valuable accession and useful finding aid to the collection.

In 1969, the American author, Trevor L. Christie, had posthumously published in England what is arguably one of the best studies of the Maybrick case to date, *Etched in Arsenic*. Christie's quite magnificent research stretched over a quarter of a century and his widow subsequently donated all of his notes and papers to the American Heritage Center at the University of Wyoming in Laramie. In June 1993 I went to Laramie and photocopied the entire collection, much of it unpublished, which Anne and Carol eventually transcribed, collated and indexed. Particularly fascinating was the surviving exchange of correspondence between Trevor L. Christie and the legendary, much respected criminologist, Richard Whittington-Egan. Richard was the editor for the British edition of Christie's book and his knowledge of the Maybrick case is profound.

So it was, in the summer of 1995, that Anne and I headed for the enchanting Malvern home of Richard and Molly Whittington-Egan, perched at the top of a hill (which I had forgotten to tell Anne about who was wearing high heels), there to talk about Florence Maybrick, examine his unique collection of her letters and sup tea out of mugs marked 'Arsenic' and 'Strychnine'. A native Liverpudlian, Richard has more than a cursory scholarly interest in the case. Battlecrease House was a familiar place of Richard's childhood. Moreover, James and Florence were frequent guests at his grandfather's dinner table. Interestingly, Richard's grandfather was convinced of Florence's 'total innocence' whereas Richard believes she probably intended to poison James and was therefore 'morally guilty'. This book, I'm quite sure, will open up the argument!

Yet all of this legitimate industry may be perceived as a smokescreen to the central question: is the Diary genuine and was James Maybrick a sexual serial murderer? The debate continues. However, whatever the final verdict, the very existence of the Diary has resulted in this deeply moving biography of Florence Maybrick. It is a book with which I am proud to be associated.

London
November 1998

INTRODUCTION

by Anne E. Graham

If it is possible to choose one's ancestors I don't think the wife of Jack the Ripper and the woman convicted for his murder would have been my first preference!

Florence Elizabeth Maybrick was a social butterfly, who courted admiration and compliments. Yet with only a dim intelligence behind her bright blue eyes, she was self-absorbed, promiscuous and a liar. She suffered from that curious Victorian malady, 'weak lungs', and developed the ability to faint at the drop of a hat, enabling her to manipulate men at whim.

Her mother, the Baroness von Roques, once admitted apologetically: 'My daughter is not a woman of much penetration,' and a close friend of the family, who knew her well, caustically remarked: 'Mrs Maybrick could hardly reach the standard of mediocrity.'

In a well-publicised trial in the summer of 1889, at the age of twenty-seven, the beautiful American was accused of administering arsenic to her ageing husband, a Liverpool cotton broker, and thereby causing his death.

In an age when middle class respectability was worshipped, Victorian society was scandalised as the sordid details of Florence's adulterous life were published in the newspapers. With dedicated hypocrisy her contemporaries convicted her on the basis of her adultery and women spectators hissed at her in the dock.

Long after the Maybrick case had been relegated to the history books and the principal actors in the drama nothing more than a memory, a hand written journal emerged. Between the frenzied scrawl of faded pages the story unfolded of a drug-induced, sadistic killer and the woman he adored.

Supposedly written by Florence's husband, James Maybrick, but concluding with the menacing signature of 'Jack the Ripper', the journal took the reader step by step through a series of crimes committed five months before the Maybrick case, to a time christened by the late Victorians as the 'autumn of terror'.

The Ripper journal first came to my father's notice during the Christmas of 1950 (though he claimed he had heard of it as far back as 1943). He came across it in a suitcase, which he had left for safe-keeping with his step-mother while he had been serving abroad for thirteen years in the British Army. It has been difficult to establish what he thought of this strange document, but for whatever reason he tossed the contents of the suitcase into a trunk and the journal never saw the light of day again until 1968.

I was a teenager in the swinging sixties, with a head full of fashion, boys and the Beatles. By 1968 my father had been widowed for some years and was embarking on a second marriage. We were moving home and I was clearing out a long and forgotten dusty closet, in what had been my grandparents' home for almost thirty years. Gingerly clawing my way through cobwebs and years of accumulated family rubbish, I discovered the journal at the bottom of a black tin trunk containing books and letters.

The journal meant little to me at the time. I only knew 'Jack the Ripper' as a Bogeyman who frightened children. Had the journal been sighed by John Lennon, I might have taken some interest in it. As it was, I simply passed it on to my father to pack away. It would not be until the early 1990s that the journal would once more enter my life, and its contents eventually published in the book *The Diary of Jack the Ripper* by author Shirley Harrison.

It never occurred to me, when my father gave me the journal, to do anything with it. At that time I still knew very little about Jack the Ripper and had no interest in the subject at all. I had a busy life with a full-time career, a child and a husband who had been ill for several years. It was also during this time that I was forced to admit that our once content, sixteen-year marriage had entered a most unhappy and destructive period.

With little thought of the long term consequences and knowing that my partner, Michael Barrett, had a burning ambition to write, I gave him the journal, via a third person, with the hope that he would take an interest in it and use its contents as a basis for a fictional book.

Its appearance in such a torturous way seemed perfectly logical to me during this unhappy and confusing time. I did not want to burden him with the knowledge that the idea for a book had originated with me. I also needed to protect my elderly father from a barrage of questions when his health was in a fragile state. Little did I realise that what had begun as a private deception in an attempt to heal a rapidly deteriorating and painful relationship, would have such far reaching consequences.

It was some two years afterwards, well after the marriage had broken down completely, that I confessed the journal's origins to Paul Feldman, who had produced the video of the book. With an agonising divorce looming ahead, a sick parent and a new life to make for myself and a teenage daughter, I had every reason to leave the past behind, and with it the journal. My foolish actions had unhappily and unwittingly touched a great many lives, causing anger and misery. Not knowing what to do for the best, I did nothing.

That was until the summer of 1994, when Paul Feldman, like an enthusiastic blood-hound, came bounding dramatically back into my life. He had personally invested many tens of thousands of pounds on researching the journal's provenance and was not a man to leave any stone unturned in his investigations. Recently his researchers had discovered that at one point in her history Florence Maybrick had called herself 'Mrs Graham' and as my maiden name is Graham, his investigations were now firmly centred on me.

His continual questioning of my friends and family left me feeling resentful and guilty, and after one particular episode he had left a kind friend close to tears. I angrily telephoned him in London. During a four hour telephone conversation which quickly developed into a verbal battle and ended in mutual respect, we arranged a meeting.

I was very much surprised when my much-loved father, now

over eighty and suffering from terminal cancer, agreed to be interviewed by Paul. During their meeting my father appeared to suggest that the reason for the journal's existence in our family was that his father was the illegitimate son of Florence Maybrick, born when she was an unmarried teenager.

Subsequent research uncovered that my grandfather had been born in Hartlepool in the January of 1879 and registered as the child of Adam and Ann Graham, a blacksmith and his wife. However, his background was an odd one. My grandfather had been very reticent about his childhood and his children had never met their grandparents. He appeared better educated than his contemporaries and had been forced to leave home as a young teenager and told to make his own way in the world.

It would later be discovered that in the year of his birth Florence was living in England, contrary to what had been previously known. The port of Hartlepool was a shipping route to St Petersburg where her step-father, a Prussian Baron, was an official at the German Embassy.

Did Florence have an illegitimate child in Hartlepool and pass him on to another family to raise? If she had was that child my grandfather? Frankly, I had been ignorant of this story before that day and I am still not completely convinced. However, if it is true it could mean that Florence Maybrick was my great-grandmother.

In the months following the interview, my father's condition rapidly deteriorated and it was necessary to nurse him at home. During what little free time I had, I developed an interest in the Maybrick case and avidly read the research material which Paul had insisted on sending me.

Within months my wonderful father was dead and the time had come for me to pick up the pieces of my own life. I threw myself with enthusiasm into the research work, and was invited to become a permanent member of the team. For some time I worked closely with my co-author, Carol Emmas, who had been conducting the Liverpool end of Paul Feldman's research. Together we became fascinated in this complicated woman who had been condemned to death for her husband's murder in 1889.

When Paul Feldman asked us to consider writing a book on the Maybrick case we learned that several good books had already been written on the subject, but none of them had the advantage of containing the information from the Home Office Files, which had only recently been opened. The temptation was too great . . .

This book has not been written to prove the contents of the Ripper Journal; that task has been left in the capable hands of others. It does, however, assume that the journal is not a old forgery, and in the last five years neither scientists nor historians have been able to prove that it is. With this in mind a new light has been shed on what the Victorian newspapers christened the 'Aigburth Mystery'.

Finally I would like to add that when we began this work neither Carol nor myself were entirely convinced that Florence Maybrick was innocent. However, the truth was out there and eventually we have found it.

Anne Elizabeth Graham

CHAPTER ONE

❧❧

Liverpool Assizes, 7 August 1889

Prisoner at the bar, I am no longer able to treat you as being innocent of the dreadful crime laid to your charge. You have been convicted by a jury of this City,* after a lengthy and most painful investigation, followed by a defence which was in every respect worthy of the case. The jury have convicted you, and the law leaves me no discretion, and I must pass on you the sentence of the law; and the sentence of the law is —

This court doth ordain you to be taken from hence to the place from whence you came, and from thence to the place of execution, and that you be there hanged by the neck until you are dead, and that your body be afterwards buried within the precincts of the prison in which you shall have been confined after your conviction, and may the Lord have mercy on your soul.[1]

---

* The jury was a Lancashire and not a Liverpool jury.

As the words of condemnation rang through the hushed courtroom, the young widow in the dock bowed her head in distress and clasped her hands. For a moment she wavered unsteadily, then, slowly regaining her composure, proudly brushed aside the assistance of the two female warders and walked down the cold stairwell to the unwelcoming cells beneath.

This was the conclusion of what had become one of the most notorious and public trials in the annals of legal history. It would echo across the Atlantic for countless years and play a major role in influencing change in English criminal law.[*] For the preceding three months, the question in the public mind had been whether or not Florence Maybrick, an attractive American aristocrat, had callously poisoned her ageing husband, by the administration of arsenic, in order to pursue an illicit relationship with a man closer to her own age.

For three weeks in the spring of 1889, James Maybrick, a fifty-year-old Liverpool cotton merchant, had been treated by his doctors for what they suspected to be a case of acute gastro-enteritis. His wife, twenty-three years his junior, had dutifully nursed him day and night, seeing to his needs and administering his medicines.

When his condition did not improve and one of the servants remembered seeing arsenic-coated fly-papers soaking in a basin in the bedroom, rumour and suspicion circulated through the household. Were the papers intended as part of the ingredients of an innocent medicinal face-wash,

---

[*] In 1889 there was no Court of Appeal to which the verdict could be referred on any grounds, and a defendant on the grave charge of murder could not give evidence in his or her own defence.

as Florence Maybrick would claim, or did she have a more sinister purpose in mind?

Still fresh in the minds of the Liverpool public was the sensational 1884 murder trial of two local married sisters. Catherine Flanagan and Margaret Higgins had been hanged for murdering four people with arsenic extracted from fly-papers in order to claim their life insurance. The Maybrick servants, remembering this infamous trial, began speculating amongst themselves about other recent curious incidents in the house.

Completely unaware that she was under suspicion, and suffering from exhaustion, Florence sent for a professional nurse to assist her in the sick-room. Soon after the woman's arrival she left the nurse with her husband and took the opportunity to write a hurried pencilled note to her lover, Alfred Brierley. She then handed the letter to her children's nursemaid to post, but it was never to be sent.

Claiming that the baby had dropped it in the mud and dirtied the envelope, nursemaid Alice Yapp opened the letter on the steps of the post office. On spying the words 'my darling', she read the contents and self-righteously hurried home to hand it to Edwin Maybrick, James's younger brother.

Astonished by the revelations enclosed, and aware of the servants' gossip, Edwin transmitted their growing suspicions to his older brother, Michael Maybrick, when he arrived the same evening from London. Within hours the doctors had been put on alert, the nurses had been given special instructions and Florence was being watched. Various items began to disappear from the sick-room to be sent for analysis, and it appeared that everyone in the household was aware of what was going on except for Florence herself.

With motive and opportunity firmly established by her brothers-in-law by a series of random events, Florence was deposed from her position as mistress in her own home. In a piteous letter to Dr Hopper, her personal physician, written shortly before her husband's death, she appeared bewildered, begging him as a friend to come and see her:

> *My misery is great and my position is such a painful one, that when I tell you that both my brothers-in-law are here and have taken the nursing of Jim and the management of my house completely out of my hands you will understand how powerless I am to assert myself . . .*
>
> *Michael now accuses me of being the primary cause of Jim's present critical state . . . I am a mere cypher in my own house, ignored and overlooked. I am too utterly broken hearted to struggle against myself or anyone else, all I want is to die too.[2]*

Was this the cry of a truly innocent woman or the clever strategy of an evil killer who had been feeding her unsuspecting spouse small doses of arsenic cunningly soaked from fly-papers?

As the trial came to an end and the prisoner left the dock, Mr Shuttleworth, Clerk of the Assize, rose to dismiss the jury amid loud hisses from the courtroom. Women spectators who had earlier been the first to condemn the prisoner wept openly at the sentence, after listening to seven days of conflicting medical testimony.

Outside St George's Hall, stretching as far as Lime Street

station, a patient crowd of several thousand people had waited in the hot August sun to hear the conclusion of the trial. The reading public, gripped by 'Maybrick Mania', had eagerly scanned the daily newspapers, after reading the word-for-word accounts of the evidence, and few outside the court now believed in the prisoner's guilt. The vast majority of observers had anticipated a 'not guilty' verdict.

One hundred and fifty policemen were brought in to restrain the crowd who, on hearing that Florence Maybrick had been found guilty, reacted with an outburst of anger and emotion.

The unpopular judgment had been reached after a seven-day trial presided over by Mr Justice Stephen, who had served as a judge on the Queen's Bench for over ten years. Although only in his sixtieth year, and young in comparison with some of his associates, he was in poor health and had only recently recovered from a stroke.

On the sixth day of the trial, the learned judge had embarked on a marathon summing-up of the case as the spectators wilted in the hot and stuffy courtroom and the jury fidgeted uncomfortably. If on occasion His Honour was inaccurate as to dates and names and referred to verbatim reports in the newspapers when he became confused about parts of the testimony, he outlined the evidence given by both the defence and the prosecution adequately and appeared on the whole in favour of the prisoner, instructing the jury that it was essential to the charge that the victim had died of arsenic poisoning.

However, the following day he appeared to have undergone a complete personality change and with it a transformation in his attitude to the case. Adopting a high moral tone, he repeatedly made inflammatory statements against the prisoner as the onlookers in the court sat open-mouthed and Mrs Maybrick cowered in the dock:

You must not consider it as a medical case in which you decide whether the man died from arsenic which was discovered as the result of chemical analysis. You must decide it as a great and highly important case, involving in itself not only medical and chemical questions, but involving in itself a most highly important moral question.

You must remember the intrigue which she carried on with this man Brierley and the feelings — it seems horrible to comparatively ordinary innocent people, a horrible and incredible thought, that a woman should be plotting the death of her husband in order that she might be left at liberty to follow her own degrading vices.

. . . There is no doubt that the propensities which lead persons to vices of that kind do kill all the more tender, all the more manly, or all the more womanly feelings of the human mind.

As the advocates of both prosecution and defence listened in amazement, His Honour added: 'It is easy enough to have conceived how a horrible woman, in so terrible a position, might be assailed by some fearful and terrible temptation.'[3]

Had some outside influence been at work after the court had retired for the evening on Tuesday 6 August? A fellow judge would later report that in the early hours of the morning he had been awoken by Judge Stephen pacing up and down his bedroom and repeating, 'That woman is guilty.'[4]

Many people would take exception to the judge's remarks,

including the newly founded Women's Franchise League organised by Mrs Emmeline Pankhurst, who echoed the Suffragette viewpoint: 'The Judge threw aside his judicial dignity and impartiality to secure a verdict of guilty against a woman on account of her sinful infidelity towards an unfaithful husband.'[5]

Florence's counsel had never denied her infidelity with Alfred Brierley, who was an associate of her husband. On the other hand, the fact that James Maybrick had kept a mistress for thirty years had been virtually ignored. Maybrick's own liaison had been touched upon during the evidence, confirming that Florence would have had grounds for a separation and thereby destroying the supposed motive for the crime, but it had not influenced the all-male jury. This simply reflected the hypocrisy of the times which accepted that a man might stray discreetly from the marital path, but condemned any woman for contemplating the same.

That James Maybrick could also be violent and had hit his wife on more than one occasion had not been revealed to the jury. However, it had been Florence's own decision not to disclose much of her husband's history; she was reported to have told her solicitors, Messrs Cleaver, 'I know he has done many wrong things, but he is dead now and I would be distressed if his life were to be made public.'[6]

With her life hanging in the balance, why was Florence Maybrick so determined to halt any investigation into her husband's background? Was it simply for her children's sake that she was reluctant to allow details of his immorality to be discussed in court, or did she suspect that an investigation might reveal a stronger motive for the crime? A motive that if revealed would destroy her children's future for ever?

With the trial now over and the cotton broker's widow condemned to death, many more questions only touched on during the inquiry were destined to remain unanswered. Who had been the sender of the mysterious bottle of medicine containing an almost fatal dose of strychnine which James Maybrick had taken a few weeks before his death? And what was the source of the large amount of arsenic deposited around the house, enough, so it had been said, to kill more than fifty people?

Why was Florence Maybrick the only person in the house to come under suspicion? And why did the police arrest her for causing her husband's death by administering poison when the original autopsy did not find any poison in the victim's body?

The legal argument would concentrate on the question: had it been proved beyond reasonable doubt that James Maybrick had died from arsenical poisoning, and if so, had Florence Maybrick criminally administered it?

On the other hand, if Maybrick had not died by his wife's hand, then how had he died? Who else had both motive and opportunity to murder the Liverpool cotton broker? Was Florence Maybrick the cold-blooded killer the jury had decided she was, or simply a convenient offering to the authorities, a woman of questionable morals sacrificed on the altar of Victorian middle-class respectability?

After the verdict had been announced, when asked if she had anything to say, Florence had replied in a voice shaking with emotion: 'My Lord, everything has been against me. I wish to say that although evidence has been given as to a great many circumstances in connection with Mr Brierley, much has been withheld which might have influenced the jury had it been told. I am not guilty of this crime.'[7]

As the echoes of the crowd's unrest filtered through the long corridors of St George's Hall, Sir Charles Russell, the sophisticated and eminent Irish counsel who had led so eloquently for the defence of Mrs Maybrick, was so astounded that he was overheard saying to his fellow barristers: 'Mark what I say, it is the most dangerous verdict that has ever been recorded in my experience.'[8]

Within half an hour of the trial ending, in an unprecedented move, a petition against the verdict was signed by every junior barrister and every Queen's Counsel attending the Assize Courts that day.

Throughout the intense excitement, Florence Maybrick had remained seated in her detention cell, waiting for the crowd to subside and the order for her removal to Walton Prison. For more than an hour the empty van waiting to transport her stood in the courtyard, surrounded by policemen, as her angry army of supporters refused to disband. Eventually the prisoner, escorted by matrons and court officials through a corridor of mounted policemen, took her place in the prison van. The cries of the crowd changed to cheers of approval as Florence Maybrick embarked on her last journey, through the streets of Liverpool to the harsh reality of Walton Prison.

To house the increasing number of felons and replace the former Borough Gaol, the authorities had, in 1855, constructed a large, gloomy prison four miles from the city in the suburb of Walton. By day, horse-drawn prison vans clattered noisily over cobblestones towards the tall, sinister building, bearing offenders for internment behind monstrous iron-studded doors.

Rules at Walton were harsh, and the diet was poor. Those who broke the regulations faced ruthless punishments of solitary confinement or half-rations. When the prisoners emerged from their cells in the early hours of the morning, the overwhelming stench of urine and faeces was unbearable, and to keep down putrid fevers chloride of lime was burned continuously in the dismal passageways.

Before her conviction, Florence had been held in one of the so-called 'association cells', which were distanced from other cells so that, for their own safety, those held on remand would not have to associate with convicted prisoners. The association cells were much larger than the other cells and were comfortable, but hardly luxurious. Some of Florence's own furniture had been supplied by friends, and she was also allowed to take exercise in the debtors' yard, where she could sit and read without having to associate with felons.

Now circumstances had changed dramatically, and after enduring the sweltering heat of the closed prison van, Florence was set to move to the condemned cell, which was always kept ready for occupation should the need arise.

The room contained a table, chairs and two hard wooden beds. Isolated and grim, only a dim hazy light filtered through a dusty grating located high in the brick wall, and when dusk fell the room was poorly lighted by a tiny gas jet which spluttered an inadequate glow. The door was encased in sheet iron and bolted all around, and as the *Liverpool Citizen* observed, 'she will be as securely fastened in as if she had been put in her coffin and the lid screwed down'.[9]

On Wednesday 8 August 1889, Florence Elizabeth Maybrick entered this joyless room. Humiliatingly stripped of her own fashionable clothing, she now wore the regulation prison dress of shapeless, coarse blue homespun fabric. Her lovely hair, once piled in elegant curls, was concealed beneath a plain white cap. A cape of stiff brown felt, marked with a broad black arrow, completed the prison costume and proclaimed her a condemned woman.

Two warders were set to guard the prisoner, and from the instant sentence was pronounced there would be at least one pair of eyes upon her unceasingly, careful to ensure that suicide should not deprive the law of its victim and the scaffold of its prey. Her every waking action was supervised, including trips to the doorless lavatory, which opened to the watchful eye of not only female warders but also that of any passing prison official.

The two women whose unhappy task it was to police the condemned prisoner were the same matrons assigned to guard the previous occupant of the death cell, Mrs Elizabeth Berry, who had been executed two years previously, in March 1887, having poisoned her twelve-year-old daughter, Edith Annie Berry. Crying bitterly, both warders had accompanied their charge to the scaffold, trying hopelessly to comfort the terrified woman as the hangman stepped forward to complete his gruesome task.

During the two-week wait for sentence to be carried out, orders had been given to move Mrs Berry to another cell while the scaffold was being erected. No such order would be received for Florence Maybrick, who was constantly tormented by the sounds of the labourers' work progressing from the place of execution, a desolate and broken-down building normally used as a coach house.

Slowly workmen erected the beams, while others noisily constructed a set of steps and fixed the trap-door through which the body would drop. From her cell Florence could hear the relentless tap, tap, tap of hammer on nails, mercilessly reminding her of her fate. If this was a ruse in order to extract a last-minute confession to justify a shaky verdict, it was unsuccessful. Florence Maybrick always maintained her absolute innocence.

The only one of her family to visit was her mother, the unconventional Baroness von Roques. No two women could have been so different. The mother, vital, energetic and a born survivor, was ready and able to do battle. The daughter, pale and hysterical, had abandoned all hope and was on the verge of collapse. After one painful interview, the Baroness spoke to a waiting reporter with an account of her visit:

When I arrived at the cell this morning Florie was sitting in a chair with her face in her hands, crying bitterly. She seems to me like a poor little rabbit who has been chased by dogs until it has neither sense or spirit left, she was sitting on a wooden chair. If there is anybody on earth who hates my daughter I wish they could have seen her there.

I was not allowed to approach Florie. A table was between us as we talked. I could not kiss her or touch her hand, since the very first day I arrived here from Paris and the very first moment we met, I have not even been allowed to kiss my child. Florie was crying, I asked her to try and control herself. I said 'It's a trying time dear, but please don't give way.' She only shook her head and all she said was 'My strength is all gone.'[10]

The post bag at the gaol was unusually large at this time, containing a number of letters personally addressed to Mrs Maybrick. Some wrote in sympathy, others to discuss the case, but after careful perusal by the Governor only a few were handed over, the remainder being destroyed.

During her confinement Florence received seven offers of marriage and a surprising proposal written to her solicitors from a working man, expressing his willingness to go to the scaffold in her place, his argument being that if an innocent life was going to be sacrificed it could make no difference whose blood was spilled. 'Mrs Maybrick is as innocent of the crime of causing her husband's death as I am,' he wrote. 'And I am ready to take her place. Surely the demands of the law would then be satisfied.'[11]

On Thursday 8 August Florence was still in a very weak state, but was able to sit up in her bed. The following day the *Liverpool Echo* reported, under the headline 'A Startling Rumour':

The Pall Mall Gazette *remarks that though there is no reference at all in the Liverpool papers to the following suggestion, it may be said that it is mentioned in several provincial journals that it is understood that another important question arises in the case and one which a jury of matrons will be empanelled to try.**

---

* A jury of matrons (married women) would be empanelled if a woman

> *Of course in the event of that jury finding that to be as it is alleged, the execution would necessarily be postponed and probably not take place at all. It is believed that there has been no instances of the execution of a woman who, at the time of her trial, was in Mrs Maybrick's 'supposed condition', since the execution of Margaret Waters* nineteen years ago.*[12]

The rumour of a pregnancy was not without foundation, though it was neither confirmed nor denied by the Home Office. In a confidential statement made almost five weeks previously, on 5 July, Dr Hopper had stated: 'On the 12th May I was sent for to see Mrs Maybrick, I found that she was suffering from a sanguinias discharge which might have been a threatened miscarriage and she told me that she had not had her monthly period since the 7th March. I was unable then to tell whether she was pregnant or not, but I think it could be ascertained now by examination.'[13]

given the death sentence claimed to be pregnant. This usually happened during the trial. The jury, a doctor and the prisoner would retire to another room and the length of the pregnancy would be established. If the gestation period was less than 140 days the prisoner would not be considered pregnant and the death sentence could go ahead. If more than 140 days then there would be a stay of execution until after the child was born. This was the fate of Mrs Louie Calvert as late as 1926 (Bernard O'Donnell, *Should Women Hang?*, 1956).

* There is no suggestion in contemporary newspaper reports or in the Metropolitan Police files (MEP03/93) that Margaret Waters was pregnant or had been before a jury of matrons before being executed at Horsemonger Jail on 11 October 1870. It appears that on this occasion the *Liverpool Echo* had the wrong information, though the confusion may have arisen with regard to her conviction, which was for killing a baby.

Florence, without doubt, had slept with Brierley on 22 March, and the Maybricks were reported to have had a full reconciliation after a serious quarrel on 30 March, implying that on that day she had slept with James for the first time since 1888. The evidence would suggest that prior to the death of her husband on 11 May 1889, Florence Maybrick was most certainly two months pregnant. Shortly after her arrest, the newspapers had coyly hinted that a miscarriage had taken place in Walton Prison, and a subsequent medical note from the prison doctor had adjourned the inquest on her husband for a week.

However, although an explanation of the nature of Florence's illness had eagerly been anticipated by the local newspapers, it had never been forthcoming, and if she had indeed miscarried during this time, why was Dr Hopper suggesting as late as July that an examination would confirm if she was still pregnant? The fact remains that there existed a strong possibility that while awaiting her execution Florence Maybrick was five months pregnant.

On the afternoon of Thursday 22 August 1889, as Florence endured her fifteenth day as a condemned prisoner, a tall, slender man aged about thirty-eight stood at the Liverpool landing stage and sadly kissed his sister a tender farewell before boarding the steamship *Scythia* with his brother en route to Boston. Having been hounded by the press, Alfred Brierley bitterly regretted the notoriety he had received due to his connection with the Maybrick case, which had left his business and his reputation in ruins.

It was not the first time Brierley had desperately tried to leave the country because of his liaison with Florence. During their affair concerned friends had advised him that his fellow cotton brokers were well aware of what was going on and were reported to have warned: 'You know James Maybrick, when he gets an inkling of this he will fill you so full of lead, you will never know what happened to you.'[14] There appears to have been clear opinion among the brokers that Florence's husband was capable of murder.

Brierley apparently thought so too. Acting on this well-meant advice, he wrote to Florence on 4 May: 'I am going to try and get away in about a fortnight and I think I shall take a round trip to the Mediterranean, which will take six or seven weeks . . .'[15]

Had Florence also convinced him that there was a darker side to her middle-aged, overweight, hypochondriacal husband? Enough to frighten him into buying a ticket for an extended trip around the Mediterranean?

In the letter that Florence had sent to Brierley and Alice Yapp had opened, she had written: 'The tale he told me was pure fabrication and only intended to frighten the truth out of me, in fact he believes my statement though he will not admit it. You need not therefore go abroad on this account . . .'[16]

What possible tale could Maybrick have disclosed to Florence which, in combination with his friends' warning, frightened Brierley so much that he immediately took the drastic action of abandoning his business, his family and his mistress to make an extended tour of the Mediterranean?

At about the same time that the *Scythia* reached the open sea, the Governor of Walton Prison approached Mrs

Maybrick as she took her morning exercise in the prison yard. In a voice heavy with emotion he said: 'Maybrick, no commutation of sentence has come down today, and I consider it my duty to tell you to prepare for death.'[17]

CHAPTER TWO

❧

It's a sort of bloom on a woman, if you have it [charm] you don't need to have anything else, and if you don't have it, it doesn't much matter what else you have.

J.M. Barrie, 1860–1937

Florence Maybrick was born Florence Elizabeth Chandler in Mobile, Alabama, during the turbulence and confusion of the American Civil War. The precise year of her birth is clouded in uncertainty, as many official records were reduced to ashes in the conflict. A passport application in her own hand states her date of birth as 3 September 1861, yet prior to this time she would declare that she had been born in 1862. What is not in dispute, however, is her colourful background as the second child of a notable and influential pioneering family whose fortune in banking, property and slaves was lost in the collapse of the Southern economy.

Her mother, who had been born Caroline Holbrook and whose third marriage had given her the title Baroness von Roques, came from an equally aristocratic old Northern family who had settled in America from England in 1628. She boasted a distinguished family tree which could be traced back to Edward II of England on her mother's side and to the first Earl of Londonderry on her father's. Prestigious American relatives included President John Quincy Adams and Chief Justice Salmon P. Chase.

Caroline Holbrook was more handsome than beautiful, with an attractive and extrovert personality. The managing editor of the *Mobile Register*, Thomas C. De-Leon, who had known her as a girl in New York, mentioned her in his book *Belles, Beaux and Brains of the 60s:* 'The lady . . . had a peculiar sway over men, from her early girlhood, scarcely accounted beautiful she could have given handicap to any prize beauty after the first half hour.'[1]

In 1856, young Carrie Holbrook travelled from her New York home to visit her uncle, the Revd Joseph Holt Ingraham, then rector of St John's Episcopal Church in Mobile, Alabama. Once the capital of French Louisiana, Mobile in the 1850s was a flourishing cotton town second only to New Orleans. With a population of almost 30,000 inhabitants, it was rich in French and Spanish culture, a repository of cotton wealth and Southern pride. Its economy, like that of towns in other slave states, had been built on the ruthless exploitation of the black men, women and children who toiled endlessly on the great plantations of the cane-brake, one of the most fertile and successful regions for cotton growing in the world.

The bustling harbour in Mobile Bay hosted ships from around the world, transporting cotton across the Atlantic to a hungry market in Britain and Europe. Rich plantation owners and overseas cotton buyers swelled Mobile's population during the cotton season, to trade, drink liquor and play stud poker in noisy, smoke-filled saloon bars. Their ladies, dressed in colourful crinolines, rode in shiny carriages along streets heavy with the perfume of magnolias, carefully guarding delicate complexions against the hot Alabama sun with parasols and veils.

Impressive public buildings and private mansions shimmering in the heat opened their doors to the rich and the aristocratic, introducing them to the reckless and extravagant world of Mobile society. Regardless of the fact that relations between North and South were strained, Caroline Holbrook slipped naturally into Southern society and took it by storm.

Among her many suitors was one William Chandler, head of the famous banking house of St John, Powers & Co. of 54 St Francis Street. Considered at the time as one of the most eligible bachelors in Mobile society, he was instantly captivated by Caroline's charms, and much to the disgust and disappointment of the home-town débutantes, he followed her to New York and married her in 1858.

The newlyweds returned to a life of wealth and privilege in the magnolia-lined streets of Mobile. They made their home in the elegant Chandler mansion at 205 Government Street, and threw themselves into the frantic life of Mobile society. It was not long before a son, Holbrook St John Chandler, was born.

In 1860, Alabama, together with other cotton states,

seceded from the Union, and the first rumblings of civil war began. However, this had little impact on the swift pace of Caroline Chandler's social life, and the gaiety continued. A family friend whose wife was Mrs Chandler's cousin gave a glimpse of the family background and the society in which they moved:

> . . . *The women in the family were considered beautiful, but were notorious for their fast imprudent conduct with men. Mrs Chandler would receive young men regardless of whether Mr Chandler was at home or not. She would meet them at the door and throw her arms around their necks and kiss them, take them into the parlour, sit down on their laps and continue to pet them.*
>
> . . . *One of the chief recreations and pleasures of the old days was for the towns which were located on the rivers and had steam boats to have what was called moonlight boat excursions on the river. The gentlemen would charter a boat, the lower deck, which was the freight deck, was cleared for dancing.*
>
> . . . *The boat would go upstream or downstream as the case may be and they would dance. At midnight refreshments would be served and the boat would return to the town about three or four a.m. These excursions were usually given on a Saturday night, so the gentlemen would not have to be at their business the next day and could sleep all day Sunday.*
>
> . . . *Mrs Chandler was right in the midst of all this and would go even if Mr Chandler did not, and on these occasions she and some of the boys would go off to the passenger cabins alone and stay for an hour or more.*[2]

The idea that Florence Chandler was in fact some other man's child was not beyond the bounds of possibility.

On 4 July 1862, either two months before Florence was born or when she was ten months old, William Chandler died from 'inflammation of the brain', reportedly caused by tension and anxiety due to the heavy financial responsibilities of his firm during the Civil War. Gossip quickly spread with regard to the circumstances of his death: ironically, Florence Maybrick's mother would soon be under suspicion of her own husband's murder.

Close relatives had complained that they had been refused admittance to the sick-room, where Caroline was his only nurse. Her explanation was that they would worsen his condition. Due to this, and her insistence on taking control over administering all his medicines, his family began to suspect that she was poisoning him.

Having built a reputation as an unconventional woman, Caroline had never been popular with her husband's family or her own sex, and the ladies of Mobile had never forgotten that she was a 'damn Yankee' who had caught one of their most eligible bachelors. Malicious rumours started to circulate and public opinion, especially the female element, soon turned against her. She was quickly ostracised from Mobile society. However, she appears to have had little motive for the crime and not a shred of evidence was ever produced against her. The authorities took no further action on the condition that she leave the city for ever, and Caroline took the opportunity to slip quietly away.

As far as we know, she never returned to Mobile, although Holbrook and Florence often visited their grandparents there. It is interesting to note that the headstone erected on the grave of William Chandler ignores the fact that he was a husband and father and reads only:

> To our beloved son William G. Chandler,
> gifted and good, the joy, the pride, the hope
> and the light of our life,
> Died July 4th 1862 in the 33rd year of his age.
> Jesus saith go thy way thy son liveth.[3]

Caroline Holbrook Chandler fled with her two small children to Macon, Georgia, and a year later, on 16 July 1863, married a dashing Confederate officer, Captain Franklin Bache du Barry, whom she claimed was the grandson of Benjamin Franklin and the son of Count du Barry, a friend of Napoleon III.

There is a possibility that Caroline and du Barry were already acquainted before the death of William Chandler; he was certainly based in Mobile at the time, and he and Caroline would undoubtedly have moved in the same social circles. A brave and conscientious soldier, du Barry was mentioned in dispatches to Jefferson Davis from Governor John G. Shorter in October 1862. Shorter complained of the weak defences of Mobile and wrote that du Barry was one of only two officers he could trust.

Caroline's marriage to du Barry was also to be short-lived. In April 1864, he applied for leave of absence to go to Europe for the benefit of his health, after being wounded in the bombardment of Charleston two months previously, and the family embarked on the British-owned blockade-runner *The Fanny*, bound for Greenock, Scotland. Two days out, du Barry died, and although the Captain offered to return to port, his widow insisted that he be buried at sea.

Losing two husbands in as many years, and both under dubious circumstances, gave cause for added speculation and gossip. Luckily for Caroline, however, she was by then out of the reach of the authorities, and she arrived in Europe once again a widow with two young children.

Living on her considerable wits, Caroline drifted through Europe. In the late 1860s, after a brief stay in Worcester, England, she returned to New York for a short time and was closely associated with her cousin, the well-known socialite the second Mrs Cornelius Vanderbilt. It was during this time that she again courted gossip after a scandal with the cousin of a famous Broadway actor.

After a few years she returned to Europe and embarked on her third and most disastrous marriage. Trapped with fellow Americans in the six-month siege of Paris at the height of the Franco-Prussian War, she, like the suffering Parisians, was brought to near starvation before Paris surrendered in January 1871.

Although Caroline was pro-French and probably politically opposed to Crown Prince Frederick, who would later briefly become Frederick III, Emperor of Prussia, the lure of a title was too strong and she literally fell into the arms of the enemy in the guise of a flamboyant Prussian cavalry officer, the Baron Adolph von Roques, of the 8th Cuirassier Regiment.

They married in 1872 and Caroline embarked on one of the unhappiest periods of her life. The couple lived in Cologne and then Wiesbaden, where in 1874 she was presented to Queen Victoria's daughter, the Crown Princess, at the Prussian Court. In June 1879, von Roques was posted to St

Petersburg, where he was military attaché to the German Embassy. Caroline claimed that he was a drinker, a womaniser and a gambler, that he beat her and frittered away what money she had.

Their life was constantly fraught with financial difficulties, and in 1879 the Baroness was sued in the common plea court by Isaac Rosenthal, a Wiesbaden banker, who claimed that she and the Baron owed him $13,015 on bills of exchange drawn by the Baron and endorsed by his wife. Although the Baroness claimed she had signed under duress, the court awarded Rosenthal a third of the money owing by attachment to a property in New York which Caroline and the children had inherited on her mother's death in 1875. The children's trustees subsequently took Rosenthal to court to force him to vacate the property, and eventually won, leaving the Baroness with a small income.

Despite the torments of this tempestuous marriage, Florence appeared fond of the Baron, who was the closest thing to a father she had ever known. One of her passions in life was horse-riding, and this she indulged in to her heart's content when residing with her stepfather. Years later she would choose to ignore the instability of her childhood and write: 'My life was much the same as that of any other girl who enjoyed the pleasures of youth with a happy heart.'[4]

By 1879 the marriage had completely broken down, and the Baron and Baroness parted with little regret on either side. In a letter to William Potter, her American lawyer, in the early 1880s, Caroline wrote: 'I am a silly and absurd little woman no doubt, but wherein I am particularly weak, I do not see. That's why women never get wise!'[5]

This statement couldn't have been more accurate: the Baroness now stumbled into an erratic life travelling between Europe and America. Her scandalous conduct and her love affairs were legendary, and one episode reported that for a short time she passed as the wife of the British attaché at the legation in Tehran. She developed an infamous reputation and over the years left behind her a stack of unpaid debts, ill feeling and broken promises to friends and acquaintances who had been taken in by her charms.

During this time her two children were placed in the custody of various friends and relatives in both Europe and America, educated by governesses and with occasional periods at boarding schools. Florence would confirm: 'I was too delicate for college life, I lived partly with my maternal grandmother and partly with my mother whose home was abroad, when not with them I was visiting or travelling with friends.'[6]

According to rumour, it was during one protracted stay in England towards the end of 1879 that Florence embarked on her first love affair. It was even suggested that she gave birth to an illegitimate son as a teenager. The account continues that she placed the child, named William after her father, in the hands of a Hartlepool blacksmith and his wife named Graham and continued to support him financially.

There is no doubt that Florence did live in England during this time. Taking into account the bohemian lifestyle and unorthodox attitudes of the Baroness, as well as future events, it would seem there was a fair foundation for the rumours.

It was from this unconventional background, lacking in sound values and stability, that the young and impressionable

Florence, travelling with her mother and brother from New York, embarked on the SS *Baltic* on 11 March 1880, bound for Liverpool, England.

As the 220 first-class passengers gathered in the bar of the *Baltic* that first evening, renewing old acquaintances and meeting new friends, the Baroness's family were introduced by General J.G. Hazard, an old friend from New Orleans, to James Maybrick, a Liverpool cotton broker. Scandalmongers would report that it was Caroline who first flirted with this eligible bachelor, who was of her own generation, but James had a different prey in mind, and was captivated by the Baroness's blonde, doe-eyed daughter.

In his forty-second year, James Maybrick was not considered conventionally attractive. Somewhat above medium height, with light sandy-coloured hair and a drooping moustache, his complexion was ruddy and his waistline reflected years of overindulgence. He was something of an opportunist, and the ruthless world of cotton broking suited his gambling instincts.

Overshadowed by a highly successful younger brother, Maybrick was emotionally insecure. In his favour, though, he had a charm of manner, friendly disposition and air of culture characteristic of the refined English gentleman, and he was a popular man amongst his contemporaries. He had established a good reputation among the cotton-broking community and had made many lasting friendships. John Aunspaugh, of Inman Swann and Company, was once reported to have said: 'James Maybrick is one of the straightest, most upright and honourable men in a business transaction I have ever known.'[7]

For her part Florence, twenty-three years Maybrick's junior, had developed into a most attractive and graceful young lady, with a shapely figure accentuated by the fashionable bustle and corset of the day. Standing at five feet two inches, she was petite, with noticeably tiny hands and feet, but her most striking feature was her eyes of piercing blue. Not a girl of outstanding intelligence, she had been reasonably well educated, although in a somewhat erratic fashion, and was fluent in both French and German. She beheld James Maybrick as a mature, knowledgeable and attractive man of the world; perhaps she was also subconsciously looking for the stable father-figure who had eluded her teenage years.

With the cotton trade in recession and his financial position unstable, James had reached a crossroads in his life. Florence's youth and vivaciousness dazzled him instantly. He desired her physical beauty and was determined to possess it. He was also more than receptive to the idea of marriage with a rich and beautiful heiress whose mother was a member of the aristocracy. Unknown to James, however, the Baroness was in an equally hopeless financial position. Although she casually mentioned ownership of a vast expanse of land in the Southern states destined as Florence's inheritance, she failed to mention that very little revenue had ever been received from any of it, or that she had been desperately trying to offload the property for the last two years.

Florence, caught up in the first heady throes of love, was unaware that her mother was attempting to manipulate the situation. Although the Baroness was genuinely impatient to see her daughter comfortably established with someone whom she perceived as a successful man of means, she was equally eager to reap her own benefits from a potential son-in-law who could help support her flagging lifestyle.

No two backgrounds could have been as different as those of James Maybrick and Florence Chandler. He had been born in 1838 in the thriving port of Liverpool, at 8 Church Alley, close to St Peter's Church where his father, William Maybrick, an engraver, held a position of considerable influence and importance as parish clerk. The Maybricks had had seven sons, two of whom died in infancy. Of those who survived, William was the eldest, quickly followed by James, Michael, Thomas and Edwin. Shortly after Edwin's birth, the family moved to a larger house, at 77 Mount Pleasant.

From this stable middle-class background, with its respect for Victorian convention, James at the age of twenty entered a shipbroker's office in London. He was eager and ambitious and embarking on a promising career when he fell in love with Sarah Ann Robertson, ten months his senior, an assistant in her uncle's jeweller's shop.

Sarah is a shadowy and elusive figure in the history of James Maybrick. Little can be discovered of her background apart from the fact that she was born in Sunderland on 22 August 1837 and lived with her aunt and uncle, Charles and Christiana Case, in the East End of London, close to Whitechapel. She would spend the next thirty years of her life with James Maybrick in an irregular relationship shrouded in mystery, calling herself 'Mrs Maybrick'. In 1865 James gave her a Bible as a birthday present, inscribing it to 'My darling Piggy' and signing it 'her affectionate husband, J.M.'.[8]

In 1868 Sarah was living in London at 55 Bromley Street, Commercial Road and was mentioned in the will of Thomas Conconi, her aunt's second husband, as 'Sarah Ann Maybrick wife of James Maybrick of Old Hall Street', confirming that her family thought the couple married. They lived together at various times in Liverpool, Manchester and Chester, and over the years she bore him five children.*

In the mid 1870s James set up Maybrick & Co., a cotton merchant company, in Knowsley Buildings, Tithebarn Street, Liverpool. His brother Edwin soon joined him as a junior partner. Business expanded towards the end of the 1870s, and he opened an office in Norfolk, Virginia, a thriving port recovering from the aftermath of the American Civil War and exporting cotton to foreign markets.

In 1877 James was stricken with malaria and was prescribed a three-month course of strychnine and arsenic. He soon became addicted to the drugs, finding them a general stimulant and also believing them to have aphrodisiacal qualities. When the treatment came to an end he continued taking the medicine and would regularly be seen mixing arsenic in with his food.

In Norfolk, where he lived during the cotton season, James plunged headlong into a carefree bachelor lifestyle, indulging his passions for drinking, drug-taking, gambling and women. He was a regular visitor to the establishment of a notorious brothel-house keeper, Mary Hogwood, whose premises he would visit two or three times a week. Some time later Mary Hogwood would confirm:

I saw him frequently in his different moods and fancies. It was a

* No marriage certificate has ever been discovered between James Maybrick and Sarah Ann Robertson. On the marriage certificate with Florence, Maybrick's status is recorded as 'bachelor'.

31

common thing for him to take arsenic two or three times during an evening, he would always say before taking it: 'Well I am going to take my evening dose', he would pull from his pocket a small vial in which he carried arsenic and putting a small quantity on his tongue he would wash it down with a sip of wine, in fact so often did he repeat this that I became afraid that he would die suddenly in my house and then some of us would be suspected of his murder.[9]

That James was an arsenic eater was confirmed by Franklin George Bancroft, an artist and writer who also visited the house of Mary Hogwood. On one occasion he asked James why he took poison: 'Longevity and a fair complexion my boy,'[10] Maybrick replied jovially.

Inevitably James's business suffered as his mental and physical condition deteriorated, and he admitted to Dr Edward C. Sequin, a New York specialist in nervous disorders, that he was a victim of alcohol abuse and other excesses.

Perhaps it was with a feeling of optimism and renewal that James embarked on his courtship with Florence, although at this stage neither party was aware that the foundations of their relationship had been built on false expectations. So enamoured were they of each other that they spent the remainder of the trip together, for the most part unchaperoned, much to the disapproval of the more orthodox matrons aboard ship. By the time the *Baltic* arrived at Liverpool, it had been decided that if they still felt the same way in one year's time, they would be married.

In order to help prolong their courtship, the Hazards kindly invited Florence to stay with them at Childwall Abbey, just outside Liverpool. James visited almost daily, business permitting. When the time came for Florence to join her mother in Paris and James's business interests took him back to America, they parted with reluctance, but with firm promises for the future.

Not everyone, however, was as receptive to the charms of the Baroness and her daughter as James had been. Michael Maybrick, for instance, considered them extravagant opportunists, and had grave doubts about the age difference.

Michael, a well-known musician of considerable talent, was the most successful of the five Maybrick brothers. At the age of fourteen he was made organist at the local parish church, and the Covent Garden Opera played one of his first musical compositions. Shortly after his coming of age he set out to study in Leipzig under Moscheles Plaidy and Carl Richter. The fine quality of his voice was soon discovered and he was strongly advised to exchange his vocation as an instrumentalist for that of a singer. In 1879 he faced his first English audience at a New Philharmonic concert, after returning from his studies at the Milan Conservatoire.

He soon made his mark in another direction under the stage name of Stephen Adams, gaining remarkable success for his 'nautical ditties' in partnership with lyricist Fred Weatherly.* Together they wrote the well-known popular song 'A Warrior Bold', while another of their compositions, 'Nancy Lee', sold 100,000 copies in less than two years, and many a diverting complication was caused at amateur musical parties by every guest producing it as their favourite song.

---

* Fred Weatherly penned the lyrics for 1,000 tunes, including 'Roses of Picardy'. It is also claimed that he wrote the words of 'Danny Boy'.

Due to his success both financially and professionally, Michael developed an imposing personality, and James, Thomas and Edwin all grew to accept his guidance. When their father died in 1870, Michael would step into his shoes as the authoritative figure in the family. But even though Michael no doubt expressed his misgivings about Florence, he supported his brother as best man at the marriage, which took place on 27 July 1881 at the fashionable church of St James, Piccadilly.

As the guests gathered at the church, the Baroness von Roques, who was standing witness for her daughter, dreadfully embarrassed the happily married John Aunspaugh by flinging her arms around his neck and shouting rather loudly, 'Oh, here is my long-lost love.'[11] The marriage ceremony was conducted by the Revd J. Dyer Tovey, and Florence floated down the aisle in a cloud of white satin and lace on the arm of her brother, who had put aside his medical studies and travelled from Paris to give her away.

When the bride and groom retired to the vestry to fill in the marriage certificate, James disregarded his relatively humble origins and gave himself the rank of 'esquire', elevating his father's status from engraver to 'gentleman'. The happy couple, with the guests' good wishes ringing in their ears, endured the traditional shower of rice and embarked on a brief honeymoon to Bournemouth.

During the twelve months between the engagement and the marriage, the Baroness had undergone a change of heart concerning the suitability of her daughter's future husband. Whether she had discovered the true state of Maybrick's financial affairs can only be conjecture, but she informed John Aunspaugh that she was 'bitterly opposed to the match and did not believe any good would come of it'.[12] A prophecy which, viewed with hindsight, would sadly become a remarkable piece of understatement.

CHAPTER THREE

*If I waited to be taken care of by my
wife, ma'am, I believe you know pretty
well I should wait till Doomsday, so I'll
trouble you to take charge of the teapot.*
Charles Dickens, Hard Times

In the second half of the nineteenth century the River
Mersey was known as 'The River of Ten Thousand
Masts'. It was a heaving mass of prosperity, vision and
promise, a gift of nature harnessed by man. In a seemingly
never-ending stream, the great packet ships and steamships
of Britain and North America sailed towards the city of
Liverpool, the focal point on which ocean and coastal
shipping routes converged to merge with river, canal and rail
networks; a pulsating channel of communication between
Britain and the world.

Under a continuous process of expansion, the dock-based industries tempted an influx of labourers seeking work. Irish, Welsh and Scots, refugees from famine, poverty and unemployment, converged on Liverpool to join a transitory force of hopeful travellers from all over Europe. For the price of four guineas, prospective emigrants in 1880 could purchase a steerage ticket on one of the many steam- or sailing-ships offering a new life in America. As many as 200,000 emigrants would pass through the port in some of its busiest years, but not everyone would make it to the New World. Some died in the dockland ghettos, while others settled in the area, making their homes on the shores of the busy estuary stretching between Bootle and Seaforth in the north and Garston in the south.

The infamous dockland area soon became a by-word for poverty, crime and infectious disease. Children played barefoot, ill clad and dirt-encrusted in fetid, overcrowded slums, where violence and vice were fostered in countless pubs, gin palaces and singing salons. Close to five hundred brothels plied their trade with little or no interference by an undermanned police force.

In the centre of the city, housing the commercial heart of the port, stood towering ornate buildings, proud monuments to human enterprise. Behind the smoke-blackened bricks and dusty windows sat an obedient and enduring army of poorly paid clerks serving the offices of bankers, insurance and shipping brokers, agents and produce exchanges.

In 1884, after following the cotton season for three years, Edwin replaced his brother as Maybrick & Co.'s buying agent in Norfolk, Virginia, and James and Florence returned to live permanently in Liverpool with their two-year-old son,* although James continued to make periodic trips to America.

They rented Beechville, a house in Grassendale Park North, a suburb protected from the city's corruptions by a green belt of public parks. It was here, two years later, on 20 July 1886, that Florence gave birth to a daughter. It was a difficult confinement, but Florence had every possible medical advantage to aid her, including the ministrations of a private nurse. Gladys Evelyn Maybrick, a sickly child, was welcomed into the nursery by nursemaid Emma Powell.

James, informing his mother-in-law in Paris, wrote: 'The doctors made a fine mess of Florie's case, but thank God she is getting on alright.'[1]

The relationship between the Baroness and the Maybricks had been somewhat tentative over the last few years, and they had only recently recovered from a serious quarrel over the ownership of her American lands, a third of which she had impulsively signed over to Florence in January 1882, shortly after her daughter's marriage. A little while before this, Maybrick had somehow managed to assume responsibility for the Baroness's business interests in America. It had been an unworkable alliance, with the Baroness and her American lawyers allowing James only limited access to information.

Land speculator and attorney David W. Armstrong, who knew both Florence and her mother intimately, had undertaken to sell the American property as far back as 1878. On

---

* James Chandler Maybrick, known as Bobo or sometimes Sonny, was born in England on 24 March 1882 at 5 Livingston Avenue, Toxteth Park, Liverpool. The local gossips noted that he was born only eight months after his parents' marriage.

1 November 1881 Florence had written to Armstrong, obviously at her husband's request, in order to nudge him into replying to one of Maybrick's many letters. Apparently worried that Armstrong might inadvertently refer to the past indiscretions of either the Baroness or herself, she had taken the opportunity to fire a warning shot of her own:

> *Before closing I wish to add, that the Baroness von Roques trusts to your honour and discretion with regard to any 'private matters' she may have confided to you and as my husband is quite ignorant of her personal affairs I must beg of you only to give information in reference to the Virginia claim and on no others!* [2]

Maybrick never really got to grips with his mother-in-law's business affairs, mainly due to the fact that everyone was keeping him in the dark. When a possible new buyer appeared on the scene, the Baroness quickly regretted her generosity in signing over part of the lands to her daughter and tried to invalidate the deed. The result was that James angrily cut off the allowance awarded to the Baroness in 1878, when the children's trustees took Rosenthal to court to vacate the New York property. The Baroness, her finances in more of a tangle than ever, was by now complaining that she was on the verge of starvation and wrote to Armstrong:

> *Mr and Mrs Maybrick have decided to deprive me of the small allowance assigned to me when the suit was decided in her and my son's favour in 1878, as she pleads by order of her husband that she was a minor at the time. I am pained to have to confide so unfilial an act and decision but I am forced to do so to show you as*

my agent that I am near starvation... My poor little girl is
completely in the power of her husband and he does not prove a son
to me.[3]

During the mid 1880s however, hostilities were briefly suspended as the Baroness, now living alone in Paris, mourned the loss of her only son, Holbrook St John Chandler. His long, lingering death from consumption in April 1885 had temporarily crushed her usually indomitable spirit, and she was eager to reforge the links with her only living family and rejoice at the birth of a granddaughter.

Unaffected by the added responsibilities of marriage and fatherhood, James had resumed his hedonistic lifestyle on his return to England and was reported to be having an affair with a woman in Liverpool. Whether or not he had also drifted back into his relationship with Sarah Robertson is speculation, but he continued to support her financially, with an annual payment of £100.

Although James Maybrick was undoubtedly a serial philanderer, he appeared on the surface an affable man, fun-loving, a good host and devoted to his children. Unfortunately, he was also the possessor of a morose and gloomy disposition and an extremely hot temper. He was frequently pessimistic regarding business conditions and often predicted future failures. John Aunspaugh once slapped him on the back and joked: 'Well Maybrick, you surely do spend a lot of money for one who is always expecting a great calamity.'[4]

As his craving for arsenic and other stimulants increased, James gained access to drugs through a relative; his cousin William, who worked for a wholesale chemist. He also started visiting the premises of Edwin G. Heaton, a dispensing chemist in Exchange Street East, and would pay calls, sometimes up to five times a day, for a 'pick-me-up' containing liquor arsenicalis.*

James complained constantly about his health. His hypochondria and the habit he had of swallowing any patent medicine recommended to him for real and imagined ills was a constant source of amusement to his friends. A business colleague once joked: 'James Maybrick imagines he is afflicted with every ailment to which the flesh has heir.'[5] Once, when James was spending time as a guest in John Aunspaugh's home in America, Mrs Aunspaugh told her husband that a neighbour had developed diabetes. 'For God's sake don't say anything about it before Maybrick,' he cautioned. 'For he will think he is dying with it right now.'[6]

Twelve months after Gladys's birth, the children's nurse, a widow in her forties, suddenly announced to the Maybricks that she was shortly to be married to John Charles Over, a Liverpool joiner, and would be leaving their employment. Surprisingly, however, Florence was not downcast at the domestic upheaval ahead, writing in a letter to her mother:

Nurse is quite changed since baby's birth. Poor little mite. It gets neither petting nor coaxing when I am not with it and yet it is such a loving little thing and ready with a smile for every cross word that nurse says to her. I cannot understand why she does not take to the

---

* If he was taking the maximum dose of seven drops of liquor arsenicalis five times a day, it would be nearly equal to a third of a grain of white arsenic.

child. I am afraid she is getting too old for a young baby and has not the forbearance and patience to look after Gladys. When she had Bobo with her it was a labour of love. With poor little Gladys it is a labour of duty only.[7]

Men of James Maybrick's standing rarely involved themselves in domestic arrangements, so when he travelled to the home of Mr David Gibson, an accountant, in Fairfield and personally interviewed a young woman for the position of nursemaid, he was seriously defying convention and many censorious eyebrows were raised.

Alice Yapp was an attractive twenty-six-year-old who had worked for the Gibsons for six years. A native of Ludlow in Shropshire, her parents had been well-to-do and she went into service as a children's nurse on the death of her father. As a nurse she was efficient and capable, but there was an underlying deviousness about her. It was reported that she snooped around Mrs Maybrick's bedroom when her mistress was out, reading her letters and delighting in ill-natured gossip about her with the other servants.

When returning to the house earlier than anticipated one evening, Florence and James discovered baby Gladys red-faced and crying alone in the dark nursery. Yapp, who had been given strict orders never to leave the children unsupervised, was discovered gossiping with her friends in the kitchen. The normally passive Florence was furious and gave the nursemaid a severe public dressing-down, leaving Yapp bitterly resenting her mistress.

With an expanding family to consider, James decided it was time to move home, and in February 1888 he took a five-year lease on Battlecrease House, a large semi-detached, buff-painted structure in Riversdale Road, overlooking the popular Aigburth cricket ground, with an uninterrupted view of the Welsh mountains and only a short walk to the railway station.

The house was set well back from the road and was surrounded by a high, ivy-clad wall, and the grounds of between five and six acres included a well-stocked orchard and a vegetable garden. The stables at the rear were occupied by a sweet-tempered hack and a shiny Humber tricycle.

The rooms were tall and spacious, and Florence spared no expense in furnishing them. Lace curtains and velvet draperies hung at the long French windows, and the heavily carved mahogany furniture was upholstered in gold and light-blue satin. Lavish lace antimacassars covered the backs of comfortable leather chairs, and small whatnot tables abounded, smothered in ornaments and the paraphernalia so beloved of the Victorian householder.

In the front and back parlours James installed two marble mantels which he had imported from Carrara in Italy. They were carved with exquisite designs so real that one visitor to the house said: 'The grapes stood out in such bold relief that you felt as if you would like to walk up and pick them off.'[8]

There was one room, however, which James claimed exclusively for his own use. Furnished with deep, comfortable chairs and always kept locked, it was only cleaned when he was there to supervise the servants. It was here he entertained his men friends and kept his liquor, cigars, cards and poker chips.

Florence related to her mother that in this room he also kept a black tin box, the contents of which she was strictly forbidden to examine. Her husband had told her it merely contained their marriage certificate, birth certificates and papers relating to cemetery lots, but she later confided to her mother: 'There were all sorts of things in there I knew nothing about.'[9]

Why did James Maybrick forbid his wife to see the contents of the box if it only contained documents with which they were both familiar? Was this the room where he retired undisturbed to write his thoughts into an old ledger, the contents of which would cause such controversy a century later as *The Diary of Jack the Ripper*? Did he keep the journal safely under lock and key in the convenient tin box for fear of having it discovered at the office by his clerk, George Smith? The writer of the journal reflected: 'If Smith should find this then I am done before my campaign begins.'[10]

Most Victorian establishments were attended by a shadowy regiment of women who lived 'below stairs', and Battlecrease House was no exception. The Maybricks employed four indoor servants: a cook, a housemaid, a waitress and the nursemaid, Yapp. Miss Williams, a peripatetic governess, was engaged in the afternoons to teach Bobo his letters, and a gardener tended the grounds and livestock. His wife, who had worked for the family at Beechville, would also help out in the kitchen when required.

Also closely associated with the household were two married sisters, Matilda Briggs and Martha Hughes, old friends of the family whose mother, Mrs Janion, was godmother to Bobo and Gladys. It was reported that Mrs Briggs had been in love with James and was keenly disappointed when he fell head-over-heels for the young American. Now separated from her husband, Mrs Briggs made it her business to spend many hours in the Maybrick household, and it was remarked upon that she exercised more control over the servants than did the lady of the house. She had also formed a close association with Alice Yapp, and the pair of them treated Florence with undisguised contempt.

During the summer of 1888 the Maybricks entertained Florence Aunspaugh, the eight-year-old daughter of John Aunspaugh, a close friend and business colleague of James who was over from America contracting business in Europe. Many years later she would recall with pleasure her stay in Liverpool and describe vividly the house and the characters who would unwittingly play such a crucial part in the drama which was about to unfold. She confirmed the relationship between Florence, Mrs Briggs and Alice Yapp which even as a young child she had sensed:

> *Both Mrs Briggs and Nurse Yapp despised and hated Mrs Maybrick and the most pathetic part about it was Mrs Maybrick did not have the brain to realise their attitude toward her. Had she sensed their enmity towards her and been more cautious conditions could have been very different and much better for her.*[11]

John Aunspaugh held James Maybrick in great regard, but had not been very impressed with his friend's chosen bride. Although admiring her beauty, he was unimpressed by her intelligence, recalling to his daughter some years later:

> *You would focus your eyes on hers with a steady gaze. They would appear to be entirely without life, or expression, as if you were gazing into the eyes of a corpse, literally void of animation or*

expression . . . At no time was there any expression of intellectuality either in eyes or face, yet there was a magnetic charm about her countenance that greatly attracted one and seemed irresistible.[12]

Fortunately, the indolent and aimless life Florence lived at Battlecrease relied little on intellectual ability. In the mornings, if she had not been up too late the evening before, she would join James at about nine o'clock for a leisurely breakfast before he left for the city. She would then retire to the parlour to write letters or reply to the continuous stream of social invitations which had arrived in the post. Nurse Yapp would duly appear with Bobo and Gladys and Florence would entertain them for an hour or so, walking in the garden or playing games in the nursery.

When she became bored she would retire to the parlour with her two cats for company and paint with her watercolours or read some light literature. In the afternoons, when not entertaining or visiting friends, she would dress and take the carriage to Liverpool, where the many shops in fashionable Bold Street would entertain her for hours on end. Sometimes she would meet James at his office and they would return together to Battlecrease to prepare for the evening ahead. The Maybricks entertained frequently and rarely spent more than one or two nights a week at home alone.

One woman friend at least thought well of Florence: 'She was one of the most good-natured and pretty women I ever met . . . She had an excellent voice; her favourite song was "Sing, Birdie Sing" and we used accordingly to call her Birdie.'[13]

Reared by the Baroness to consider her health as 'delicate',

Florence accepted without question this fashionable affectation of middle-class femininity. However, when the need arose, she responded to the needs of her children with all the spirit, energy and determination of her pioneering ancestors.

When scarlet fever raged in Liverpool during the summer of 1886, Bobo fell victim to the dreaded disease, which had little regard for class and was proving fatal to young children all over Liverpool. James, at the first sign of infection, fled with the new baby and the nursemaid to the safety of Wales, abandoning Florence to nurse the child alone. Discharging all the servants except the cook, who prepared her food and set it out in front of the bedroom door, Florence tenderly nursed her son for six nerve-racking weeks until he had made a complete recovery.

There is no doubt that Florence loved her children, but generally she was immature, self-absorbed and frivolous. Her greatest pleasure was in the clothes she wore and the admiration she received from her contemporaries. Young Florence Aunspaugh recorded one incident which illustrated the child-like quality of Florence's nature:

> One day she was in Liverpool walking on a street with low shoes and discovered she had a hole in her stocking. This was the most distressing calamity that could have happened to Mrs Maybrick, in her opinion. Mr Maybrick was a great tease and thoroughly enjoyed a good joke and this was too good a one to let pass.
>
> That evening at dinner, Mrs Maybrick was deploring her tragedy. Mr Maybrick said, 'Yes, Bunny, it was awful. I saw that hole four blocks away,' and made other ridiculous remarks about the hole in the stocking.

> *Mrs Maybrick was badly spoiled and she could not stand it any longer, she burst into tears. When Mr Maybrick saw that he had carried the joke too far, he got up from the head of the table, went over behind her chair at the foot, put his arms around her, kissed her and told her he was only teasing and told her not to worry about the hole it was of no importance. He did not see the hole and no one else did.[14]*

Few could have anticipated the tragic events the future would hold for what seemed on the surface to be a straightforward Victorian household. But Battlecrease House was proving to be a not very happy home and this was clearly remarked upon in the Ripper journal: 'A dark shadow lays over the house it is evil.'[15]

Cracks had begun to appear in the Maybricks' relationship as early as 1887, after Florence had discovered the existence of Sarah Robertson and her children. Disappointed in her marriage, she indulged in her own liaisons, with her husband's brother Edwin and a London solicitor named Williams.*

It was not unusual for a man in Maybrick's position to maintain a mistress. Traditionally, married men found discreet sexual pleasure with the women they kept or with prostitutes, and wives had little choice but to turn a blind eye to a husband's infidelities. But Florence had a more independent spirit, inherited from her mother, and she contacted her American solicitors to procure a separation. Whatever advice

---

* Williams was known to John Aunspaugh and Alfred Brierley and his affair with Florence was confirmed in letters written by both men. However, nothing else is known about him, although it is probable that he worked for a law firm which was used by the cotton brokers' association.

she was given was obviously not followed up. Perhaps James indicated that he would end the relationship with Sarah and Florence decided to let matters rest, but the marriage remained rocky and by July 1888 they were occupying separate beds.

Another contributing factor to their problems was that James had informed Florence that they were living far beyond their means. His friends on the Exchange assumed that Mrs Maybrick had a considerable income of her own, because they did not believe his business could possibly support them in the style in which they lived. But Florence's income was not considerable, merely genteel, and like her mother, she had never been taught how to economise.

Florence's housekeeping was subsequently reduced to £7 a week to cover staff wages and household expenses, which inevitably resulted in an uncomfortable interview with the cook, asking her to be as frugal as possible.

Once a month, the mistress of Battlecrease House would wrestle with the household accounts, staring vacantly at the stack of invoices and wondering how the family could possibly have consumed so many joints of meat or pints of cream. Impossible numbers, which refused to add up, would blur before her eyes, while the ink, combined with her tears of frustration, deposited huge blots on the paper.

Bills bearing the compliments of milliners and dressmakers would be stuffed hastily into drawers in a forlorn attempt to make them disappear, and Florence was reduced to applying to various moneylenders and pledging her jewellery for additional funds. She was even forced to borrow £100 from Mrs Briggs, confiding that her husband was in financial difficulties. In an emotionally charged letter to her mother she wrote:

> *I am utterly worn out and in such a state of overstrained nervousness I am hardly fit for anything. Whenever the doorbell rings I feel ready to faint for fear it is someone coming to have an account paid, and when Jim comes home at night it is with fear and trembling that I look into his face to see whether anyone has been to the office about my bills. My life is a continual state of fear of something or somebody. There is no way of stemming the current.*
>
> *Is life worth living? I would gladly give up the house tomorrow and move somewhere else, but Jim says it would ruin him outright. For one must keep up appearances until he has more capital to fall back on to meet his liabilities since a suspicion aroused all claims would pour in at once, and how could Jim settle with what he has now?*[16]

But was James being less than honest with Florence about his financial situation? Before they took on the added expense of Battlecrease House, James had undergone a period when he had been reduced to living off his capital, though it had not stopped him moving the family into a larger home. But some time between late 1887 and his death in 1889, his finances had undergone a dramatic recovery. On his death he left the considerable sum of £5,016.1s. 0d.* – the equivalent at today's prices would be in the region of £220,000 – but he did not appear to have informed his wife,

---

* This was the gross amount; the net value was £3,770. 16s. 6¾d. When the will was resworn in 1893, the amount was £6,816. 1s. 0d.

who was trying to economise and getting herself even deeper in debt.

However precarious Florence believed their financial circumstances to be, it never interfered with the Maybricks entertaining in the grand manner. Towards the end of Florence Aunspaugh's visit, when her father returned from Europe to take her back to America, they held a formal dinner party in his honour.

As the Maybricks stood in the hall to ceremoniously receive their guests, none of the men passed without commenting on Mrs Maybrick's beauty, referring to her as a 'goddess' or a 'Greek statue'. 'Maybrick,' one man complimented him, 'you have the prettiest wife in England.'[17]

Florence, tightly laced into a whalebone corset, was looking her most attractive. She triumphantly greeted her guests, graciously accepting their compliments with a dazzling smile and a slight inclination of her head. Any habits of economy she had been desperately trying to develop were certainly not reflected in the gown she had purchased for the evening's entertainment, as Florence Aunspaugh remembers:

These were the days of the spider waist, the well-developed bust and hips and the bustle. The material was of grey silk or fawn of a heavy rich quality trimmed in dark purple velvet and ecru Brussels lace. The back of the skirt was unusually attractive, it was in three large puffs, one below the other and the last terminating in a long train.[18]

That evening twenty couples sat down for dinner and the conversation was forced into groups due to the length of the table. Edwin Maybrick, who had returned from Virginia at the end of the cotton season, was flirting outrageously with his sister-in-law, and John Aunspaugh and James overheard Florence laughingly say to him: 'If I had met you first things might have been different.'[19] James dropped his knife and clenched his fists, his face flushed the colour of fire and his eyes glazed. In a second, however, he had recovered himself, and everything passed on smoothly.

For some time the gossip at the Exchange had been that Florence and Edwin had more than a brotherly and sisterly interest in one another. James had already suspected that Florence had a lover – perhaps he was aware of Williams, the London-based solicitor – but had he ever for a moment anticipated that she could be having an affair with his own brother?

Would this evening and the overhearing of an indiscreet remark be the catalyst that would change a world of secret fantasies into sadistic reality? Had the constant use of drugs channelled his unpredictable and fluctuating emotions into a journey of revenge down London's filthy backstreets and alleys, looking for a scapegoat on whom to focus his aggression?

The Ripper journal reflects the thoughts of a pathological liar, consumed with hatred, jealousy and the desire for a wife whom he knows has another lover. Was it possible, as is claimed in the journal, that James Maybrick was responsible for the progressive sadism which resulted in five mutilated victims in and around Whitechapel in the autumn of 1888?

As stated in one of the journal's earliest paragraphs,

before the killings had started: 'I finally decided London it shall be. And why not is it not an ideal location? Indeed do I not frequently visit the Capital and indeed do I not have a legitimate reason for doing so?'[20]

CHAPTER FOUR

❧❧

> *Prostitution is caused not by female depravity or man's licentiousness, but simply by underpaying, undervaluing and overworking women so shamefully that the poorest of them are forced to resort to prostitution to keep body and soul together.*
>
> *George Bernard Shaw, 1856–1950*

In the early hours of Friday 31 August 1888, Police Constable 97J John Neil found the body of a Whitechapel prostitute lying in the gutter in Buck's Row, and accidentally stepped into a chapter of British criminal history.

From the light of his bull's-eye lamp he noted that the woman's throat had been cut, but it wasn't until the corpse had been removed to the local mortuary and the police discovered she had also been disembowelled that the hunt for the most notorious killer of all time would be under way.

The mutilated body was later identified as that of Mary Ann Nichols, known as Polly Nichols, an alcoholic and the mother of five children. She had been living from prostitution since being deserted by her husband in 1880, and spent her nights in common lodging houses or the casual ward of the local workhouse.

At least three people had seen Polly in the early hours of Friday morning looking for a customer in order to earn her fourpence 'doss money', the price of a warm bed in an overcrowded, lice-infested lodging house. She was last seen at 2.30 a.m. on the corner of Osborn Street and Whitechapel Road, much the worse for drink and boasting that she had earned her rent money three times that day, and spent it. Her last client probably strangled her from behind before cutting her throat as she positioned herself against a convenient wall in order to earn fourpence from a 'knee-trembler'.

The following day the *Liverpool Echo* published a report stating that coffee stall keeper John Morgan had given a description fitting that of the murdered woman. She had called at his stall, situated a few minutes away from Buck's Row, in the early hours, accompanied by a man whom he recalled she addressed by name. The headline of the article asked: 'Who is Jim?'[1]

Concealed beneath a veneer of wealth and the thriving business of England's capital city there existed a population of close on a million slum-dwellers in London's notorious East End. Murder was no stranger in the dingy back alleys and courts, where men, women and children survived in poverty on filthy streets, separated both spiritually and economically from their more fortunate neighbours.

The residents of Whitechapel grew accustomed to the pungent aromas from the Aldgate slaughterhouses which competed with foul-smelling liquid sewage flooding from cellars and the general corruption rotting on the littered streets. Bad sanitation, poor nutrition and impossible housing conditions contributed to the high mortality rate among East End children, fifty-five per cent of whom died before reaching the age of five.

Some inhabitants tried to make a meagre but honest living, while others were driven to a life of crime and vice. Excessive drinking, a traditional escape from poverty, resulted in a proliferation of drunken brawls, with senseless men and women falling out of the doors of public houses at closing time. Ragged street Arabs mingled by day with pickpockets, cut-throats and prostitutes, sleeping at night in common lodging houses, the age old place of shelter for the impoverished.

Prostitution among the women was rife. It was estimated by the police that in 1888 there were sixty-two working brothels and a street population of 1,200 prostitutes in the Whitechapel area alone. Women sold their bodies through economic necessity: in some cases it was looked on as akin to having a part-time job to supplement low-paid work in sweatshops or when the market for casual labour was flooded; for others it was their primary occupation.

Whitechapel was an area well known to James Maybrick. Bromley Street was where he had met and seduced Sarah Robertson, and he now regularly visited the offices of Gusavus A. Witt, in Cullum Street, whose business he ran. It was a simple matter to catch the train from the station located practically at the bottom of his Liverpool garden; the five-hour journey took him into the very heart of London.

James also visited his brother Michael on many occasions, staying with him at his flat in Wellington Mansions, close to London's Regent's Park. Was James Maybrick a regular client of London prostitutes? He was certainly no stranger to their American cousins when he had resided in Virginia, as Mary Hogwood had confirmed.

The Ripper journal would disclose that the killing of Polly Nichols was the Ripper's second murder; the writer claimed to have strangled a woman in Manchester some time before. This new killing had simply whetted his appetite: 'The bitch opened like a ripe peach,' the journal reflected. 'I have decided next time I will rip all out. My medicine will give me strength . . .'[2]

At 6 a.m. on 8 September, an excited crowd gathered in the back yard of 29 Hanbury Street behind a dilapidated lodging house. The lacerated corpse of forty-seven-year-old Annie Chapman lay on the ground covered by a sack, ready to be removed by the police. Her abdomen had been opened, her uterus removed and her intestines slung over her left shoulder like a bloodied scarf. The murderer had made an unsuccessful attempt to sever her head. At her feet lay part of a torn envelope with the letter 'M' handwritten along one side.

Annie, stout and only five feet tall, was already close to death with a chronic disease of the lungs when she fell into the hands of the Ripper. She only occasionally prostituted herself and mainly worked at selling her own crochet work or hawking matches and flowers. She had picked the envelope up off the floor of her lodging house prior to placing two pills in it before leaving home for the evening. Did the Ripper simply use the convenient 'M' on the envelope to tease the police? The writer of the Ripper journal certainly suggested that this was the case: 'I have left the fools a clue.'[3] He would also claim that he had removed something from the woman's body, and wrote: 'I intend to fry it and eat it later.'[4]

Annie's murder had taken the writer even deeper into a bottomless pit of perversion, occasionally tempered by melancholy. He had a desperate need to repeat his evil crimes. Three weeks later he would prowl the London streets again, and this time it would be a double event, with two murders taking place within three-quarters of an hour of each other.

Driving his horse and cart into Dutfield's Yard in Berner Street at 1 a.m. on Sunday 30 September, Louis Diemschutz was just too late to save the life of Elizabeth Stride. His horse reared in the darkened yard, anticipating an obstruction in its path, and on investigation with his long-handled whip, Diemschutz discovered her warm, blood-soaked body. Only seconds earlier, 'Jack the Ripper' would have been caught in the frenzy of his murderous attack.

Forty-four-year-old Swedish-born Elizabeth Stride had not been saved, but neither had she been mutilated. The murderer would later record in his journal his feelings of panic and relief: 'To my astonishment I cannot believe I have not been caught. My heart felt as if it had left my body. Within my fright I imagined my heart bounding along the street with I in desperation following it . . . I had no time to rip the bitch wide.'[5]

Frustrated by his failed attempt to release his pent-up craving to 'rip', the shadowy figure hurriedly moved on, looking for the opportunity to seize his next victim. With either cunning or knowledge he passed over the border dividing the Metropolitan Police from the City Police and headed for Aldgate High Street.

The residents of Whitechapel were becoming agitated and wary of being out late, but the 'sisters of joy' had to earn a living, and prostitutes nervously continued to walk the streets looking for trade.

The last recorded words of prostitute Catharine Eddowes were 'Good-night old cock'[6] as she was released by an amiable policeman from Bishopsgate Police Station at 1 a.m. She had been arrested earlier in the evening for being drunk and disorderly, having caused a fracas by attempting to imitate a fire engine.

Two days previously, after returning from hop-picking in Kent, Catharine Eddowes was reported to have told the superintendent at the Shoe Lane Workhouse, who knew her well: 'I have come back to earn the reward offered for the apprehension of the Whitechapel murderer. I think I know him.' He warned her to take care that she was not herself murdered. 'Oh, no fear of that'[7] was her reply. Had James Maybrick been a client of Catharine Eddowes?

A man described later in the *Times* as having a fair moustache, being about thirty years old and wearing a cloth cap was seen talking to her thirty-five minutes after her release from the police station. Ten minutes later she was dead.

In a corner of Mitre Square, Catharine's killer carried out an unrestrained and depraved attack. After strangling her and cutting her throat, he proceeded to mutilate her face, cutting eyelids, jaw and lips and partially removing her nose and ears. Below each eye he carved two triangular

'V'-shaped flaps. Observing them upside-down they formed the letter 'M', and the Ripper journal would confirm that that was just what he meant: '. . . had a go at her eyes, left my mark.'[8]

He then turned his attention to her abdomen. Slashing at the intestines and colon, he scooped them into a pile and laid them at her side.

The murder caused confusion within the London police forces. The Metropolitan Police were responsible for all of the city except for one square mile which was under the jurisdiction of the City Police, but both forces were baffled and embarrassed by their unsuccessful attempts to arrest and charge the man who was committing these grisly murders under their very noses.

On 29 September, Scotland Yard received a letter written in red ink and forwarded from the Central News Agency. Dated the 25th and addressed to 'Dear Boss', it taunted the police, describing the Eddowes murder and promising another. It was signed, chillingly, 'Jack the Ripper'.

The mysterious killer, who had hitherto been universally known as the 'Whitechapel Murderer', had impudently rechristened himself, and the Ripper journal would take the credit for it: 'Before I am finished all England will know the name I have given myself. It is indeed a name to remember.'[9]

The newspapers revelled in the gruesome details of the recent bloodshed, describing the crimes graphically with words never seen before in public broadsheets. The Victorian public, fed on a diet of sexual repression since the 1860s, eagerly anticipated each edition as the exciting melodrama unfolded.

There were several descriptions of the suspect reported in various newspapers. The *London Echo* suggested that the wanted man was of education and means, probably about forty years of age, with dark clothes and a dark silk handkerchief around his neck, and likely to be wearing a stiff dark bowler. The *Telegraph* went one better and published an artist's impression of the wanted man.

After the double murder, 80,000 hand-bills were sent out asking for information, followed by a house-to-house investigation. A suspicion began to develop that the murderer was not living in the district of Whitechapel, and perhaps not even in London at all.

On 11 October the *Liverpool Daily Post* ran a report under the heading 'Alleged Liverpool Clue':

> *A certain detective of the Criminal Investigation Department has recently journeyed to Liverpool and there traced the movements of a man, which have been proved somewhat of a mysterious kind.*
>
> *The height of this person and description are fully ascertained and amongst other things he was in possession of a black leather bag. The person suddenly left Liverpool for London and for some time occupied apartments in a well known first class hotel in the West End.*
>
> *He was in the habit of visiting the poorer part of the East End and that he left behind in the hotel his black bag containing certain items of clothing, documents and prints of an obscene description.*[10]

According to the report, the person referred to had possibly landed in Liverpool from America.

The Charing Cross Hotel had not been named in the article, but on 14 June they had advertised in the *Times* an appeal to owners of lost property to claim their belongings. Among the names listed to come forward was the unusual S. E. Mibrac. It has been suggested that if you swap the second and fifth letters the name spells Mabric. Perhaps the owner of the bag, the Liverpool suspect and the writer of the journal were one and the same person.

Several arrests had been made in London, one being that of a Polish Jew nicknamed 'Leather Apron'. John Pizer unfortunately fitted the melodramatic description given by a local woman who said the murderer had a repulsive smile and gleaming eyes. No evidence was found, and Pizer was soon released.

Two nights after the double murder, Police Constable Robert Spicer of the Metropolitan Police claimed he had arrested 'Jack the Ripper' whilst on his beat. He had noticed a man sitting on a wall with blood on his shirt cuffs and talking to a young woman, and took him back to the police station for questioning. The suspect claimed he was a doctor and was quickly released by the CID without his bag ever having been searched. Described as being about five feet nine inches tall and around twelve stone, with a fair moustache, high forehead and rosy cheeks, he wore a high hat and a black suit with a gold watch and chain, and was carrying a brown bag.

Spicer then found himself in trouble for arresting someone who was thought to be a respectable doctor, and the CID allowed him to take no further part in the investigation of the man's story. The officer was said to have been so disappointed that he claimed his heart was no longer in his police work, and in April 1889 he was discharged from the police force for being drunk on duty.

Spicer stood by his story, and even wrote to the *Daily Express* as late as 1931 reiterating his claim. Is it possible that for a short time the police actually had the Whitechapel murderer in their clutches?

It was reported that at the time of the man's arrest the officers at the police station were running about in a state of near panic, and the Ripper journal would reflect: 'They remind me of chickens with their heads cut off running fools with no heads ha ha!'[11] With each episode the Ripper had become more confident, ghoulish and brutal, while the thoughts of the writer of the journal communicated increasing sadistic pleasure and sexual gratification.

In the Ripper journal Florence Maybrick is constantly referred to as a whore, but after the double event she is called 'a whoring mother'. Was this perhaps related to a conversation James had with one Dr Richard Humphreys which confirmed his wife's unfaithfulness? The doctor had been called to Battlecrease House to see Florence, and he later informed James that she had suffered a miscarriage of between four and five months. The husband's response was: 'it could not possibly be mine'.[12]

At the beginning of November, the Ripper vented his anger on his next victim, a turning point which temporarily frightened him back into sanity. It was a most vicious, grotesque and depraved outrage which on reflection shocked even the perpetrator of the deed, or at least the writer of the Ripper journal: 'God forgive me for the deeds I committed on Kelly, no heart, no heart.'[13]

In the early hours of Friday 9 November, on the rain-swept streets of the East End, the dim rays of gas lamps shimmered in deep black pools between the cobbled stones. Over the muted sounds of a hard-working barrel organ and a hearty chorus of late-night revellers, the pure sound of a young woman's voice was heard singing a sentimental Victorian ballad. As the strains drifted on the wind outside 13 Miller's Court, Mary Kelly's shout of 'Murder!' was heard but ignored by two women in the room above her lodgings.

At 10.45 a.m. Thomas Bowyer, an Indian Army pensioner, discovered the mutilated corpse of the twenty-four-year-old prostitute. On looking through the grimy window of Mary Kelly's room when he called to collect the overdue rent, he saw a sight he would take with him to his grave.

It was not until 1.30 p.m. that the police finally entered the room after breaking down the locked door. The victim's clothing had been laid on a chair at the foot of the bed, and other clothes had been burned in the grate. The remains of a woman later confirmed as Mary Jane Kelly lay on the bed wearing the remnants of a chemise. The corner of the sheet was heavily bloodstained and may have covered the face during the attack.

The body had been subjected to a veritable autopsy, with the abdominal cavity emptied of most of the viscera. Kelly's arms and legs were mutilated, her breasts removed and her face hacked beyond recognition.

With frightening detachment, the police surgeon, Dr Thomas Bond, reported to Dr Robert Anderson, head of the Metropolitan Police CID:

The tissues of the neck were severed all round to the bone. The viscera were found in various parts viz; the uterus and kidneys with one breast under the head the other breast by the right foot, the liver between the feet the intestines by the right side and the spleen by the left side of the body. The flaps removed from the abdomen and thighs were on the table . . . The face was gashed in all directions the nose, cheeks, eyebrows and ears being partly removed.[14]

The police took an official photograph of the crime scene, but it would not be until a hundred years later that crime researcher and writer Simon Wood would notice in the photo that written on the wall above the bed there appeared to be two initials. Closer examination discovered that one was the letter 'M', which was clearly visible, while to the left was a letter 'F'. Both were assumed to be written in blood. The killer would chillingly confirm that he had written them himself: 'An initial here and an initial there would tell of the whoring mother.'[15]

Had the Ripper revenged himself on the woman in Miller's Court because he identified her with his young and beautiful wife – the woman who had betrayed him with his own brother? Was this why he carefully covered the victim's face with part of the sheet and leaned across the bloodied corpse to daub his wife's initials on the wall in the dead woman's blood?

The Whitechapel prostitutes had been living in fear of Jack the Ripper, but for some reason the man Mary Jane Kelly invited into her room that evening, and who she was heard entertaining for a number of hours, must have been someone she felt she could trust. Was it because he appeared a gentleman and in her eyes not capable of committing such atrocities?

All went quiet after November 1888. The press continued to sensationalise the Whitechapel murders, convinced that the Ripper would strike again, and the police persevered in their attempts to hunt him down, but the identity of Jack the Ripper would remain undisclosed, and the few months of terror he inspired would become part of English folklore.

Within six months of the last Ripper crime, the press would have another sensational murder to report. This time, James Maybrick was the victim . . .

CHAPTER FIVE

❦

*If you are afraid of loneliness, don't
marry.*

Anton Chekhov, 1860–1904

A thick blanket of fog engulfed Liverpool on
31 December 1888, muffling the distant sound of
foghorns drifting in from the river and dulling a vibrant
chorus of church bells greeting the New Year. Like the
weather, recent events in the Maybrick household would
suggest there would be no agreeable start to 1889. On New
Year's Eve, as the winter fog closed in around Battlecrease
House, Florence wrote indignantly to her mother:

*In his fury he tore up his will this morning, as he had made me sole
legatee and trustee for the children in it. Now he proposes to settle
everything he can on the children alone, allowing me only the
one-third by law! I am sure it matters little to me as long as the*

children are provided for. My own income will do for me alone. A
pleasant way of commencing the New Year![1]

Towards the end of 1888, the Maybricks' relationship had deteriorated rapidly after Florence had miscarried what could have been Edwin's child, and the couple had been living together for the most part in frosty politeness.

The tormented outpourings of the Ripper journal had continued since the last of the Whitechapel killings, and the writer had taken macabre credit for another murder, probably in Manchester. However, the entries were growing fewer and James's thoughts were beginning to drift more towards his wife.

The previous August, Edwin had returned to America on board the SS *Adriatic* and Florence had been casting around for comfort and romance elsewhere. At a ball held at Battlecrease House in November, she found a new and dangerous outlet for her affections with cotton broker Alfred Brierley, a friend and close associate of her husband.

A senior member of the firm Brierley and Wood, Alfred was the son of a wealthy Liverpool family. At thirty-eight, and still a bachelor, the handsome cotton man was considered quite a catch within the Maybrick social circle. Gertrude Janion, Mrs Briggs's spinster sister, had been making sheep's eyes at him for some time, but much to her annoyance it was on Florence that he began bestowing all his attention.

The cotton men of Liverpool were a close-knit community, and gossip was like mother's milk to them. They had watched with interest Florence's romantic attachments to Williams and Edwin Maybrick, and were now speculating on Alfred Brierley becoming her next conquest. On 22 November 1888, Charles

Ratcliffe, a mutual friend of the Maybricks and John Aunspaugh, concluded a business letter to his friend in America with the line: 'I think Alf is getting the inside track with Mrs James' affections.'[2]

His words would be chillingly if somewhat crudely echoed in the Ripper journal: 'The whore is not satisfied with one whore master she now has eyes for another.'[3] It appears that James Maybrick had also noted Florence's preoccupation with the wealthy Liverpool bachelor.

It is unlikely that Maybrick confronted Florence with her new affair. Entries in the Ripper journal about this time suggest that humiliation was an essential ingredient in sharpening the Ripper's sexual appetite and he was secretly delighted at the thought of his wife taking a new lover. Of more immediate importance to him was finding a new and regular supplier of arsenic in order to feed his growing addiction.

In January 1889, in an incredible piece of luck, James met an inventor named Valentine Blake, who was attempting to launch Ramine Grass, a substitute for cotton, on to the British market. Initially interested in its business potential, James invited Blake to the offices of Maybrick & Co. for a meeting. To his delight he discovered that one of the ingredients employed in the manufacture of the product was arsenic, and he admitted to Blake: 'I take it when I can get it, but the doctors won't put any into my medicine except now and then a trifle, that only tantalises me.'[4]

Maybrick asked the inventor to sell him any arsenic he had left over from his experiments, but Blake had no licence to sell drugs and suggested that they should make it a quid pro quo deal. Maybrick promised to do what he could in promoting the venture, and the inventor presented him with 150 grains of arsenic in three separate paper packets. One was white and the other two black.* When handing the packets over, Blake warned: 'Be careful, you have almost enough to kill a regiment.'[5]

James now had an unlimited supply of what he called his 'medicine' and Florence became aware that he was taking a white powder which he prepared himself. Worried about the effect it was having on both his constitution and his temper, which was at times becoming violent, she subsequently wrote a letter to Michael Maybrick informing him that she thought his brother was taking strychnine.

She also confided her concerns to Dr Humphreys, who had been attending the children. He coldly dismissed her worries and added jokingly: 'Well, if he does die suddenly you can say you told me about it!'[6]

The Maybricks' social life had not diminished with marital conflict, and in March 1889 they joined a group of friends at the Palace Hotel in Birkdale for a race meeting. Among the party, which included Alfred Brierley, were some new friends, a recently married young couple, Charles and Christina Samuelson.

During a card party on their last evening together, an argument broke out between the newlyweds and in a fit of temper Christina shouted at her husband, 'I hate you!' Florence turned to Charles in an effort to mediate and said bluntly: 'You must not take a serious note of that, I often say I hate Jim.'[7] This well-intentioned but candid advice would

---

* Arsenic sold by chemists had by law to be mixed with soot or indigo; the black arsenic from Blake was mixed with charcoal.

have far-reaching repercussions for Florence.

It was probably also during this fateful stay at the Palace Hotel that Florence took the opportunity of teasing Alfred Brierley into joining her on a reckless adventure in a London hotel.

On her return home, in an unbelievable piece of brainless mismanagement, Florence proceeded to book rooms for a week at Flatman's Hotel in Henrietta Street under the names of Mr and Mrs Thomas Maybrick of Manchester. Not only was this an establishment where she had stayed previously with her mother, it was also the meeting ground of cotton brokers from all over England and the Continent. It was a foolish and indiscreet move and one that both she and Brierley would live to regret.

Unwisely, Florence contacted the manager of the hotel several times in order to confirm her requirements, even going as far as arranging the menu for an evening meal. Letters and telegrams moved at lightning speed between Flatman's Hotel and Battlecrease House.

After resolving to her satisfaction the tangled maze of arrangements, she then found it necessary to concoct an equally elaborate and complex web of lies in order to cover up her week away in London, and foolishly told three separate stories in order to cover her tracks.

First she told her husband that her godmother, the Countess de Gabriel, who was over in England from Paris, had asked her to accompany her to see Sir James Paget, an eminent surgeon, and that they would be staying at the Grand Hotel. Then, writing to her mother in Paris, she glibly informed the Baroness that she was going for a week's stay in London with Mrs Briggs.

Lastly, in order to get her post forwarded while she was away, she told Alice Yapp that she was staying in the Grand Hotel with her mother.

Two evenings before she journeyed to London, Florence wrote a letter to an old family friend, John Baillie Knight. He had known her since his two maiden aunts had befriended the Baroness and her daughter more than ten years ago in Switzerland, and Florence had since stayed with the family many times, before and after her marriage. She appealed to Baillie Knight to meet her at Flatman's on Thursday 21 March as she wanted his advice. It appears that Florence had more than a secret assignation in mind when she planned her visit to London.

Leaving her two children, who were recovering from whooping cough, to the tender mercies of Nurse Yapp, Florence arrived at Flatman's on the afternoon of 21 March and occupied a bedroom and sitting room in the part of the hotel situated at 9 Chapel Street. At 6.30 p.m. John Baillie Knight duly arrived and they dined together at the Grand Hotel. She confided to him the true purpose of her trip to the capital and asked him to recommend a good solicitor, as she was seeking a separation from James. She had discovered, she said, that her husband had been keeping another woman in Liverpool. He was also cruel and had struck her.

With brotherly concern, Baillie Knight advised her to go to her mother in Paris and gave her the address of London solicitor Markby and Stewart. He then treated her to a trip to the theatre and dropped her off in a cab at Flatman's at 11.30 p.m.

The following afternoon saw the arrival of Alfred Brierley. For some unaccountable reason he and Florence decided to

A very young Florence Chandler, showing the emerging beauty for which she was to become noted. (*Richard Whittington-Egan*)

Florence's mother, the Baroness von Roques: 'I am a silly and absurd little woman, no doubt.' (*Richard Whittington-Egan*)

Florence's birthplace and childhood home, Mobile, Alabama. (*Carol Cain*)

Mobile, Alabama, as it was before the civil war, showing some of the boats in the background on which Florence's mother would go on her scandalous 'moonlight excursions'. (*Carol Cain*)

James Maybrick. A colleague described him as 'one of the straightest, most upright and honourable men I have ever known', but is this in fact the face of the notorious murderer, Jack the Ripper?

The *SS Baltic*, the transatlantic liner on which Florence first met James Maybrick in 1880. (*Stewart Evans*)

Michael Maybrick, James' successful and charismatic brother. What role did he play in the strange events of spring 1889?

Thought to be a photo of Edwin Maybrick, James's youngest brother and business partner. Did Edwin become one of Florence's many lovers? (*John Harrison*)

BATTLECREASE
House
The Residence of the Maybricks at Aigburth, Liverpool.

Battlecrease House – the Maybrick's family home in Liverpool. As the writer of the Ripper journal described it: 'A dark shadow lays over the house, it is evil.'

The Exchange Flags: the cotton trading square in Liverpool. (*Richard Whittington-Egan*)

Florence's lover, Alfred Brierley, who deserted her when she needed him most. (*Richard Whittington-Egan*)

The inscription in the fron of the Bible that James Maybrick gave to his mistress, Sarah Robertso (a.k.a. 'Piggy'), in which he describes himself as h 'husband'. (*Keith Skinner*)

Florence Maybrick, circa 1887, just before her imprisonment. (*John Harrison*)

James Maybrick aged 48, in 1887. The twenty-three year age gap between him and his young wife is clearly visible. (*John Harrison*)

STUART CUMBERLAND'S ILLUSTRATED MIRROR

A REFLECTOR OF PEOPLE, POLITICS, FINANCE, the DRAMA, etc.

No. 15.—One Penny.   LONDON, MONDAY, SEPTEMBER 23, 1889.   [Registered at G.P.O. as a Newspaper

THE GREAT WHITECHAPEL PUZZLE.

Find "Jack the Ripper" and his Knife.

An 1889 newspaper headline, showing the hunt for the Whitechapel murderer in full force. Was he in fact living 200 miles away, in Liverpool?

change their rooms, thereby drawing even more attention to themselves. Their new accommodation consisted of a bedroom and sitting room in the part of the hotel in Henrietta Street. That evening they dined together in the public dining room. The following morning they were seen by the waiter when he arrived with the breakfast.

Although Florence had booked to stay at Flatman's for seven days, the visit was cut short on the Sunday and the couple left the hotel abruptly. Brierley paid the bill of £2 13s. 1d. and told the manager that he had received a telegram from his brother. According to Brierley, he and Florence resolved never to meet again, 'chiefly in consequence of my having repeated to her an avowal of my attachment to another lady.'[8]

Florence would later confess:

He piqued my vanity and resisted my efforts to please him, I told him I was going to London and taunted him with being a coward and afraid to meet me, unwilling to let such a chance slip by. I was however momentarily infatuated. Before we parted he gave me to understand that he cared for somebody else and could not marry me and that rather than face the disgrace of discovery he would blow his brains out. I then had such a revulsion of feeling I said we must end our intimacy at once.[9]

Brierley slunk back to Liverpool determined that the affair had ended, and Florence, no doubt upset and rejected, continued with her visit to the capital. She stayed the rest of the week with Margaret Baillie Knight, the aunt of the friend she had dined with on her first evening in London. Still resolute in her intention of procuring a separation from James, Florence asked Margaret to accompany her on a visit to Markby and Stewart, the solicitors recommended to her. At the dictation of Mr Markby, Florence wrote a letter to James stating that in consequence of his connection with another woman, she could no longer live with him, and going on to suggest that he grant her an annual allowance and that she continue to live in Battlecrease House.

It is not known if she confided her troubles to Michael Maybrick when he escorted her to dinner at the Café Royal on the Monday evening, or what explanation she gave him for her journey to London. However, on the evening before she was due to return to Liverpool, she showed the solicitor's letter to John Baillie Knight, who again took her to dinner and a show. He would later confirm its contents, but he was unable to say whether it was a copy or the original.

Florence at this point appeared determined to ask James for a separation. She must have learned the correct way to go about it either from Mrs Briggs (who had been through the procedure herself) or when she had contacted her American solicitors in 1887. A woman who left her spouse in 1889 was at a decided disadvantage in law. Had Florence simply left James before obtaining a separation, she would have been guilty of desertion and could have lost all rights to maintenance and custody of her children.

Florence returned to Liverpool on the Thursday in order to prepare for one of the prime social events of the sporting calendar, which was taking place the following day. The Aintree Grand National was a pleasant opportunity for the women to parade in new and colourful spring clothes and the men to gamble on the big race. This year was the fiftieth anniversary of the event and was to be particularly favoured by the presence of His Royal Highness the Prince of Wales. James Maybrick had organised an omnibus to leave from outside his office in Tithebarn Street and had invited a number of friends, among whom were the Samuelsons and Alfred Brierley.

During the afternoon Brierley generously bought tickets for the grandstand, from where some of the party watched the big race. The going was good and the day was clear as twenty runners tackled the legendary Beecher's Brook, and the excited crowd cheered enthusiastically in what was the fastest race for sixteen years. Frigate won at 8–1, Why Not came second at 100–9 and MP third at 20–1.*

Whatever feelings of revulsion Florence had felt for Brierley after his suicide threat and their abrupt departure from Flatman's Hotel had obviously evaporated. Tripping gaily arm in arm with him, she returned to the omnibus to be met by an angry, red-faced husband on the point of apoplexy. He reproved her in front of their friends, and turning to Mrs Samuelson, Florence hissed angrily: 'I will give it him hot and heavy for speaking to me like that in public.'[10]

Burning with indignation, Florence returned home at about seven o'clock, closely followed by her angry husband. A violent argument soon ensued, witnessed by the servants. James was heard shouting from the bedroom, 'Such a scandal will be all over the town tomorrow,' and, 'Florrie, I never thought you could come to this.'[11] Had Florence, resentful

---

* His Royal Highness the Prince of Wales had two horses running: the first, Magic, at 25–1 came fifth, and Hettie, an outsider at 66–1, fell.

about being reproved in public, taken the opportunity to thrust the solicitor's letter at him?

Elizabeth Humphreys, the Maybricks' cook, would give a colourful eye-witness account of the proceedings:

> *It began in the bedroom, Mr Maybrick sent Bessie Brierley [the housemaid] for a cab to send his wife away. She came downstairs into the hall to go to the cab, he followed her and raved and stamped like a madman, waving his pocket handkerchief over his head.*
>
> *The button holes of Mrs Maybrick's dress were torn with the way he had pulled her about. She had on a fur cape he told her to take it off as she was not to go away with that on as he had bought it for her to go up to London in.*[12]

Flying to her mistress's aid, the kindly cook pleaded with James: 'Oh master please don't go on like this, the neighbours will hear you.' But James, in no mood to be told what to do by one of his servants, shouted: 'Leave me alone, you don't know anything about it.'[13]

Undaunted, the cook begged him not to send Florence away that evening as she had nowhere to go. James, suddenly regretting his bravado, did a comic about-turn and threatened, 'By heavens Florie, be careful. Once you go through this door you shall not enter the house any more.'[14] He then fell dramatically across an oak settle in the hall and went quite stiff. Cook Humphreys did not know if he was drunk or in a fit, but she used the opportunity to send the cab away.

Alice Yapp put her arm around her mistress's waist and coaxed her back up the stairs, saying, 'Come up and see the children.'[15] She then made up a bed in the dressing room, and Maybrick petulantly spent the remainder of the night in the dining room after Alice told him that Florence had gone to bed.

The following morning, sporting a black eye, Florence went to Mrs Briggs complaining of her husband's cruelty and the two women went to see Mr Donaldson, the solicitor who had arranged Mrs Briggs's own separation.

They then went on to see Dr Hopper. Florence told him she could not bear her husband to come near her, and that she did not care to have any more babies. Although Hopper was aware of this, as James had previously complained to him of his wife's coldness, he was shocked at the suggestion of a separation and tried to persuade her against such a course. Later that day he took it upon himself to go to Battlecrease House in order to mediate between the warring couple:

When I went to the house the same day Mr Maybrick told me that his wife had gone off with a man on the course yesterday contrary to his expressed wish. That he had afterwards reproved her in public and that she had cut up rough. That they had a further quarrel in the evening and that he had struck her.* He seemed to want to be reconciled and I sent him to fetch Mrs Maybrick in.

He brought her in and then repeated in her presence what he had previously accused her of. She said that he was absurdly jealous and that he had cross-questioned her about her visit to London, but I persuaded them both and they agreed to be reconciled. She had

---

* Although Hopper was told about Florence flirting with Brierley on the racecourse, he apparently was not told about the letter proposing a separation.

> *also told me when we were alone that there was an obstacle to a*
> *reconciliation viz debts, Mr Maybrick agreed to pay all her debts*
> *whatever they might be.*[16]

Satisfied with his efforts to pacify the unhappy couple, Hopper
was unaware that the following day Mrs Briggs would come to
stay and would be the cause of a further argument. Again it was
the cook who graphically described the whole affair after James
demanded that Florence come down from her bedroom:
'There was some quarrelling and shouting and Mr Maybrick
and Mrs Briggs appeared to have both been very much excited.
Mrs Maybrick said something about never having invited anyone to the house without Mr Maybrick's knowledge and then
she went upstairs again.'[17]

At six o'clock Mary Cadwallader, the waitress, went to her
mistress's bedroom to take her up a cup of tea and found that
Florence had fainted. The waitress and the cook hurried for
James, and both he and Mrs Briggs rushed upstairs. According
to the cook, James Maybrick suddenly became very affectionate, crying out, 'Bunny, Bunny,* here's your hubby,'[18] and
dispatched a servant for Dr Humphreys, who lived locally.

It was two hours before Florence recovered consciousness,
and all in the household thought her dead. Dr Humphreys
travelled backwards and forwards four or five times during the
night; as soon as he went away, the panic-stricken husband
sent for him again.

Mrs Briggs made repeated visits to the kitchen for beer, as

---

* He called his wife Bunny and his mistress Piggy – did James look on all
  women as animals?

80

'she was put out about the quarrel and must have something to keep her up.'[19] At about 9 p.m. she was unsteady on her feet and half undressed, having put on a gown of Florence's which was much too small for her. She was standing in this condition when Dr Humphreys snapped at one of the servants, 'Who is that woman?'[20]

The following day, yet another catastrophe would follow for Florence as a repercussion of her London visit. James intercepted a letter from his mother-in-law written half in French and half in English. The Baroness had written: 'I cannot understand your movements in London. I thought you were with Mrs Briggs. It was ridiculous having your letters addressed to the Grand when you were not there. Your conduct has been indiscreet, but I cannot believe you have done wrong.'[21] This time Dr Hopper was called, and found Florence in bed indulging in a fit of hysteria.

Florence somehow managed a glib explanation about her godmother dining at the Grand and living in lodgings. Both men appeared to believe her, and the three of them went on to discuss the reconciliation, with James promising to pay the debts his wife had run up with two money-lenders. By the time an exhausted Dr Hopper left the house, it appears peace had once again been restored.

When Florence and Brierley had parted at Flatman's Hotel they had undertaken not to meet again except in public unless she had problems associated with the trip. Although apparently now reconciled with James, after a week of being confined to bed suffering from nervous prostration Florence made a clandestine trip to Brierley's lodgings on 6 April.

Was Florence really reunited with James, or did she have her own reasons for feigning the reconciliation? Future events would suggest that she was still infatuated with Brierley and wanted to run away with him. She had, however, now realised she was pregnant again and was sleeping with her husband in order to provide the child with a legitimate father should Brierley not come up to scratch.

A week later, Florence called to see Dr Hopper at his surgery and complained to him that she was 'not right internally', which was probably a delicate way of referring to the fact that she thought she was pregnant. Unfortunately, Dr Hopper was in a hurry and couldn't examine her, and he suggested she see another doctor, but whether she did or didn't is not known.

In blissful ignorance of his wife's continual problems, well aware of the Flatman's affair but content with the apparent restored harmony in their married life, James embarked on a trip to London in order to pay his wife's debts. It must have come as a severe shock to discover that Florence had been borrowing from a money-lender at an interest rate of sixty per cent.

Justifiably worried about his health after a lifetime of abuse, James was also taking the opportunity of making a long-promised appointment with Michael's London doctor, Charles Fuller. While he was away, Florence received two letters, one from Knightly, the money-lender, requesting the payment of her debt, and the other from her recent hostess, Margaret Baillie Knight.

The latter had uncovered inconsistencies in Florence's movements in London and had become considerably worried when letters continued to arrive at her house after Florence had returned home. Concerned for her welfare, she had written to the Baroness and then made enquiries at the Grand Hotel, only to discover that Florence had never stayed there. Displeased with her young friend, the elderly lady ended her letter with a genteel scold:

> *The forwarding of the letters was quite an innocent thing. When you were with your friend it did not matter where you were living, but you expressly stated it was at the Grand Hotel, and this want of accuracy you see misled us. We are plain people and accustomed to believe what is told us.*[22]

Frightened of further revelations and desperately trying to keep control of an ever-worsening situation, Florence sat down and wrote a feeble, guilt-ridden letter of apology to her husband, a further insight into the child-like and naïve side of her nature:

> *My Own Darling Hubby,*
>
> *The enclosed letter has come this morning from Mr Knightly, nothing from Mr Shore who may be out of town also.*
>
> *I have had a terrible night of it and try as hard as I will to be brave and courageous because Jim thinks I may yet be of comfort to him and the . . . of my physical weakness overcomes what remains of my mental strength.*
>
> *I have not sufficient self-respect left to lift me above the depth of disgrace to which I have fallen. For now that I am down I can judge better how very far above me others must be morally.*
>
> *I despair of ever reaching that standard again, although I may receive some of your confidence by living a life of atonement for yours and the children's sakes alone. Nothing you can say can*

make me look at my actions but in the most degrading light, and the more you impress the enormity of my crimes upon me the more hopeless I feel of ever regaining my position.

I feel as though for the future I must be an eye sore and a perpetual reminder of your troubles and that nothing can efface the past from your memory. My agony of mind last night was just awful and as I promised Jimmy not to take chloral I did not, but I took some lavender instead or bromide, I don't know which or I would have gone mad.

Please darling put me out of my pain as soon as you can. I have deceived and nearly ruined you, but since you wish me to live, tell me the worst at once and let it be over.

Has Blucher [Michael Maybrick] refused his help and have you been able to settle satisfactory with Knightly and Shore? Are the shares safe and what time will you be home?

Darling try and be as lenient towards me as you can. For notwithstanding all your generous and tender loving kindness, my burden is almost more than I can bear. My remorse and self contempt is eating my heart out and if I did not believe my love for you and my dutifulness may prove some slight atonement for the past I should give up the struggle to keep brave.

Forgive me if you can dearest and think less poorly of your own wifey.

Bunny

The children are well. I have been nowhere and seen no one.[23]

While in London James had lodged with his brother Michael at his luxurious Regent's Park flat, and it was there that he had consulted with Dr Fuller. He complained to him of pains in his head and numbness in his hands and legs, and also confessed that he was apprehensive of being paralysed. However, he did not disclose to the doctor his increasing reliance on dangerous medicines.

Fuller listened gravely and after an examination lasting an hour assured him that there was very little wrong with him apart from indigestion. Maybrick returned to Liverpool feeling more cheerful, contentedly clutching a handful of prescriptions the doctor had written up. The medicine was little more than a placebo, consisting of an aperient and a tonic with liver pills. He returned to London the following week to consult Fuller again. The doctor was pleased with his progress and reduced the prescriptions.

The atmosphere on the whole was now much more pleasant at Battlecrease House, and it was beginning to be reflected in the entries in the Ripper journal. The passionate, angry scrawl of the previous months had become more restrained, and the writer was much calmer in word and deed.

Overcome with remorse, and desperately trying to understand his hellish actions, his pen now reflected his new-found feelings for the woman James had always really loved. Florence, who in previous pages had always been referred to as 'the whore', was now transformed to 'my dear Bunny'. The writer also made a pathetic attempt in a mawkish outpouring of verse to justify to himself his reasons for creating the terror in the East End:

> *tis love that I yearn for*
> *tis love that she spurned*
> *tis love that will finish me*
> *tis love that I regret* [24]

Two important developments now happened over a short period of time. On 25 April Edwin Maybrick returned from America; and on the same day James hurriedly redrafted his will:

> *Liverpool 25th April 1889. In case I die before having made a regular and proper will in legal form, I wish this to be taken as my last will and testament.*
>
> *I leave and bequeath all my worldly possessions, of whatever kind or description, including furniture, pictures, wines, linen and plate, Life Insurances, cash, shares, property, in fact everything I possess in trust with my Brothers Michael Maybrick and Thomas Maybrick, for my two children James Chandler Maybrick and Gladys Evelyn Maybrick. The furniture I desire to remain intact and to be used in furnishing a home which can be shared by my widow and children, but the furniture is to be the children's. I further desire that all moneys be invested in the names of the above Trustees (Michael and Thomas Maybrick) and the income of same used for the children's benefit and education such education to be left to the discretion of said Trustees.*
>
> *My widow will have for her portion of my Estate the policies on my life, say £500 with the Scottish Widows' Fund and £2000 with the Mutual Reserve Fund Life Association of New York, both Policies being made out in her name. The interest on this £2,500 together with the £125 a year which she receives from her New York property will make a provision of about £125* a year, a sum although small will yet be the means of keeping her respectably.*

* He obviously wrote this in such a hurry he never added the interest to the £125 income from the New York property.

> *It is also my desire that my Widow shall live under the same roof with the children so long as she remains my Widow.*
>
> *If it is legally possible I wish the £2,500 of Life Insurance on my life in my wife's name to be invested in the names of the said Trustees, but that she should have the sole use of the interest thereof during her lifetime, but at her death the principal to revert to my said Children, James Chandler and Gladys Evelyn Maybrick . . .*[25]

Whatever possessed James Maybrick to draft this terrible will, cutting Florence off without a penny and treating her with such contempt and condescension when he was apparently reconciled with her? Everything he owns is handed over to Michael and Thomas Maybrick, lock, stock and barrel, including the couple's two children. There is no provision in the will which could secure for his son and daughter even the expense of an education if Michael and Thomas did not desire it, or any suggestion of an inheritance when they come of age. There are no covenants as to how the children are to be brought up except at the discretion of the two trustees, who, if they wished, could spend all the money and send the children out to earn their living as chimney sweeps.

As for his widow, he treats her almost with mockery, even denying her motherhood by referring to their son and daughter as 'my two children'. He graciously allows Florence to live under the same roof as the children, but only for so long as she remains his widow. However, when the children are grown, apparently she is to be made homeless without so much as a blanket and a knife and fork. Not only is Florence robbed of her guardianship and her third of the estate required by law, but he even tries to give to his brothers the life insurance that is legally hers.

It had been four months since James had torn up his previous will. Is it significant that he drafted the new one only three days after he had returned from completing the payment of his wife's debts in London? In her letter to James, Florence referred to 'shares' and asked: 'Has Blucher refused his help?' It appears that James's money was tied up in investments and that he intended asking Michael to advance him a loan in order to settle with Knightly and Shore. Dr Hopper had been told that Florence owed something in the region of £1,200, a considerable amount.

Had Michael subsequently lectured James on Florence, convincing him that she was too irresponsible to be trusted with the children's future? Was the new will the price James had to pay to Michael for getting him out of financial hot water and settling Florence's debts?

Towards the end of April, within a week of Edwin's return and the drafting of the infamous will, Florence twice purchased a number of fly-papers, remarking to the chemist that flies had been troublesome in the kitchen. Some time later a curious housemaid made a strange discovery. Lifting a towel covering the washstand in the Maybrick bedroom, she discovered a number of arsenic-coated fly-papers soaking in a bowl.

CHAPTER SIX

❦

*Depend upon it, sir, some circumstantial
evidence is very strong, as when you find
a trout in the milk.*

Henry David Thoreau, 1817–62

On 26 April 1889, four days after James Maybrick had
returned from London, a mysterious parcel of medicine
postmarked London was delivered to Battlecrease House.
Mary Cadwallader, the waitress, handed the small pasteboard
box to her master shortly after it arrived.

The following morning James Maybrick looked grey and ill,
and the cook would recall that he was sick before leaving for
the office. Florence told Nurse Yapp and the housemaid that
her husband had taken an overdose of the London medicine
and was in great pain. She subsequently threw the remains of
the package down the sink.

On his arrival at his office, James took morbid delight in

relating to his clerk, George Smith, a strange experience he had suffered that morning: 'He said that he had taken an overdose of medicine and there was strychnine in it, that he was on the WC for an hour and all his limbs were stiff and he could not move.'[1]

Recovering slightly in the afternoon, James attended the Wirral Races on horseback. William Thomson, a friend who spoke to him on the racecourse, remarked, 'You don't seem to be able to keep your horse.' James complained to him of not feeling well and admitted that he had 'taken a double dose that morning'.[2]

At one point in the afternoon the weather changed suddenly and the spectators were caught in a violent storm. James stayed at the race meeting, but by the time he arrived for dinner at his friend Hobson's house he was soaked to the skin. The following day, after a disturbed night's sleep, he felt quite ill and Florence, who assumed he had drunk too much the evening before, gave him an emetic and called the doctor. 'Do take this mustard and water,' she was overheard saying. 'It will remove the brandy and make you sick again if nothing else.'[3]

By the time Dr Humphreys eventually arrived at 11 a.m., Maybrick was complaining of palpitations in his heart and had convinced himself that he was on the verge of paralysis.

Although Dr Humphreys had visited Battlecrease many times in the past, he had never attended James as a patient. On previous occasions he had taken care of Florence or the children and he was not familiar with Maybrick's constitution, his degree of hypochondria or his appetite for poisonous medicines.

James complained to Humphreys of feeling in a dazed condition when at the races the previous day, and claimed that afterwards, when dining with a friend, his hands were unsteady and he upset some wine and was greatly distressed lest his friend would think he was drunk. He never disclosed to Humphreys his previous day's overdose of the London medicine containing strychnine and convinced the doctor that his symptoms were due to a strong cup of tea he had taken in the morning.

Humphreys prescribed some dilute prussic acid and advised James to drink nothing but soda water and milk that day. Over the following few days he visited his patient on a number of occasions, consequently coming to the conclusion that Maybrick was an acute dyspeptic and advising him on a new diet.

Although James's condition appeared to improve over the next few days, he took great pains to describe his symptoms in a long letter to his brother Michael on 29 April:

My Dear Blucher,

I have been very very seedy indeed. On Saturday morning I found my legs getting stiff and useless, but by sheer strength of will shook off the feeling and went down on horseback to Wirral Races and dined with the Hobsons.

Yesterday morning I felt more like dying than living so much so that Florry called in another Doctor who said it was an acute attack of indigestion and gave me something to relieve the alarming symptoms, so all went well until about 8 o'clock I went to bed and had lain there an hour by myself and was reading on my back.

Many times I felt a twitching but took little notice of it thinking *it would pass away. But instead of doing so I got worse and worse and in trying to move round to ring the bell I found I could not do so but finally managed it, but by the time Florry and Edwin could get upstairs, was stiff and for five mortal hours my legs were like bars of tin stacked out to the fullest extent, but as rigid as steel.**

The Doctor came finally again but could not make it indigestion this time and the conclusion he came to was the Nuxvomica I had been taking. Dr Fuller had poisoned me as all the symptoms warranted such a conclusion I know I am today sore from head to foot and layed out completely . . .[4]

The mild tonic Fuller had prescribed for James on his recent visit to London had indeed contained nux vomica, which in turn contained strychnine and brucine, a mild stimulant. But this medicine, like the others prescribed by Fuller, had been made up for James by the chemist Clay and Abrahams on his return to Liverpool and was not the mysterious medicine containing strychnine to which James ascribed his symptoms after taking an overdose of it on the morning of 27 April.

Was James under the impression that Fuller had sent him more nux vomica by post? Fuller would later confirm that the only medicine he had prescribed to James had been in the Liverpool prescriptions. But if Fuller had not sent him the mysterious parcel of medicine, which had undoubtedly contained a dangerous dose of strychnine, who had?

During his conversation with the London doctor, James had been asked if he had been taking any other medicine.

---

* James was correct when he complained to George Smith that his illness was the result of ingesting an overdose of strychnine, as muscular twitchings and stiffening of the knees are classic symptoms.

After his patient's death, Fuller would report: 'He told me he had been taking a pill which he said I had prescribed for his brother [Michael]. This however, was not the case. I had not prescribed it.'[5] Fuller examined the pills superficially at the time, identifying them as a herbal recipe containing powdered rhubarb, extract of aloes and extract of camomile flowers. But did they also contain an ingredient of which the doctor was not aware?

Friends on the Exchange would say later that James had been seen taking some pills around this time, and that they had made him ill. Why had Michael Maybrick been feeding his brother pills, and why had he lied to him as to their origin? And what of the mysterious parcel? Who else but Michael could have sent it from London and given James the impression that it had been prescribed by Fuller?

The life James had been leading, with its increasing reliance on drugs, had been a thorn in Michael's flesh for many a long year. There was also his expensive and frivolous wife and her tortuous mismanagement of money, and Sarah Robertson, with her brood of illegitimate children. James was a scandal just waiting to break. Had Michael also recently learned of his brother's involvement in the recent horrors in Whitechapel? The writer of the Ripper journal thought so: 'George* knows of my habit and I trust soon it will come to the attention of Michael. In truth I believe he is aware of the fact.'[6] Had Michael, in 1889 at the peak of his career, decided that James was a luxury he could no longer afford? Had James also played right into his hands by redrafting his will and making over everything he owned to his brothers?

---

* 'George' was George Davidson, James Maybrick's best friend in Liverpool.

The letter to Michael of 29 April had continued: 'What is the matter with me? None of the doctors can make out and I suppose never will, until I am stretched out and cold and then future generations may profit by it if they hold a post-mortem which I am quite willing that they should do . . .'[7]

While James lay in bed dreaming grimly of furthering the cause of medical science, Florence had briefly consigned her troubles to oblivion and was enthusiastically getting ready for a masked ball which was being held in Wavertree the following evening. With James too ill to attend, Florence had begged him to allow Edwin to be her escort for the evening, and was now determined to be the belle of the ball. She had been preparing for the event for days and had happily written to her mother to ask her advice on her costume:

> *We are asked to a 'bal masque' which, being given in Liverpool and the people provincials, I hardly think likely to be a success. A certain amount of 'diablerie', wit and life is always required at an entertainment of this sort; and as it will be quite a novel innovation people will hardly know what is expected of them.*
>
> *However, we are requested to come in 'dominoes and masks', and I should like to know how the former is made and if the latter are not procurable in gauze instead of papier mache. I think I read something of the kind in an article about the 'bal masque' at the opera in Paris.*[8]

With her costume arrangements completed, Florence found it necessary to make one further preparation before the night of the ball. Besides all her other woes, she had been horrified to discover that her face had broken out in spots and intended giving herself a medicinal face-wash. Having been unable to find a prescription which she had been given years before by a New York doctor, Florence listed the ingredients she could remember and subsequently made a purchase of tincture of benzoin and elderflowers.* One ingredient she had already prepared, some days before. This was the liquid remaining after she had soaked the fly-papers, hopefully now containing enough arsenic to complete the mixture.

The 'bal masque' was apparently a great success and Florence and Edwin merrily danced the night away, returning to Battlecrease in the early hours. As this was only the fifth day since Edwin's return to England, it may also have been the first opportunity the couple had had to discuss their future behaviour. It appears unlikely, however, that Florence would have disclosed to him her ongoing and increasingly tangled affair with Alfred Brierley.

The morning after the ball, James appeared to be feeling a little better and departed for the office. Some time later, Edwin followed after picking up a parcel from Florence containing a jug of liquid food which James intended to warm up for his lunch. After eating it he felt ill and complained to Edwin that the cook had added sherry to it. 'She knows I don't like it,'[9] he grumbled.

In the office that afternoon the Maybrick brothers were joined by an old friend from Norfolk, Virginia, Captain Irving of the White Star Line. He would remember James taking a

---

* Both are herbal recipes. Elderflowers, from the elder plant (sambucus nigra), soften the complexion and are helpful as a skin cleanser. Benzoin, which comes from the plant styrax (styracaceae), relieves skin problems. Arsenic was used as a face-wash and for removing unwanted hair.

small packet from his pocket, mixing the contents in a glass of water and drinking it down.

Irving joined the Maybricks for dinner that evening at Battlecrease House, and in a private conversation with Edwin some time afterwards he asked, puzzled: 'What on earth is the matter with Jim?' Edwin replied: 'Oh, he's killing himself with that damned strychnine.'[10]

Two days later, on 3 May, James visited his office for what would be the last time. This would also coincide with the final entry in the Ripper journal, perhaps written in his den before he left the house at 11 a.m. The emphasis of the last few entries had changed dramatically. The author no longer appeared to be writing for his own gratification and had developed a style reflecting that of a badly written Victorian novel. It appears that Jack the Ripper was now writing for an audience:

> *I pray whoever should read this will find it in their heart to forgive me. Remind all, whoever you may be, that I was once a gentle man. May the good lord have mercy on my soul, and forgive me for all I have done.*
>
> *I give my name that all know of me, so history do tell, what love can do to a gentle man born.*
>
> *Yours truly*
> *Jack the Ripper.*
> *Dated this third day of May 1889.*[11]

The writer, apparently reconciled to the prospect of death, had previously admitted that 'Bunny knows all'.[12] Had James really confessed to his wife his atrocious crimes, and had she in turn told her lover? Or, what is more likely and is suggested by the evidence, did Florence tell Brierley, but, on reflection, decide that the father of her children could not possibly be Jack the Ripper and refuse to believe it herself, reassuring her lover: 'The tale he told me was pure fabrication and only intended to frighten the truth out of me . . . You need not therefore go abroad on this account . . .'?[13]

On the other hand, was this just part of the author's dramatic story-telling, what he wanted his future readers to believe? One more important question would also remain: what had he done with the journal? Was it still locked up in the tin box in his den?

After a visit to a Turkish bath in the afternoon of 3 May, James returned home feeling very ill, and at midnight Florence called in Dr Humphreys, who found his patient suffering a gnawing pain from his hips to his knees. He was told that James had been sick twice during the day, and administered a morphia suppository.

The following day James was unable to retain food in his stomach, and the doctor advised him not to take any fluids, suggesting that he suck ice or a damp cloth to abate his thirst.

Florence was certainly behaving in a very strange and muddle-headed way during this time. She had managed to entangle herself in a further complicated deception with Alfred Brierley. Convincing him that she had left her husband, who was supposedly making enquiries to discover the name of the hotel they had stayed in together in London, she advised her now terrified lover to write to her via her London friend John Baillie Knight. He duly replied on 4 May, a fateful letter which she hid away in her dressing table:

I suppose now you have gone I am safe in writing to you. I don't quite understand what you mean in your last about explaining my line of action. You know I could not write, and was willing to meet you although it would have been very dangerous. Most certainly your telegram yesterday was a staggerer,* and it looks as though the result was certain, but as yet I cannot find an advertisement in any London papers.

I should like to see you, but at present dare not move, and we had better not meet until late in the Autumn. I am going to try and get away in about a fortnight and think I should take a round trip to the Mediterranean, which will take six or seven weeks, unless you wish me to stay in England.

Supposing the rooms are found, I think both you and I would be better away as the man's memory would be doubted after three months. I will write and tell you when I go. I cannot trust myself at present to write about my feelings on this unhappy business, but I do hope that sometime hence I shall be able to show you that I do not quite deserve the strictures contained in your last two letters.

I went to the D and D and of course heard some tales, but myself knew nothing about anything. And now dear, goodbye, hoping we shall meet again in the autumn. I will write to you about sending letters just before I go.[14]

After convincing Brierley that she had left James, she realised she had pushed him too far and was now forced into a further lie to make him believe that she had returned. With the perfect

---

* What was said in the telegram Brierley described as a 'staggerer' has never been discovered, but it seems likely that Florence told him that James had been trying to discover the rooms they had stayed at in London. James, however, had been doing no such thing.

excuse that James was ill, she immediately dispatched another telegram: 'Recalled owing to May's critical state, name of street now known, have secured Henrietta's* silence, but left John to provided [*sic*] against further contingencies.'[15]

Meanwhile, in London, John Baillie Knight had become rather annoyed about being used as a go-between, and he wrote to Florence remonstrating with her about her actions and what he knew about the London affair:

At last I am glad to find you tell me to write fully. I have of course been afraid to do so before both for your sake and my own. In consequence I have had to submit without being able to reply to several rather censorious letters.

You certainly did make a mess of it when you were last in London, and really it was quite unnecessary and still worse most impolite to tell so many fibs; when one gets into the meshes of these the least contretemps is quite enough to spoil everything. I told my aunts the truth as it seemed to me at the time the best thing to do. I said we dined at the Grand Hotel, went to the Gaiety and came home in a cab, they were very unhappy about you thinking all sorts of absurd things and they were distinctly relieved to find things were as I said.

But the worst of it is you told them a long story about dining with friends etc., and I think there will be some difficulty about your reception at their house again. Aunt M, after the return of the letters also wrote to your mother in Paris, who replied that you had been staying with friends in London.

I forgot to say my aunts also discovered that you did not stay at

* Flatman's Hotel stood partly in Henrietta Street.

the Grand. Your mother has also written to me once or twice for
information about you to which letters I have replied to the best of
my ability. I have a great admiration for your mother's sagacity, she
understands things very quickly.

And now once and for all, I am not going to be led into telling
any more lies or doing any underhand or dangerous missions. I am
quite in the dark now as to what all this mystery is for. And am I
to receive letters for you? Why cannot they be sent to your own house
now? I am obliged to speak what I think because I am tired of all
this scheming which only seems to me to endanger your reputation at
a most critical time and not to serve any further end. If I could see
that I was serving your interests in any way I should not perhaps
speak as strongly. Besides I have my own interests to think of and
though I daresay you will think me very selfish, I shall take the
utmost care of them . . . I should be glad to have a long letter from
you in reply to this, but I will stand no abuse remember . . .[16]

Under increasing mental pressure, and juggling with the web
of intrigue she had tied herself into with Alfred Brierley,
Florence dutifully continued to nurse James. Whether she
loved him or not, she appeared to be solicitously tending him
on his sick-bed.

On Sunday 5 May, Dr Humphreys attended his patient,
whose condition had fluctuated day by day. He advised him
again not to take any fluids except for a little iced water. Cook
Humphreys entered the sick-room and insisted on making
James some lemonade, but Florence, strictly following the
doctor's orders, refused to allow him to drink it. The cook
remembered: 'He looked very wistfully after the glass.'[17]

Edwin, on the other hand, thought little of the doctor's

instructions, and after giving his brother some medicine, encouraged him to drink a brandy and soda. The patient was promptly sick.

By Tuesday Florence had become increasingly concerned about her husband's condition, and she telegraphed Edwin to send for another doctor. Edwin initially attempted to arrange for his friend Dr McCheane, a well-known consultant, to attend his brother. However, McCheane was seriously ill and recommended his colleague, Dr William Carter, a respected Liverpool toxicologist.

Had Edwin also told Dr McCheane that James was 'killing himself with that damn strychnine', as he had confided to Captain Irving? Was this why the doctor had recommended the services of Dr Carter, a specialist in cases of poisoning?

Carter received a telephone call at the Royal Southern Hospital at 3.30 in the afternoon requesting that he attend Battlecrease House that evening in order to consult with Dr Humphreys. He arrived at 5.30, and as he entered the house a storm which had been gathering for some time broke with great violence. A portent of things to come, perhaps?

As the wind and rain crashed against the bedroom window and thunder rumbled in the background, Carter, with Dr Humphreys present, examined his patient for the first time. James appeared restless during the examination and groaned that his mouth was 'as foul as a midden'.[18] He also complained of vomiting, and of extreme dryness and irritability in his throat, which Dr Carter noticed was red and inflamed.

Carter enquired as to Maybrick's 'habits of life', and from the information received from Edwin came to the conclusion that his patient was suffering from acute dyspepsia, caused by a grave error of diet while away from home. He prescribed a careful diet and small doses of antipyrin and tincture of jaborandi. For reasons best known to himself, Edwin failed to mention to either of the two doctors that his brother regularly took strychnine.

On the morning of the following day, two uninvited visitors arrived at Battlecrease House. Mrs Briggs, accompanied by her sister Mrs Hughes, had been alerted by a telegram from Michael Maybrick, who, aware of his brother's illness, had asked her to visit James. Why Michael, with his brother Edwin practically living at Battlecrease House, should find it necessary to telegraph for information to a woman he hardly knew would never be explained.

Alice Yapp excitedly met the two women in the garden and beckoned them across the lawn, reportedly saying: 'Thank God Mrs Briggs you have come for the mistress is poisoning the master. For goodness' sake go and see him for yourselves.'[19] She then went on to tell them about the discovery of the fly-papers, and suggested that Mrs Maybrick had tampered with her husband's food.

Both women claimed to be so astounded by what Yapp had suggested that they tiptoed up the back stairs to see James for themselves. However, Florence, who had been entertaining her friend Mrs Kennah in the morning room, heard their arrival and followed them up. Confronting the women angrily in the bedroom, she told them that they had no right to be there and demanded they go downstairs immediately.

Mrs Briggs advised Florence in no uncertain terms that in her considered opinion James was seriously ill, and suggested that she telegraph for a nurse. She did not know that Dr Humphreys, at Florence's request, had that morning telegraphed for Mrs Howie, the nurse who had previously looked after Florence in her confinements.

Florence, however, was terrified at the older woman's prognosis, and she allowed Mrs Briggs to send a telegram to the Nurses' Institute. She was not aware that Mrs Briggs had taken the opportunity to dispatch a dramatic message to Michael Maybrick, declaring: 'Come at once strange things going on here.'[20]

In the afternoon of the same day, a professional nurse arrived from the Nurses' Institute. Four years previously, Ellen Ann Gore had completed her one-year training at the Liverpool Royal Infirmary and was now engaged on private nursing duties based at the Dover Street institute. She was a pale, thin, ghostly-looking woman who, in her severe nurse's uniform, appeared older than her twenty-seven years. Florence found her rather intimidating, unlike the comfortable Mrs Howie, and complained that on their first meeting, 'She was so long in changing her clothes, and he seemed so much worse that I went in several times and asked her to hurry.'[21]

Nurse Gore, like Mrs Briggs, thought her patient very ill, and her first words to Florence were: 'Yes, he is very ill, he is almost pulseless.'[22]

As the concerned wife left the sick-room, Edwin Maybrick instructed the hospital nurse that she was now in sole charge of the patient, promising her that he would arrange for another nurse to assist her as soon as possible. It is unlikely that Edwin was suggesting at this time that Florence was the cause of James's illness. He was probably under the impression that she was too tired and not capable of continuing with much more of the nursing.

After visiting the Dover Street institute to make the necessary nursing arrangements, Edwin went to see Dr Carter and asked him what he thought of his brother's condition. Once again, Edwin neglected to mention anything about his brother taking strychnine, although it was a perfect opportunity, and Carter advised him that although James was very ill, he trusted that he would make a full recovery.

Meanwhile, at Battlecrease House Elizabeth Humphreys, the cook, was concerned for her mistress and told Florence that she was looking worn and tired. Jaded and dispirited, but completely unaware of the suspicions and ill-natured gossip of Mrs Briggs and the servants, Florence took the opportunity to write a hurried letter to her lover. Full of exaggerations and inconsistencies, it was a desperate attempt to stop him leaving the country:

Your letter undercover to John K came to hand just after I had written to you on Monday. I did not expect to hear from you so soon and delayed in giving him the necessary instructions. Since my return I have been nursing M day and night. He is sick unto death. The doctors held a consultation yesterday and now all depends on how long his strength will hold out.

Both my brothers-in-law are here and we are terribly anxious.* I cannot answer your letter fully today my darling, but relieve your mind of all fear of discovery now and for the future. M has been

---

* Only one brother-in-law was at the house. Michael did not arrive until later in the evening, Thomas was in Manchester and William had not been seen by the family for years.

delirious since Sunday and I now know that he is perfectly ignorant
of anything even to the name of the street, and also that he has not
been making inquiries whatever.

   The tale he told me was a pure fabrication and only intended to
frighten the truth out of me. In fact he believes my statement
although he will not admit it. You need not therefore go abroad on
this account dearest, but in any case please don't leave England
until I have seen you once again.

   If you do wish to write to me about anything do so now as all
the letters pass through my hands at present. Excuse this scrawl my
own darling, but I dare not leave the room for a moment and I do
not know when I will be able to write to you again.

   In haste yours ever Florie.[23]

Determined to dispatch the letter to Brierley as soon as
possible, Florence handed it over to Nurse Yapp, who was
playing in the garden with the children, and asked her to take
it to the postbox. Yapp would later claim that she gave the
letter to baby Gladys to carry and that the child dropped it in
the mud. Alleging that the envelope was dirty, she took it into
the post office in order to transfer it to a clean envelope.

Unable to resist the temptation, the nursemaid read the
letter not once, but twice, on the post office step. Realising its
potential for mischief, she returned it to her pocket and
hurried home to Battlecrease House, dragging the two children in her wake.

From her vantage point at the nursery window, Alice Yapp
waited impatiently for Edwin to return. As he approached the
house, she ran down to meet him in the garden. As the two sat
side by side on a convenient garden bench, she gave him

Florence's ill-judged letter to Brierley. While Edwin recovered from the shock of discovering that Florence was in love with another man, the servant spitefully whispered to him tales of food being interfered with and fly-papers soaking in a bowl.

CHAPTER SEVEN

❧

There is so much good in the worst of us
And so much bad in the best of us
That it hardly becomes any of us
To talk about the rest of us.

Anon

The London train slowly ground to a halt at Edge Hill Station with a groan and a long, exhausted spit of black ash and steam. A tall, thick-set figure emerged from a first-class carriage amid a swirl of ghostly grey smoke to be greeted enthusiastically on the bustling platform by his brother. Alarmed by the contents of Mrs Briggs's surprising telegram, Michael Maybrick had immediately packed his bags and taken the next available train to his home town.

Even with his hair slightly receding and a curly moustache standing to attention on either side of fleshy pink cheeks, the famous composer still bore a striking resemblance to his brother James. Physically taller and more muscular, his appearance and demeanour was that of a fastidious, well-dressed military man rather than a popular singer and musician.

At forty-nine years old and still unmarried, Captain Maybrick of the Artists' Volunteers, was an enthusiastic member and serving officer in the local yeomanry. He was also a rising star in the secret world of British Freemasonry. He was a founder member and first principal of the Orpheus Lodge for musicians, Master of the Athenaeum Lodge, Master of St Andrew's Lodge and a member of two other chapters. Since the time of his initiation, his rise in the brotherhood had been meteoric and he had not long since been created 'Grand Organist of England' and 'Grand Organist of Grand Chapter'. The speculation was that he would soon be admitted as a member of the 30th Degree, an honoured position which would set him on the path to becoming one of the most important and powerful Freemasons in the country.

Clever and talented, Michael knew his own worth, but he was arrogant and not universally liked. Years later, John Aunspaugh's daughter Florence would write, somewhat caustically, of how success had gone to his head:

> He had been courted by royalty, the Pope and all the celebrities of the world and it had 'turned his head'. My father did not like or admire him at all. He said his success had endowed him with a 'superiority complex', and thought that he had forgotten more than anybody else ever did know . . . he thought he should be classed with Shakespeare, Byron, Milton and Tennyson. My father often

laughed and said 'Michael had already engaged a tomb in Westminster Abbey'.[1]

On the station platform, Michael received Edwin's puppy-like adoration as his due and treated him in return with brusque affection. They journeyed to Battlecrease House by carriage, arriving at 9.30 p.m., by which time Michael had listened patiently to a confusing story from his younger brother concerning fly-papers and arsenic and been shown the letter Florence had written to Brierley.

With Mrs Briggs, Alice Yapp, Edwin, the servants and heaven knew who else forming the opinion that James's illness was being deliberately caused by his wife,* Michael Maybrick was now faced with a dilemma he had not anticipated: James dead now threatened a scandal even more dangerous than James alive.

Unfriendly speculation had given Florence motive and opportunity, but there was, as yet, no direct evidence that she had administered poison to her husband. However, Michael could not rule out the possibility that once suspicion was raised an investigation might follow, and a subsequent post-mortem would reveal not the expected arsenic, but strychnine.

An enterprising policeman could put two and two together over the mysterious parcel of medicine that James had received, and Michael would have to ensure that he had covered his tracks. He was now in a position to arrange

---

* Gossip was already spreading. In an interview with the *Liverpool Daily Post* on 9 September 1889, Captain Irving confirmed that he had been kept fully informed by a mutual friend about the sickness of James Maybrick and the suspicions surrounding it.

much firmer evidence against Florence in order to make certain that any resulting investigation would be centred only around his sister-in-law. At the same time, once James died, and die he must, it would be in Michael's interests to contain any possible evidence of his brother's scandalous life and homicidal excursions into Whitechapel.

Within an hour of entering the premises, Michael Maybrick was firmly in control of the household. Florence, who like all the Maybricks was a little in awe of her famous brother-in-law, appeared not to question his authority in her own home. After visiting the sick-room, he interviewed the professional nurse. Alerting her to the need for caution, he instructed her to prepare all the patient's food and drink herself and taste everything before giving it. Considering that the entire household was of the opinion that Florence was trying to poison her husband, Nurse Gore, in complying with his instructions without question, was either a very dedicated nurse or a very foolish one.

On seeing his sister-in-law, Michael curtly accused Florence of neglecting James and complained that a second doctor and a nurse should have been brought in sooner. It did not seem to occur to Florence to defend herself by replying that neglect had never crossed Edwin's mind, and he had been practically living at the house for the last two weeks.

It was not in Michael's interests for Florence to be put on her guard by becoming aware of the suspicions surrounding her. Although the opportunity presented itself, he did not mention to her that her letter to Brierley was sitting comfortably in his pocket, or that it had been opened and the contents read by at least two other people. Neither at any time did anyone in the household tell Florence that she was under suspicion of poisoning her husband. Mrs Briggs would later confirm: 'We were in a delicate position being told not to speak to her about the suspicions which pointed to her.'[2] And only Michael Maybrick had the unquestioned authority in the house to give such an order.

Florence was distressed that Michael thought she had neglected James, and Elizabeth Humphreys, the cook, found her in the dining room. 'I am blamed for all this,'[3] she lamented, telling Humphreys that her position in the house was not worth anything and that Michael Maybrick had always had a spite against her since her marriage. Perhaps another woman with a stronger character would have thrown Michael's suitcase out of the front door, with him following behind, adding Mrs Briggs and Alice Yapp for good measure. Florence, though, meekly accepted his right to rule Battlecrease House while her husband was ill, and had never, in any case, asserted much control over the servants or Mrs Briggs.

Others in the household, however, had realised the danger posed by Michael Maybrick's arrival, and some time later a strange smell impregnated the passageway leading from the servants' quarters. Elizabeth Humphreys and the waitress, Mary Cadwallader, had found every fly-paper remaining in the house and burned them in the kitchen stove. Mary had cautioned the cook that it might be the best thing to do before the police arrived.

Meanwhile, at 10.30 p.m., Michael left the house to make an impromptu visit to Dr Humphreys, who lived close by. The interview was lengthy, but the doctor did not appear to think

Michael's revelations of enough importance to return to the house until the next morning.

By 11 a.m. on the following day, Nurse Gore had worked a gruelling twenty-hour shift with a difficult and restless patient and had had plenty of opportunity to think about the strange circumstances surrounding James Maybrick. She gratefully handed over her responsibilities to Nurse Callery, her relief, who arrived just before lunch.

Meanwhile, after having made a visit to Mrs Briggs, who confirmed how ill she thought James was, and no doubt gave her opinion of 'strange goings on', Michael returned to the house. He hovered about the sick-room for the rest of the day, and dispatched a telegram to Dr Carter, requesting his attendance.

Carter and Michael Maybrick met for the first time late in the afternoon. Michael was at his most arrogant: 'Now, what is the matter with my brother?'[4] he demanded gruffly. The consultant did not appear overly impressed with Michael's haughty manner and simply repeated the opinion that it was acute dyspepsia.

'But what is the cause of it?'[5] demanded Michael. Dr Carter gently replied that his conclusion was that James had committed a grave error of diet by taking some irritant food or drink, or both, which was thought to have set up inflammation.

Had Michael been innocent and only concerned with his brother's welfare, why didn't he take the opportunity of informing Carter that James had written to him and suggested that his illness had been caused by taking what he had believed was Dr Fuller's medicine? Even at this late stage the doctor may have been able to administer an antidote. Michael, however, turned to Dr Humphreys, who had just entered the room, and asked him if he had informed Dr Carter of their conversation the previous evening.

'God forbid that I should unjustly suspect any one,' boomed Michael, striding energetically across the room, 'but do you not think if I have serious grounds for fearing that all may not be right, that it is my duty to say to you?'[6]

Both men agreed, and Michael then informed the two doctors that James had been subject to attacks since the middle of April; that he had been able to eat ordinary food when away from home, but was sick soon after returning to Battlecrease; and that this contrast had been widely remarked upon.

Was it Mrs Briggs who had informed him of this when he had visited her earlier in the day? If so, was she repeating something she had heard from Alice Yapp? James had certainly not suggested this contrast to his brother when he had written to him on 29 April describing his symptoms.

Carter listened attentively as the story emerged of a serious estrangement between James and Florence; of how she was known to have been unfaithful, and had purchased fly-papers before the commencement of her husband's illness. Michael then dramatically presented Carter with a bottle of Neave's food (a digestive drink) from the sick-room and asked him to analyse it.

Although rather shaken, the doctors appeared less than convinced that their patient's wife had been trying to murder him, and Carter privately thought Michael Maybrick rather theatrical. However, they decided that they would surround James with safeguards to prevent anyone tampering with him.

Dr Carter, who could be as pompous as Michael on

occasion, promised that they would 'maintain an attitude of great vigilance',[7] while the more practical Dr Humphreys subsequently took a sample of the patient's urine and faeces to analyse. Neither doctor, however, suggested administering to the patient any form of antidote for arsenic poisoning; informing the victim of his brother's suspicions; or challenging the suspect.

On the evening of the same day, when the housemaid took a cup of tea to Florence in the sick-room, she noticed Michael removing what looked like a small bottle from the wash-stand. Is it possible that he had retrieved the medicine bottle which had been sent to James in the post from London? Florence said she had thrown away the contents, but did not confirm she had disposed of the bottle.

At 11.00 p.m., Nurse Gore, who had just returned to duty, opened a fresh bottle of Valentine's Meat Juice,* an easily digested, simple meat extract popular with people on a convalescent diet. Following her instructions from Michael to the letter, she reduced and tasted some before giving it to her patient.

Not long afterwards, in a whispered conversation, James complained to Florence of feeling very sick and depressed, and begged her to give him one of his powders. She had already refused to do it once that day and knew Nurse Gore would not allow her to give him any medicine without careful supervision. However, he continued to press her and promised faithfully that the powder could not harm him. He suggested that she put some in the food he was taking.

---

* Valentine's Meat Juice was brown in colour and sold in onion-shaped bottles each containing about nine teaspoonfuls of liquid.

Some time later the nurse saw Florence taking the bottle of Valentine's Meat Juice and disappear into the dressing room for a little over two minutes. On her return she asked Gore to fetch some ice, but the nurse was suspicious and refused haughtily, saying she would wait until her patient was awake. Florence then covertly returned the bottle to a small table, but the nurse observed her. Later, when James awoke with a burning sensation in his throat, Florence was anxious that he should not take the food and removed the bottle of meat juice from the table to the wash-stand, where James was unable to see it.

When Nurse Callery came on duty the following day at 11 a.m., Nurse Gore asked her to take a sample of the meat juice. Then, instead of retiring to bed, she put on her bonnet and cloak and departed to the Nurses' Institute to speak to the Lady Superintendent. She had not mentioned anything about the meat juice or her suspicions to Dr Humphreys when he had called to see the patient in the early morning. However, before leaving the house she spoke to Michael Maybrick, which resulted in him removing a bottle of brandy from the bedroom and putting it under lock and key. She did not take the opportunity of telling him about the meat juice, which was still on the wash-stand in the bedroom. It had not been given to James since Florence had touched it.

Whatever Nurse Gore's real reason was for visiting the Lady Superintendent, it resulted in Nurse Callery being dismissed and replaced by a new nurse, Wilson. In the meantime, on her return at 1.30 in the afternoon, Gore instructed Nurse Callery to dispose of the sample of the meat juice and then spoke again to Michael Maybrick, who removed the bottle of Valentine's Meat Juice from the bedroom and later in the day gave it to Dr Carter.

If Michael had been trying to secure evidence against Florence, she had now unwittingly played right into his hands. With Nurse Gore having witnessed her acting suspiciously with the meat juice, if that meat juice was subsequently found to contain arsenic, Florence would be the obvious suspect.

Meanwhile, while Florence was helping in the sick-room, she was asked by Nurse Callery to pour the contents of one medicine bottle into another. Michael walked into the bedroom just as she was carrying out the task and bellowed: 'Florence how dare you tamper with the medicine!' Startled, she turned and replied: 'It is on account of the thick sediment, which cannot be properly shaken in the smaller bottle.'[8]

Michael made quite a song and dance about the matter, telling Florence he was very much displeased and that he would have the prescription remade immediately. It is unlikely that Florence would have added poison to the medicine in full view of the nurse and anyone who happened to walk into the bedroom, but Michael had now established his own concern for his brother's welfare and a further suspicion against his sister-in-law. In time the original medicine bottle would be tested and found to contain no impurities. However, what of the one Michael had remade?

Still shaken, Florence left the house for some fresh air and met Michael in the garden. She timidly asked him why he had not called in Dr Fuller. Michael replied tersely that it was rather late in the day for that. In fact Dr Fuller was the last person Michael would want to see at Battlecrease House. He knew he had not prescribed the tablets that James had been taking, and that he had not sent him any medicine in the post, and might ask some awkward questions. Meanwhile the bottle of Valentine's Meat Juice lay in Michael's pocket, waiting for the arrival of Dr Carter.

It was with an intense feeling of relief that Carter reported finding nothing wrong with the Neave's food or the brandy which Michael had given him to analyse. Humphreys had also found the patient's urine and faeces free from poison. However, both doctors had tested only for the expected arsenic, not strychnine. As for the meat juice, Carter promised that he would analyse it that evening.

On examining James, he told them he felt much better, although both doctors now thought him much worse. Dr Carter noticed a whiteness on the patient's right hand* and James complained to him of having diarrhoea. The tenesmus† he had been suffering from over the previous few days had not abated, and the doctors decided to give him a nutrient suppository, a nitro-glycerine tablet and a dose of sulphonal. He was also ordered to continue with regular doses of brandy and champagne.

By the evening of Friday 10 May, Florence was being closely watched by everyone in the household. Her every action was noted and would be given as evidence in the great trial which was drawing closer with each passing minute.

---

* At a later date a contemporary doctor writing for the *Lancet* would suggest that perhaps James had been suffering from the first signs of Raynaud's Disease, a disorder of the blood vessels affecting the fingers and toes.

† Straining of the lower bowel.

That evening, Nurse Wilson, Callery's replacement, overheard James saying to Florence: 'Oh Bunny, Bunny. How could you do it? I did not think it of you.' He said this three times, and Florence replied: 'You silly old darling, don't trouble your head about things.'[9]

At 7 p.m. George Smith, the clerk from Maybrick & Co., arrived at the house, bringing with him a piece of paper which Edwin took up to the bedroom. The servants could hear James shouting: 'Oh Lord if I am to die why am I to be worried like this?'[10] The ever-present Alice Yapp informed her fellow servants that they were trying to get James to sign a will. Had Michael been unable to find the original will which had left everything to him and Thomas? At a much later date Florence would argue that 'Unlawful pressure and influence had been brought to bear upon the testator.'[11]

During the night, James's condition deteriorated and he became delirious. For the first time since the onset of his illness, Dr Humphreys arrived at the conclusion that his patient would not recover. Florence, fatigued beyond belief, went to the servants' bedroom to wake the cook. She asked Humphreys to send one of the servants to fetch Mrs Briggs, as their master was dying. In the early hours of the morning, the children were brought to the bedside to kiss their father goodbye, but James would linger for many hours yet.

In the morning, after taking an overdose of chloryl, Florence collapsed on the floor of the bedroom and was carried into the dressing room by Edwin. Laid on the bed, she was left neglected and forgotten.

Dr Carter arrived in the afternoon and gravely informed Michael that he had discovered a 'metallic irritant' in the

Valentine's Meat Juice and that he intended to send it for further analysis. He concluded: 'If things turn out to be as I fear the matter must pass entirely out of our hands.'[12]

The hot and stuffy bedroom was now full of people. Mrs Briggs and her sister Mrs Hughes had arrived in the early hours of the morning. Thomas, the other Maybrick brother, had journeyed from Manchester, and George Davidson and Charles Ratcliffe, both close friends of James, had been at the house all day. The servants and nurses stood respectfully at the door while Michael and Edwin bent over the dying man's bed. At 8.30 p.m. on Saturday 11 May 1889, as his wife lay in a drug-induced sleep in another room, suspected of his murder, James Maybrick drew his last breath in the arms of his best friend, George Davidson.

When the Home Office analyst eventually investigated the bottle of meat juice it would be discovered that arsenic had indeed been added to the contents. However, in his opinion, the arsenic contaminating the meat juice had been added 'in solution', as he had been unable to find any solid arsenic particles, either settled at the bottom or floating to the top of the liquid. So whatever the powder was that Florence had put in the meat juice, it had certainly not contained arsenic.

Apart from the two professional nurses, only two other people had been in contact with the meat juice: Florence and Michael Maybrick.

On the Saturday afternoon, before James Maybrick died, Michael had told Mrs Briggs and Mrs Hughes that the meat juice contained arsenic. However, Dr Carter at that stage had only reported that he had discovered a 'metallic irritant' and would not identify it as arsenic until he returned home later on the Saturday evening. Only one person could possibly know that the meat juice contained arsenic, and that was the person who had put it there. That person was Michael Maybrick.

CHAPTER EIGHT

❧

Teach thy necessity to reason thus;
There is no virtue like necessity.
     William Shakespeare, 1564–1616

In a darkened bedroom at Battlecrease House, Edwin Maybrick had a tight grip on Florence's arms and was shaking her violently. From far away she could hear his persistent angry voice demanding an answer: 'I want your keys. Do you hear? I want your keys.'[1] As her head swam and an overwhelming feeling of nausea threatened to engulf her, she gratefully abandoned herself to unconsciousness.

Within minutes of James Maybrick's death, Edwin had carried Florence from the dressing room to the spare bedroom. There she remained insensible throughout Saturday night and most of Sunday morning until Edwin tried without success to awaken her.

Battlecrease House was in turmoil. Dr Carter and Dr

121

Humphreys had refused to sign the death certificate, and matters were now in the hands of the coroner. Michael, in his role of law-abiding citizen and loving brother, had made sure that there would be more than enough evidence to give to the authorities when they arrived. On the Sunday morning, he gave instructions to Edwin, Mrs Briggs and Mrs Hughes to search the house for the keys to the safe. With the corpse of James Maybrick hardly cold and discreetly covered with a sheet, they ransacked the bedroom and dressing room. Within a short time various incriminating items had been discovered, including some bottles of arsenic and Florence's letters, which Michael immediately took into custody.

Some time later Charles Ratcliffe wrote to John Aunspaugh in America:

> ... *in her room they claim to have found quantities of arsenic, thirteen love letters from Edwin, seven from Brierley and five from Williams. I always knew the madam was dumb, but I must frankly admit I did not consider her that dumb as to leave her affairs accessible to any who choosed to penetrate ... Michael says Edwin's letters will never be produced in court ... If they had only found the arsenic in Mrs Maybrick's room, as James was such an arsenic dope I don't think they could have proven anything on her, but finding all those love letters as a motive it is going hard with her.*[2]

According to Florence's mother there had also that morning been found a packet of compromising letters by women to James Maybrick. These, claimed the Baroness, were suppressed and later probably destroyed by Michael.

What else was found that day? Did one of the searchers discover the journal that James had been writing? And if so, what was done with it? Michael would undoubtedly have destroyed it, and Mrs Briggs, Mrs Hughes or Edwin would very likely have passed it on to him. However, the house was in chaos, and Alice Yapp, like a squirrel storing nuts for winter, was collecting together anything she could get her hands on before leaving with the children for Mrs Janion's.

During the trial Alice was seen with Florence's umbrella, and years later monogrammed teaspoons and a silver locket which had once belonged to the owners of Battlecrease House turned up at her home. It seems likely that there were other objects the nursemaid had taken a fancy to, and she may well have discovered the journal during her search. On the Sunday morning she said to Elizabeth Humphreys: 'I will tell all I know, if only to prevent Mrs Maybrick having the children.'[3] Was she perhaps referring to the journal, the contents of which would have given Florence an even stronger motive for killing her husband?

Well pleased with the progress of events so far, Michael decided to catch a train to London, leaving Edwin in charge to wait for the arrival of the police. This was an ideal opportunity for him to remove from the house anything which would incriminate him. Perhaps he also took the opportunity to visit the mysterious Williams. Charles Ratcliffe wrote: 'Williams says his letters to Mrs Maybrick will never be brought into Court.'[4]

Before leaving the house, Michael visited Florence in her bedroom shortly after she had been examined by Dr Hopper. Nurse Wilson was present, and ignoring his sister-in-law, Michael spoke directly to her attendant: 'Nurse, I am going up to London, Mrs Maybrick is no longer mistress of this house, as one of the executors I forbid you to allow her to leave this room. I hold you responsible in my absence.'[5] He had obviously decided to put Florence under house arrest even before the police had arrived.

In the evening of the day Michael left for the capital, Inspector Baxendale arrived from Garston Police Station. After inspecting the body, he was taken by Edwin to various places around the house and shown a variety of bottles, which he took away with him. He was also given three letters, and a telegram from the proprietor of Flatman's Hotel.

On Monday 13 May, a post-mortem was conducted on the body of James Maybrick in the bedroom of Battlecrease House. Dr Humphreys and Dr Carter were assisted by Dr Alexander Barron, a professor of pathology at the Royal Infirmary. The stomach of the deceased was removed, tied at both ends and placed in a bottle, as was the tongue and the upper portion of the gullet. The doctors then removed the intestines and six ounces of the liver.

While the three doctors were sealing the various jars, Superintendent Isaac Bryning was directing the removal of parts of the pipes and drains from outside the house, and under his direction Dr Humphreys was taking samples of sediment and liquid for analysis.

Over the next few days a hundred and thirty-nine jars and bottles containing various medical products, ranging from laudanum to corn-plasters, were taken from the house. Inspector Baxendale also received a pan, a basin and a jug from Edwin Maybrick, and a further twenty-six bottles from James's office.

Mrs Briggs, under Michael's instructions, had been turning away visitors to the house since Sunday morning. Most of the cotton-broking families had called to convey their condolences to the widow, as good manners and custom demanded. All had been told by Mrs Briggs that Florence was too ill to receive visitors.

Meanwhile, Florence had been enduring the constant presence of either Nurse Gore or Nurse Wilson. When she asked to see her children, Nurse Wilson tartly informed her that they had been removed from the house, and that Michael Maybrick had given instructions that she was not to see them.

Michael returned from London on the Monday and the following day the inquest was opened by Coroner Brighouse at the Aigburth Hotel. Michael formally identified his brother's body and passed to Inspector Baxendale a number of Florence's letters.

The Coroner began by announcing that 'The result of the post-mortem examination was that poison was found in the stomach of the deceased in such quantities as to justify further examination.'[6] He then adjourned the inquiry for a fortnight. However, his statement was completely untrue. No poison whatsoever had been found in James Maybrick's stomach during the post-mortem conducted by the three doctors the previous day.

The medical men had agreed that their patient had died from an irritant poison, but they had been unable to tell whether that had been caused by a poisonous substance or impure food. The contents of the various jars had been passed on to Mr Davies, the county analyst, only that morning, and he had not yet completed the analysis. When he did, he found no weighable portions of arsenic in any part of the viscera. Who then had given what amounted to false information to the Coroner?

A short time afterwards, a grim-faced Dr Humphreys visited Florence in her bedroom. He took her pulse, then left the room without a word. Presently a crowd of men entered. One of them stepped to the foot of the bed and introduced himself: 'I am the superintendent of police, and I am about to say something to you.' Clearing his throat and looking directly at the woman in the bed, he continued: 'Pray listen to what I say and consider before you reply, if you do reply. You are in custody on suspicion of causing the death of your husband, Mr James Maybrick, on the 11th May . . .'[7]

For two and a half days Florence had been a prisoner in her own home at the instigation of her brother-in-law, unable to contact anyone or see any of her friends. Michael had not arranged any legal representation for her, and now she was officially under arrest with a police officer standing guard outside her bedroom door.

If she had been given the benefit of legal advice, perhaps she would not have listened to Mrs Briggs when the woman she had once considered her friend suggested that she write to Alfred Brierley for help. The pitiful entreaty, once written, was handed over by Mrs Briggs to the police, who kept it as evidence against Florence:

I am writing to you to give me every assistance in your power in my present fearful trouble. I am in custody, without any of my family with me and without money. I have cabled to my solicitor in New York to come here at once. In the meantime, send some money for

present needs. The truth is known about my visit to London. Your
last letter is in the hands of the police. Appearances may be against
me, but before God I swear I am innocent.[8]

Brierley never received the letter, and as it transpired, the
police had also refused to send the cable to Florence's
American solicitor. Fortunately, Dr Humphreys, realising that
she was desperately in need of legal assistance, arranged for
the solicitors Messrs Cleaver to represent her.

However, Michael had no intention of making things easy
for Florence, and when Arnold Cleaver arrived at Battlecrease
House he refused to admit him, informing the solicitor that
he would require a permit from the Superintendent of Police.
An angry Mr Cleaver went to see Dr Humphreys, who
explained to him the circumstances under which he had
withheld the certificate of death. 'Suspicion had been aroused
against the prisoner by the contents of the intercepted letter,'
the solicitor would recall. 'And by the results of the analysis of
a bottle of Beef Juice, a proportion of the contents of which
I was then given to understand she had administered to the
deceased. I subsequently ascertained that she had not done
so.'[9]

The following day, Mr Cleaver obtained the necessary
authority from the police and returned to Battlecrease to
consult with his client, but he was unable to speak to Florence
in private:

My communications with her on this occasion were made under
great difficulties, being in the presence of a nurse and virtually of a
police officer who was at the open door, and were therefore carried

*on in a low tone and I was unable to make any note of her
statement, having been warned that all written statements were
examined by the police.*[10]

On Thursday afternoon the stillness of Battlecrease House
was broken by the sound of whispering voices and hurrying
footsteps. In her bedroom Florence asked the nurse what was
happening. 'The funeral starts in an hour,' she replied acidly.
'But for you he would have been buried on Tuesday.'[11]

Dragging herself to the bedroom window, Florence looked
down on to the driveway, where four magnificent jet-black
horses harnessed to an ornate hearse stood restlessly anticipating the arrival of the coffin. As the servants and hushed
mourners hurriedly formed a pathway leading from the house,
James Maybrick's brown oak coffin covered with white flowers was laid reverently in the back of the vehicle.

As the horses moved off at a steady pace, a light breeze
danced through the ornamental black feather head-dresses
towering over the animals' heads. Nine other carriages accompanied the hearse as James made his last journey through the
streets of Liverpool to Anfield Cemetery. From her place at
the window, his widow, overcome with grief, beat hopelessly
on the glass and collapsed in a dead faint.

At her house in Paris the same morning, the Baroness von
Roques was sitting down to breakfast when she received a
telegram from Florence: 'Jim passed away on Saturday.'[12] Half
an hour later a second telegram followed: 'Come at once. Serious
charges against me. Did not know when I telegraphed before.'[13]

Past differences forgotten, the Baroness threw a few things
in a suitcase and left Paris the same day. Forty-eight hours later

she arrived in Liverpool, exhausted, bedraggled and completely baffled. On leaving the railway station to look for a carriage, she walked straight into Michael Maybrick, who was again on his way to catch the London train.

'This is a nice state of affairs,' he snarled. The Baroness asked him what he meant. 'I mean a question of murder, and there is a man in it.' She tried to question him further but he ignored her and shouted: 'You had better go up to the house, she is in a dying condition. Edwin will tell you everything.'[14] Before she had collected her wits to reply, he was lost in the crowds in the busy station.

The Baroness arrived at Battlecrease House in a whirlwind of black bombazine and French perfume and met Edwin in the vestibule. Marching him into the morning room, she demanded an explanation of why she had not been sent for earlier. Edwin, in a state of great agitation, replied weakly that nobody had known her address.

'Oh, everyone knew it, Paris would have found me,' she boomed confidently. 'Tell me what has happened.' Sweating nervously, Edwin told her a long, confusing story made even more bewildering by the Baroness's endless interruptions. 'How could you deliver her up to the police in this way and not a friend by her...?' she accused him angrily. 'Oh,' he exclaimed, 'I have been very fond of Florrie. I would never have believed anything wrong of her. I would have stood by her, and I did until the letter to a man was found. I wish I could meet Brierley.'

'Yes,' the Baroness shouted, 'that is just about the best thing you could do. In my country and among the men I have known, they would have met Brierley instead of calling in the police!'[15]

After effectively reducing Edwin to a quivering wreck, and in despair at his disjointed story, she abandoned him and went in search of Florence, whom she eventually discovered in bed, attended by Nurse Wilson and Inspector Baxendale. On entering the room, the Baroness greeted her daughter in French and asked: 'What are these people doing here?'

The Inspector jumped to his feet and cautioned her to speak English, as he said he intended writing down everything she said. The Baroness gave him a withering look and replied: 'You may write as much as you like my friend. I have nothing wrong to say; but it strikes me as very strange to see you in this room.'

'Do mammy dear, don't excite yourself, the inspector is only doing his duty,' cried Florence. 'But,' exclaimed the Baroness, 'what is the nurse for and the people outside? I consider it infamous; and Edwin seems to have lost his head!'[16]

Ignoring both the Inspector and the nurse, the Baroness dragged a chair across the room and sat down to question her daughter. 'They think I have poisoned Jim,' Florence told her. 'Why if he is poisoned he poisoned himself, he made a perfect apothecary's shop of himself, as we all know,' replied the Baroness with spirit. 'Dr Hopper, Mrs Briggs and Michael believe me guilty,' Florence sobbed. 'But, Mammy I am innocent.'[17]

Nurse Wilson then demanded that the Baroness leave the room, and having already decided to question Edwin again she mildly complied. Her second interview with Edwin, however, was no more successful than the first had been, and she decided that the best thing for her to do would be to see her daughter's solicitor the following day.

In the evening Florence was reduced to hysterics by some incident or other, and her mother discovered her being held down on the bed by the two nurses and two policemen. Outraged that the men had hold of her bared arms and legs, the Baroness tried to intervene, promising them that she would be able to calm her daughter if they would only allow her to.

However, authority had gone to Nurse Wilson's head, and she refused to allow the Baroness to interfere, threatening to have her evicted from the room by the policemen. Finding it useless to resist, the Baroness recovered her dignity and retreated from the bedroom, but she was determined to have the last word and hesitated dramatically at the doorway to deliver the immortal line: 'Better death than such dishonour'[18] before slamming the door behind her.

Alice Yapp, on her way to fetch more of the children's clothes, was the next person to receive the sharp side of the Baroness von Roques' tongue, when they met on the stairs. 'Are you the one who has caused additional trouble to that poor young thing by showing letters you find?' snapped the Baroness. 'She weren't a poor young thing then,' Alice replied with spirit. 'Well you are an ungrateful, disloyal servant,' hissed the older woman.[19]

The following day Florence was allowed to see her mother for a few minutes, and the Baroness took the opportunity to question her discreetly in French. 'Tell me, have you really done anything wrong my dear to your husband?' 'No mama,' Florence replied. 'I swear to you I am innocent. I did put a powder he asked for in the meat juice, but he did not have it.'[20]

In the afternoon the Baroness took a carriage to the city to see Arnold Cleaver. She had been in the office for only five minutes when a telegram arrived which took the solicitor by surprise, and he said hurriedly: 'They are going to meet in half an hour, and if you wish to see her before she is removed you had best hurry.'[21]

It would be the *Liverpool Daily Post* who would give an account of what happened next, under the headline 'Extraordinary Magistrates' Proceedings': 'Previous to entering the house a long conversation took place between the magistrate, the police, the doctors and Messrs Cleaver, during which the nature of the evidence against the prisoner was disclosed. On hearing this Messrs Cleaver at once said they would offer no objection to a remand.'[22]

The court was now officially opened in Mrs Maybrick's bedroom and Superintendent Bryning addressed Colonel Bidwell, the magistrate: 'This person is Mrs Maybrick, wife of the late Mr James Maybrick, she is charged with having caused his death by administering poison to him. I understand that her consent is given to a remand and therefore I need not introduce or give any evidence.'

The magistrates' clerk replied: 'You ask for a remand of eight days?' Superintendent Bryning replied in the affirmative, and Mr Cleaver said: 'I appear for the prisoner and consent to a remand.'[23]

It is likely that the conversation outside the house had included the information that arsenic had been discovered in the victim's body, which was probably why Mr Cleaver had consented to a remand. However, the charge had now changed from 'on suspicion of causing the death of your husband', to 'having caused his death by administering poison'.

Having rushed back to Battlecrease, the Baroness was refused permission to see her daughter. She discovered from Dr Hopper that her remark, 'Better death than such dishonour,' had precipitated Florence's removal to prison, as it was thought that the Baroness was going to poison her daughter rather than allow her to stand trial.

Florence was ushered from the house in such haste that she was unable to pick up her bag of toiletries or so much as a change of clothing. Her mother's cloak, which had been left on a chair in the hall, was thrown hastily around her shoulders. Accompanied by Dr Humphreys, Superintendent Bryning and one of the nurses, she was carried to the waiting cab in a chair while her mother watched helplessly from a bedroom window.

As she looked down at the departing party, the Baroness heard the key being turned in the bedroom door. Flying across the room and pulling at the handle, she shouted and kicked the door in fury. Once the cab had left, she was released by a red-headed policeman who would remember to his dying day the dressing-down he received from the furious matron.

Now that Florence had left the house and the police had departed, Michael made it perfectly clear to the Baroness that her continued presence at Battlecrease was not acceptable, and she departed resentfully to find herself a hotel. The astonished servants were rounded up and told that they would have to leave by Monday. It appears that Michael was not expecting Florence to return to Battlecrease House.

Within a week Florence Maybrick had lost her husband, her children, her home and her freedom. After a long drive she arrived exhausted at Walton Prison and was received by the Governor. Escorted across a small courtyard and through a narrow passage, she came to a dark and gloomy reception area where the stench of the enclosed community made her retch.

Before being taken to a cell for sick prisoners, she was weighed, and relieved of her valuables: a watch, two diamond rings and a brooch. As he left, Dr Humphreys gave her a few shillings for her immediate needs. Left with nothing but the clothes she stood up in and some loose change, Florence in her first few days of imprisonment was at a great disadvantage, as prisoners on remand were allowed certain concessions. Why the Baroness never saw her during this time is not clear, but under the circumstances perhaps she had been refused entry to the prison. However, Florence was not entirely without friends, as Charles Ratcliffe would confirm in a letter to John Aunspaugh:

Mrs Sutton and Mrs Holloway came to my house in Mrs Sutton's carriage. My wife and I got into the carriage and we four at once went to the jail. Mrs Maybrick presented a most pitiful and deplorable picture. She showed she had been very ill and was yet a sick woman, eyes were sunken, hair dishevelled, dirty and filthy.

She told a most pathetic story and her appearance surely did substantiate the proof of her statement. She said when Michael took possession and put Mrs Briggs in charge she was subjected to all kinds of insults and ill treatment by Mrs Briggs and the servants.

She was not allowed to have any communication with her friends. She was cursed and given impudent answers whenever she made a request of them. That she would lay in bed all day with only being given a cup of cold coffee and cold dry toast. They would not help her out of bed when she needed attention. She was not able to get out of bed alone and she just layed there in her own filth and they would not change her bed. Filth was all over her and she smelled horrible.

Mrs Sutton went home at once, got a tub and some clean clothes. She and my wife gave Mrs Maybrick a good hot bath and put clean clothes on her. We got her a good soft mattress for the jail bunk and clean bed clothes. The cotton brokers' wives take it turn about to go every day to the jail, carry her a good meal and see that she is kept clean.[24]

On Monday 27 May, sixteen days after the death of James Maybrick, the inquest was again opened, this time at the Wellington Reading Room, which had been the old police court, in Garston. The newspapers were well represented and between thirty and forty reporters squashed into the crowded courtroom. In an article published the following day, the *Liverpool Daily Post* bewailed the difficult conditions the press representatives had had to endure:

The pressmen experienced the utmost difficulty in hearing, and for twelve mortal hours over which the proceeding extended many of them had to take notes in all sort of positions, standing up between serried ranks of policemen, on their knees, sometime almost on the back of learned counsel, and in various other awkward positions, for it was found impossible to hear at the tables assigned to them.[25]

Florence was not present in the courtroom that day, as Dr Beamish from Walton Prison testified that she was too ill to attend. Although Mr Davies had completed his analysis of the parts of the body which the medical men had sent him after the post-mortem, he was not called to give his evidence.

It appears that in the excitement of what had become a very public case, everyone had forgotten that a coroner's court is called in order to determine cause of death. In the mean time, the coroner's jury had their minds poisoned with all sorts of stories about Florence Maybrick. Michael Maybrick took the stand and spoke of how he had accused Florence of not attending her husband properly. Nurse Yapp happily related the fly-paper incident and the quarrel after the Grand National, and Nurse Gore informed the crowded courtroom that Florence had interfered with the meat juice.

The last of the twelve witnesses called was Mrs Christina Samuelson, who delighted the waiting reporters by telling the crowded courtroom how Mrs Maybrick had told her that she hated her husband. By the end of the first day of the inquest, cause of death had still not been established.

By now, aware that Mr Davies had been unable to find any weighable traces of poison in the viscera, the Coroner adjourned the inquest for a week and took the unusual step of ordering an exhumation of the body. The *Liverpool Courier* expressed its surprise: 'The disentombing of remains which have, prior to interment, been subjected to a post-mortem examination, is unusual, and it was believed that the Coroner had considered this step necessary because the result of the analysis of the viscera had not been such as expected.'[26]

The evidence collected around Battlecrease House to date would perhaps have been enough to send Florence to trial for attempted murder. However, was someone in the background pushing for the capital charge?

The Coroner had already been manipulated once, having been lied to about the result of the original post-mortem. Had Michael Maybrick been using his Masonic influence with the authorities, who, after having discovered adultery and opportunity, were now determined to find arsenic? Was Michael concerned that Florence knew more about her husband's secrets than he had given her credit for? Would Florence Maybrick be the Ripper's final victim?

CHAPTER NINE

❧

*No lesson seems to be so deeply incul-
cated by the experience of life as that
you never should trust experts...*
                    Lord Salisbury, 1830–1903

On 1 June 1889 the *Liverpool Daily Post* treated its readers
to a highly colourful, allegedly eye-witness account of
the exhumation of the body of James Maybrick. Guaranteed
to send shivers down the spine of anyone with a nervous
disposition, it boasted the headline 'The Aigburth Mystery – A
Midnight Mission'.

*... The night was perfectly black and the stillness of the cemetery
appalling. Across the gravel path which runs past the grave there
had been placed two forms or benches obtained from the adjacent
catacombs. Here the party who were silent and pre-occupied stopped
and the grave diggers lighted their naphtha lamps, the light from*

which cast a faint and sickly glow over the surrounding tombstones.

However the men got quickly to work, ropes were fastened to the handles of the coffin, and in a moment afterwards it was raised over the ground, its mountings scarcely yet tarnished with rust. It was placed with its ends upon the two benches then commenced the operation of unscrewing the lid.

This of course, did not take long, but there was scarcely anyone present who did not feel an involuntary shudder as the pale worn features of the dead appeared in the flickering rays of a lamp held over the coffin by one of the medical men. The body was not removed from its receptacle.

What everyone remarked was that although interred a fortnight the corpse was wonderfully preserved. There were scarcely any signs of corruption, the only thing noticeable was that whilst the extremities, the feet and the lower part of the legs and hands had remained their natural colour the rest of the body had turned a dark hue.

As the dissecting knife of Dr Barron pursued its rapid and skilful work there was, however, whenever a slight breath of wind blew an odour of corruption. The doctor removed in succession his lungs, heart, kidneys and part of the thigh bone; coming to the head he cut out the tongue* and opening the skull removed one half of the brain.

Each part as it was removed was placed in a large stone jar, which was covered over securely with a canvas cloth and then sealed with Dr Barron's seal. This done, the remains were re-covered, the coffin silently and expeditiously lowered again into the vault, and

---

* The tongue had already been removed in the first post-mortem, so unless the unfortunate man had two, this is incorrect.

the benches were replaced in the catacombs; the jar was taken into one of the vehicles, which about midnight moved slowly and in silence towards the entrance of the cemetery. The others who had been engaged in the horrible business left immediately afterwards glad that it was over.[1]

With the county analyst busy once again with the remains of James Maybrick, Florence was remanded for another week at Walton Prison. Meanwhile the newspapers had discovered the selling power of the 'Aigburth Mystery' and were reporting the most amazing stories, some of which even had a basis in truth:

We have it upon the authority of a gentleman who affirms that he saw the document that prior * *to his visit to London in April last, the late Mr James Maybrick wrote to his brother Michael, a letter which in view of the present circumstances, is extraordinary. The deceased gentleman said that he could not understand exactly the nature of his illness, and he thought it would be desirable, in the event of his illness proving fatal, if his body was subject to medical examination.*[2]

Michael had certainly not mentioned this letter from James in the coroner's court, so who was disclosing such private information, selectively choosing only that which could hurt Florence? It appears that a hungry press was being fed information from someone very close to home.

The inquest had been called in order to look for anything which could have contributed to James Maybrick's death. In

---

* The letter was written after the London visit, not before.

this same letter James had written to Michael that 'Dr Fuller had poisoned me as all the symptoms warranted such a conclusion'. If Michael was an innocent party in the crime, why had he not disclosed this essential evidence to the Coroner? Because he was not an innocent party and he knew very well that Dr Fuller had not sent James the medicine containing strychnine which had almost killed him two weeks before he did eventually die. Why also had the mysterious 'gentleman' who had claimed to have seen the letter not divulged this important sentence to the press? Was it possible that Michael and the 'gentleman' were one and the same person?

The *Liverpool Courier* also published details of two insurance policies James had opened in the October of 1888 and the January of 1889. They then threw out suggestions that money matters might furnish a clue to the mystery:

> . . . *Mrs Maybrick had frequent transactions with private loan offices. Some of these date back as late as 1887 and although at first these only represented moderate amounts they were, it is alleged, gradually increased until they involved considerable sums.*
>
> *It was only a fortnight before his death that the late Mr James Maybrick became by accident aware of his wife's monetary dealings. A letter to his wife requesting repayment of a loan of over £50 fell into his hands, and it is said that he called at the loan office and paid the amount . . .*[3]

On the morning of 5 June Florence was taken from Walton Prison to attend the adjourned inquiry at Garston. She was escorted by Dr O'Hagan, one of the prison physicians, a female attendant and a burly policeman. There is little doubt that the widow had been very ill during her time in prison. Had she miscarried the child she had been carrying, or had the medical staff been able to save it? Although the newspapers had been throwing out hints with regard to her mysterious illness, nothing would be disclosed in court as to its nature.

Draped from head to toe in black crêpe, Florence was taken on arrival to an anteroom so that she could be formally identified by the proprietor and staff of Flatman's Hotel. In a letter written in the following January to a Scottish lawyer, the hotel waiter, Alfred Schwieso, gave his impression of the proceedings:

> . . . *I am aware that everyone for the prosecution was dead against her, especially those whose duty it was to go no further than seeing that justice was done, but they proved to me to be very much two faced.*
>
> *. . . When I arrived at the Coroner's Inquest I met an inspector; this was the conversation that passed between us, he asked: 'Will you be able to recognise Mrs Maybrick?' I said I should not, he said: 'Keep with me and I will take you so as you can see her', or words to that effect, 'because you will be sworn whether you recognise her or not, when you are called.' I saw her twice before I was taken to recognise her, by order of the Coroner.*
>
> *Now with regard to Mr Brierley of course I should not have recognised him at all if it had not been for the police, but as I was for the prosecution I went by their orders, which I am sorry for now, for they acted in a very shameful manner.*[4]

After being identified by Schwieso, Florence was not brought into court, but sat in an adjoining room listening to the evidence through an open door. Edwin took the stand and denied categorically that his brother had taken arsenic, failing to mention that he knew he had taken strychnine.

At three o'clock Florence was again remanded and taken to the Lark Lane county police station, where she was to spend the night. The *Liverpool Echo* reported that 'During her detention at Lark Lane she will have the most comfortable of quarters.'[5] Florence, on the other hand, had a different story to tell: '. . . the cell contained only a plank board for a bed, it was dark, damp, dirty and horrible. A policeman taking pity on me brought me a blanket to lie on. In an adjoining cell, in a state of intoxication two men were raving and cursing throughout the night. I had no light, there was no one to speak to . . .'[6]

Florence's non-appearance at the inquest the following morning disappointed the waiting newspaper reporters and fuelled the rumour that she was insane. She was in fact sitting out of view of the court in an anteroom. One of James's friends* sat with her, speaking words of encouragement as they listened to the evidence through the open door.

As the only evidence heard at this time was sensational stories touching on Florence's personal character, the minds of the coroner's jury were being slowly poisoned against the widow. At last her legal advisers woke up to this fact and her counsel addressed the Coroner: 'I think that we should before going further in this case have some evidence as to the cause of death.' To which the Coroner made the extraordinary

---

* It was always thought that all of James's friends had deserted her, but one at least had the courage and kindness to stand by her, as she would later confirm. She did not, however, mention his name.

reply: 'It is a pity, Mr Pickford, that this application was not made before.'[7]

Eventually Mr Davies, the analyst, surrounded by numerous jars and bottles, was called to give his evidence. He had found no weighable portions of arsenic within the selection of the viscera removed at the original post-mortem. However, he had since discovered 1:50th of a grain in part of the liver, nothing in the stomach or its contents, but traces not weighable in the intestines.

Although there was little arsenic found in the corpse, there had certainly been a large amount discovered sprinkled liberally throughout the house.

Around 9.30 p.m. on the Saturday evening, shortly after James had died, Michael had ordered Nurse Yapp to pack the children's clothing, as he had arranged to send them to stay with their godmother, Mrs Janion. Acting on instructions, Alice Yapp and Bessie Brierley carried an unlocked trunk, which normally contained bedroom towels, from the linen closet into the night nursery and left it there.

At midnight, Nurse Yapp returned to the night nursery, accompanied by one of the hospital nurses, and opened the trunk, the side of which bore the initials F.E.M. As she lifted the lid, a rolled-up cot-sheet fell out, exposing a packet of yellow insect powder and a chocolate box. On opening the chocolate box, Yapp found five items which would provide damning evidence against Florence.

Yapp removed the box and carried it to Michael Maybrick who, together with Edwin, inspected the contents. It contained a bottle of solution of morphia, with the chemist's name erased; a bottle with no mark on it containing a saturated solution of arsenic of about two grains; a bottle of vanilla essence and a small packet of black powder consisting of a mix of charcoal and arsenic, labelled on one side 'Poison' and on the other 'Arsenic – poison for cats'. Lying on the top of the contents was a handkerchief with Florence Maybrick's name embroidered on it.

Michael instructed Edwin to consult the Maybricks' next-door neighbour, who was a solicitor, and he recommended that the box be put under lock and key immediately. Michael wrapped the contents in paper, sealed it with his personal seal and locked it in the wine cellar.

The 'poison for cats' packet would be found to contain 65.2 grains of arsenic mixed with a fine powder of charcoal, enough to kill more than twenty people. There is now little doubt that this package was one of the three sachets totalling 150 grains given to James by the inventor Valentine Blake the previous January. Unfortunately for Florence, this evidence would not be produced until 1894, almost five years after her arrest. Blake would then confirm that he had not mixed the compound he had given James with the usual soot or indigo required by law for over-the-counter chemist sales, but with charcoal.

It appears that an organising hand had discovered James Maybrick's store of arsenic and had put part of it in the cot-sheet parcel, adding anything else that looked remotely like dangerous poisons and throwing in for good measure a handkerchief embroidered with the principal suspect's name. The insect powder would prove to be perfectly harmless, as was the vanilla essence. However, this latter had a connection with a morsel of gossip which had emerged from the kitchen some weeks earlier when James had been eating a diet of bread and milk for breakfast.

After half of his meal had been returned uneaten to the kitchen, one of the servants suggested that it tasted sweeter than when it had left. An open packet of vanilla essence was then discovered and it was assumed that Florence had added some to the dish. Alice Yapp, in her garden conversation with Mrs Briggs when she claimed that Florence was poisoning her husband, had recalled this incident and interpreted it as food having been 'interfered with'.

Florence's accusers would suggest that she had purchased this arsenic mixed with charcoal and hidden the parcel herself in the linen closet. Why, however, would she have added to a box intended as a store of poison a perfectly harmless bottle of vanilla essence? More to the point, perhaps, is why she would have bothered with the clumsy and time-consuming procedure of extracting arsenic from fly-papers when she already had such a large store at hand.

The housemaid, whose job it was to look after the bedroom linen, had been in and out of the trunk on an almost daily basis fetching clean towels for the bedrooms. Why then had she not discovered the cot-sheet parcel before midnight on the Saturday?

The last person to arrive to stay at the house had been Nurse Wilson, on the Thursday afternoon, and it is likely that the housemaid would have supplied her with clean towels. It is therefore reasonable to suppose that the parcel had been put there after Thursday afternoon or, more likely, while the trunk was in the night nursery on the Saturday evening. This parcel was nothing less than a theatrical attempt to incriminate

Florence, but unfortunately it would be taken at face value.

On the morning following the discovery of the 'poison for cats' evidence, Michael had joined Mrs Briggs, Mrs Hughes and Edwin in the search for the keys to the safe. Whether or not they ever found them is unclear, but they did find yet another store of arsenic.

On the evening of the same day, Edwin disclosed to Inspector Baxendale two hat boxes which had been uncovered in the corner of the dressing room during the morning's search. Inside one of the boxes was a rag later identified as another of Mrs Maybrick's handkerchiefs, and a glass containing a milky liquid. In this concoction the analyst was to discover twenty grains of arsenic.

In the other hat box was a smaller box containing four bottles, yet another of Florence's handkerchiefs and a second bottle of Valentine's Meat Juice.

The meat juice was analysed and found to be clear of poison. However, three out of the four small bottles contained various quantities of arsenic in solution: in the first, fifteen grains of arsenic mixed with charcoal; in the second, two grains; and in the third, twenty grains.

The following day, Mrs Briggs handed to the Inspector a fourth handkerchief belonging to Mrs Maybrick and a bottle. On analysis it was found that the bottle held no arsenic, but the handkerchief, covered in a reddish-brown stain, contained approximately twenty grains.

Altogether the arsenic discovered on the Sunday morning and that handed over by Mrs Briggs on the Monday amounted to seventy-seven grains. Added to the arsenic previously discovered in the 'poison for cats' parcel and the half-grain found in the meat juice, the overall amount of arsenic discovered in the house was approximately 142.7 grains.

With the benefit of hindsight, it now seems certain that all the arsenic discovered in the house could be traced back to three parcels given to James by Valentine Blake five months before. The 7.3 grains unaccounted for had probably been taken by James himself.

If all the arsenic discovered in the house had come from the same source, it is reasonable to suppose that the person who made up the 'poison for cats' parcel also distributed the rest of the arsenic around the house in order to incriminate Florence.

According to the analyst, the third bottle found in the second hat box, containing twenty grains of arsenic in solution, had been the source of the arsenic used to contaminate the bottle of Valentine's Meat Juice which Michael handed to Dr Carter. So whoever planted the evidence must have been the same person who contaminated the meat juice. Since Michael Maybrick almost certainly contaminated the meat juice, then only Michael could have planted the evidence.

One other very interesting discovery was a small round bottle found in the linen closet the day before Florence was taken to prison. This contained a trace of arsenic, believed to be in a solution of what the analyst described as 'scent'. It appears that this was the face-wash that Florence had made up containing the arsenic from the fly-papers. Mr Davies searched the body carefully for traces of fibre from fly-papers, but failed to find any.

Not surprisingly, after the disclosure that so much arsenic had been discovered in the house, the defence was not entered on and the coroner's jury returned a verdict by a majority of thirteen to one after a deliberation lasting half an hour. However, it was still by no means clear, for all the arsenic found at Battlecrease, that James Maybrick had died of arsenic poisoning.

Florence was brought into the open court for the first time, in order to hear the verdict. On seeing the all-male jury from beneath the folds of her long veil, she recognised most of them as one-time guests in her home. The Coroner then stood to deliver the verdict and spoke to the prisoner directly: 'Florence Elizabeth Maybrick, the jury have inquired into the circumstances attending the death of your husband, and they have come to the conclusion that he was wilfully murdered by you. It is my duty to commit you to the next assizes, to be held at Liverpool, there to take your trial on that charge.'[8]

Deathly pale, Florence was returned to the dubious comfort of Lark Lane police station to await the magistrates' hearing, which was delayed due to the Whitsuntide holiday. She was not entirely forgotten over the holiday period, however. Mrs Pretty, a local greengrocer, sent her each day a gift of her best produce, with a note of sympathy. Meanwhile the cotton-broking wives ensured that her meals were sent in from a nearby hotel.

Transported to the Islington courthouse the evening before the hearing, Florence spent the night in the company of a policeman's daughter, who remained with her while her father stood guard outside the door. She would remember gratefully the young woman's kindness: 'That night on going to bed as I knelt weary and lonely to say my prayers, I felt a hand on my shoulder and a tearful voice said softly, "Let me hold your hand Mrs Maybrick and let me say my prayers with you." A simple expression of sympathy, but it meant so much to me at the time . . ."[9]

Only two magistrates – Sir William B. Forwood and Mr W. S. Barrett – sat to hear the evidence the following morning. The witnesses called had been heard at the inquest and their evidence was substantially the same. However, Mrs Christina Samuelson, who had excited the spectators with her revelation that Florence hated her husband, was not present. It was later discovered that she had fled to Paris.

When the court adjourned, the *Liverpool Daily Post* recorded:

When Mrs Maybrick rose to leave the court, in order to reach the door she had to meet full-face a tier of lady spectators at the back, and the moment she turned round the ladies started hissing her with unmistakable signs of disgust – Mrs Maybrick made haste to get away – the presiding justice immediately shouted to the officer on duty to shut the door, while the burly figures of several policemen who made forward towards the hostile spectators effectually put an end to the outburst.[10]

The following day, after listening to the rest of the evidence, the magistrates retired. After a brief consultation they returned, and Sir William Forwood addressed the court: 'Our opinion is that this is a case which ought to be decided by Jury.' Mr Pickford, who was defending Florence, replied: 'That being so, it is no use my occupying the time of this court in giving my defence and I shall reserve it.'[11]

However, the medical evidence was still contradictory as to whether or not James had died from arsenic poisoning. Some

two years later, Alexander MacDougall, a Scottish barrister
who had followed the case very closely, wrote a rambling,
indignant thesis on the subject. After giving a blow-by-blow
account of the evidence, he summed up the magistrates'
hearing:

> *Well I think my readers will find it somewhat difficult to*
> *understand why these Magistrates committed Mrs Maybrick to trial*
> *for murder on that evidence. There was certainly not sufficient*
> *evidence that the cause of death was arsenic! The doctors could not*
> *say so.*
>
> *The analyst had found no arsenic in the stomach, the appear-*
> *ances of which, at the post-mortem, Dr Humphreys said were*
> *consistent with either poisoning or ordinary congestion of the*
> *stomach, but he had found a minute quantity of arsenic after*
> *examination in the liver, certainly not enough to cause death, the*
> *appearance of which, at the post-mortem, Dr Humphreys said*
> *showed no evidence of any irritant poison, and Dr Carter agreed*
> *'but in a more positive manner' and Dr Barron did not exactly*
> *agree with Dr Carter!*
>
> *The analyst had found arsenic and traces of arsenic in some*
> *bottles and things which had been found in the house after death, as*
> *to which, where they came from or who had put them there, nobody*
> *knew anything about. However, there had been some evidence that*
> *Mrs Maybrick had committed adultery with Brierley, at an hotel*
> *in London in March, and so the Magistrates committed Mrs*
> *Maybrick for trial for murder in May!*[12]

Returned once again to further long days of boredom at
Walton Prison, Florence awaited the date of her trial. On

22 June the *Liverpool Review* noted a few short lines published by one of its competitors during the week: 'All creditors in the estate of James Maybrick deceased late of Knowsley Buildings, Tithebarn Street, Liverpool and Riversdale Road Aigburth are requested to forward on or before Saturday next the 22nd instant particulars of their claims with dates and items to the undersigned. Layton Steel Springman . . .'[13]

One of the creditors who subsequently made claim on the estate was a dressmaker with a bill for several dresses amounting to £10. It was subsequently discovered that it was James Maybrick's mistress and not Florence who had ordered the dresses. The bill was discreetly paid by the estate's trustees, who discovered at the same time that the woman had in her possession a quantity of jewellery which James had given her as collateral for a small loan when he had been in a financial crisis.

Michael and Thomas Maybrick, the trustees of James Maybrick's estate, had also been busy in other areas, and on 8 July, contrary to the will and before it had been proved, the entire contents of Battlecrease House were put up for auction. Everything was sold, including the children's toys. Florence's clothes were put in store, with one or two small items sent to her solicitor. Any evidence which had lain in the house on her behalf had now completely disappeared.

On 21 July Florence wrote to her mother from Walton Prison:

> *I am feeling better on the whole, but my whole faith in human nature is at an end. I did believe, however, that blood was thicker than water under no matter what circumstances, but the Maybricks*

*have effectually cured me of that illusion, since they have forsaken
me, their blood relation, and for such stagnant water too! I could
have believed it of Michael, but I did think Edwin was true and
returned some of the trust and affection I have thrown away upon
him for so many years. His day of retribution will come, for God is
just.*[14]

The Liverpool assizes opened on 26 July with Mr Justice
Stephen presiding. Born in 1829, James Fitzjames Stephen
came from a wealthy family background with a strong
puritan streak. His father, who had been an under-secretary
at the Colonial Office, had reared his children in an austere
household, teaching them that life was only for duty and not
for pleasure.

Stephen had been educated at Eton and Trinity College,
Cambridge, which he left without a degree. He was called to
the Bar in 1854 after obtaining an LL B at London University.
A Liberal and a Utilitarian in his early years, he eventually
turned to Conservatism, and Benjamin Disraeli once said of
him: 'It is a thousand pities that Stephen is a Judge, he might
have done anything and everything as a leader of the future
Conservative Party.'[15]

Something of a loner, Stephen was respected but not
popular on the circuit, and his success as a barrister had only
been moderate. In 1868 he spent three years in India as the
law member for the Governor-General's ruling council, and it
was probably there that he acquired the habit of opium
smoking. It was perfectly legal at that time and opium could
be bought openly from a licensed shop or druggist. In a
private letter to Lord Lytton at the time of the trial, Stephen

wrote: 'I do still now and then smoke an opium pipe as my nose requires one occasionally and is comforted by it.'[16]

He became a judge on the Queen's Bench in 1879, and used the criminal court as if it was his own school of morality. It was well known that he had a particular dislike of women in court.

In his opening speech to the Grand Jury,* Stephen said:

> *The next case I will mention to you is a case which I have reason to believe has excited very great attention in this country and certainly if the prisoner is guilty of the crime alleged to her in the charge, it is the most cruel and horrible murder that could be committed.*
>
> *. . . I hardly know how to put it otherwise than this: that if a woman does carry on an adulterous intrigue with another man, it may supply every sort of motive . . . It certainly may quite supply — I won't go further — a very strong motive why she should wish to get rid of her husband.*[17]

His Lordship's opinion proved enough for the all-male Grand Jury, who brought in a 'true bill' against Florence Maybrick, fixing the date of the trial for 31 July 1889.

Meanwhile, in Walton Prison, Florence, suffering from insomnia and stress, was relieving the never-ending boredom by reading, and writing innumerable letters. She knew that her children had returned to the city after six weeks with Alice

---

* The Grand Jury was a tribunal of no fewer than twelve and no more than twenty-four men, to decide whether the magistrates were justified in exposing the accused person to the trouble and risk of a trial by jury. This Grand Jury consisted of twenty-one members, including Mr E.H. Cookson, Mayor of Liverpool.

Yapp in Betws-y-coed, a Welsh holiday resort, but not aware that they had then been spirited away by Edwin. She had also been allowed to read the *Liverpool Post* and the judge's address to the Grand Jury. To a friend she wrote: '...it is enough to appal the stoutest heart. I hear the police are untiring and getting up the case against me regardless of expense.'[18]

Concerned at the thought that her trial was to be held in Liverpool, Florence wrote an emotional letter to her mother:

> *I sincerely hope the Cleavers will arrange for my trial to take place in London. I shall receive an impartial verdict there, which I cannot expect from a jury in Liverpool where minds will virtually be made up before any evidence is heard. The tittle-tattle of servants, the public, friends and enemies, and from a thousand by-currents, besides their personal feelings for Jim, must leave their traces and prejudice their minds no matter what the defence is.*[19]

It was perhaps unfortunate that her solicitors, Messrs Cleaver, had decided not to apply to move the trial to Manchester or London, but they had managed to engage the services of Sir Charles Russell, a famous advocate at the zenith of his career. A Liberal Member of Parliament, in 1886 he had been appointed Attorney-General in Gladstone's short-lived administration, the first Roman Catholic to hold the office since the Reformation.

Russell was a large, good-looking, flamboyant Irishman in his late fifties, driven by boundless energy and enthusiasm for the law and politics. The *Review of Reviews* would say of him: 'He made money rapidly and squandered it as quickly. No man made more money at the bar ... he loved the green table and the green turf and although he played well and had an Irishman's good eye for a horse, you heard more of his debts than of his savings.'[20]

On arrival in Liverpool, he took what was considered the unusual step of visiting the prisoner and talking to her at length before the trial. He would later write that '... he was perplexed by the instructions in the brief'.[21]

Russell's usual fee was a staggering £500, with a daily retainer of £100, a huge amount at the time. It was rumoured that he had negotiated a smaller fee for the Maybrick case because of the public interest. However, the Cleaver brothers, who had been working for Florence since May, also had to be paid, as did her American firm of solicitors, Rowe and Macklin. Arnold Cleaver had travelled to America to rally support, and considerable expenses were mounting from Rowe and Macklin, who had been tracking down witnesses in America and shipping them to England. The Baroness, no stranger to financial disaster, was desperately trying to raise funds for the defence and was borrowing money at an alarming rate from English and American friends.

No money from the sale of the Maybrick estate had been received from Michael, who would later say that as a witness for the prosecution he could not fund Florence's defence. However, with the Baroness's permission, a mortgage of $5,000 was applied to the lease of the already heavily mortgaged property in New York, and signed over to Mr Cleaver.

The Mutual Reserve Fund paid out £200 as a good-will gesture against an insurance policy on James made out to Florence, but they intended to reserve their rights on the remainder until the outcome of the trial. It was the mounting expenses and tightening finances that had probably decided the defence against moving the trial to London.

As the trial date came closer, Florence's nerves sharpened and her correspondence showed how the strain was beginning to tell. In a letter to a friend dated the eve of the trial, she wrote:

> *I feel so lonely — as if every hand were against me. To think that for three or four days I must be unveiled before all those uncharitable eyes ... so far the ordeal has been all anticipation. Pray for me, my friend, for the darkest days of my life are now to be lived through. I trust in God's justice, whatever I may be in the sight of man.*[22]

CHAPTER TEN

❦

What sort of a doctor is he? Oh, well, I
don't know very much about his ability;
but he's got a very good bedside manner!
                                    Punch 1884

When Florence Maybrick's trial opened on 31 July, she
was not aware that it had turned into the social event of
the season. Liverpool society, who had been fighting for
tickets to sit in the public gallery, arrived at the Crown Court
armed with luncheon boxes and opera glasses.

Since the outcome of the Grand Jury, the under-sheriff and
police authorities had been besieged with applications from
public and press alike to gain admission to St George's Hall,
the impressive home of the law courts. One of the finest
Neoclassical buildings in the world, the 500-foot-long structure stood aloof from the commercial heart of the busy port,
towards the north end of the city. Supported by sixteen

elegant Corinthian columns, and completed in 1854 to house the Triennial Music Festival and the assize courts, the building had once been acclaimed by Queen Victoria as 'worthy of ancient Athens'.

The Crown Court was situated at the south end of the building and had seating for 400 people. Part of the public area had already been reserved for one-day ticket holders, and the whole of the old jury box and some seats behind the barristers' table had been made available for the local and international press.

Finding suitable quarters away from the court for the unusually large number of witnesses had resulted in them being split into two groups. Those wanted for the prosecution were sent to wait in the Grand Jury room, while the defence witnesses occupied the sheriff's court. The administrator's office had been a hive of activity for days, and Mr Jennings, Keeper of St George's Hall for the last five years, was seen to throw up his arms in despair and declare that he had never seen anything like it.

Over the seven days of the trial, refreshment contractors Galt and Capper did a roaring trade in tea and sticky buns, as more than 7,000 excited spectators were ushered in and out of the public gallery. The women in the main admitted frankly that they had come to have a 'peek' at Mrs Maybrick; the men, on the other hand, declared that they had come to hear the famous advocate Sir Charles Russell.

Early on the morning of the first day of the trial, as the crowds began to gather outside St George's Hall, Florence's barrister, eating a leisurely breakfast at a local hotel, was joined at the table by an old friend, Sir Henry Lucy, the distinguished parliamentary journalist. Although Russell told Sir Henry that he was confident of his client's acquittal, the barrister was reported to be looking pale and haggard after having, only four months earlier, concluded the most notable and exhausting achievement of his career. As leading counsel with the Parnell Commission, he had faced 340 witnesses over sixty-three bitter and sometimes violent sittings to successfully defend Charles Stewart Parnell, who, with sixty-five Irish Members of Parliament, had been accused of sedition.

In a remarkable, colourful and ruthless cross-examination, Russell had vindicated Parnell by exposing a witness named Piggot as a forger. The poor wretch shot himself a few days later, and the commission ended with Sir Charles fervently pleading the cause of his country in a speech lasting six days. He concluded with genuine tears in his eyes and collapsed dramatically into his seat as the court exploded into rapturous applause. But the long battle had left him thoroughly exhausted, and he was still not completely recovered by the time the Maybrick trial began.

While Sir Charles was enjoying a tasty breakfast, Florence was leaving Walton Prison for the criminal courts in a closed prison van. Better known as a Black Maria, the vehicle looked like 'a sort of hearse with elephantiasis'.[1] The unfortunate prisoners were accommodated in stuffy closed boxes running either side of a central aisle.

A large, unruly crowd had gathered outside the gates of the dismal gaol, jeering and shouting obscenities at the passengers as the top-heavy vehicle lumbered out from the prison yard. In the confined space inside, Florence would remember with horror: 'I felt as if I were already buried.'[2]

Accompanied to the court by a female warder, Florence was dressed in customary mourning. However, the black of her dress was relieved by two white cuffs, and she had substituted the heavy veil worn at the magistrates' court with a more fashionable black bonnet draped with a lighter veil and black silk streamers. A smart crêpe jacket and long black gloves completed a stylish, though somewhat dismal, ensemble.

Long before their arrival at St George's Hall, Florence could hear the noise of the gathering crowds over the clatter of the horses' hooves on the cobblestones. The sunny plaza which fronted the law courts was already thronged with the curious. Street hawkers, singers, beggars and thieves plied their trade amid a carnival atmosphere. Colourful javelin men in cream and crimson uniforms, part of the traditional assizes procession, had been drafted in to assist the police in managing the rapidly increasing mass of people.

The prisoner was ushered with a little difficulty through a side entrance via the warders' kitchen into an underground holding cell. It was a dim, dreary and chillingly cold place in winter and summer alike, separated from a draughty dark passage by a door of iron bars. A little fresh air penetrated through a meagre grating halfway down the whitewashed wall and the cell was lit by a flickering candle secured out of reach within a wire-mesh box. Sitting alone in the semi-darkness on the uncomfortable wooden bench which encircled the room, Florence waited to be called into the dock.

At ten o'clock a blare of trumpets playing 'Silver Threads Among the Gold' filtered into the underground chamber, heralding the entrance of Mr Justice Stephen into the crowded courtroom above. As the echoes died away, it was followed by the call: 'Put up Florence Elizabeth Maybrick.'

Stepping carefully up a winding stone stairway into a well of light, Florence entered the dock in the centre of the hushed court. Blinding sunshine poured in from the domed glass roof, and the sharp colours of the panelled courtroom, in stark contrast to the greyness of Walton Prison, momentarily took her breath away.

On the judge's bench opposite, high above the room, Mr Justice Stephen sat grim-faced in full-bottomed wig, resplendent in scarlet and ermine robes beneath a canopy of gold and crimson. On one side of him, in his role as Deputy-Lieutenant of the County, sat the High Sheriff, wearing a bright scarlet uniform. Lord Sefton and the court chaplain sat on his other side. Below them and to their right, Florence noted the pulpit-like witness box, where the secrets of her life would be exposed by friends and enemies alike. To their left, enclosed within a box-like structure, were two empty rows of hard, high-backed benches, soon to be filled by the jurymen.

Beneath the judge's bench, surrounded by piles of books and brief papers, sat Florence's counsel, Sir Charles Russell, and Mr William Pickford. Opposite them, deep in conversation, were the members of the prosecution, Mr Addison and Mr McConnell. Also present, under a sea of bobbing dusty-white wigs, sat interested members of the Bar, while at the side of the dock a busy line of press representatives were already taking innumerable shorthand notes.

From behind her Florence could feel the uncharitable eyes of the spectators in the gallery burning into the back of her neck. To her left, directly opposite the jury box, in several rows of seats, were the more favoured ticket-holding observers, among them James Maybrick's friends, Liverpool dignitaries and Florence's mother, the Baroness von Roques.

In the dock, Florence was flanked on one side by a female warder and on the other by the Governor of Walton Prison. Towering over her from behind stood a beefy policeman, who indicated that she should approach the front. The court then rose as the chaplain read the opening prayer.

When the court had settled amid a rustle of silk, paper crackling and subdued throat-clearing, the Clerk of the Arraigns stood to read the charge in a loud clear voice: '. . . having at Garston on the 11th of May, 1889, feloniously, wilfully and of her malice aforethought killed and murdered one James Maybrick by the administration to him of poison'.[3] Peering at the prisoner from over the top of gold-rimmed spectacles, he asked: 'How plead you?' Florence replied resolutely: 'Not guilty,' and sat down in the cane-bottomed chair provided for the occasion.

It took under an hour to swear in the all-male 'common jury', which was made up of three plumbers, a wood-turner, two farmers, three shopkeepers, a milliner, a house-painter and a baker. At least one of them could not read or write, and another, it was later discovered, had recently been before the magistrates for beating his wife. Afterwards Florence would remark cynically: 'They were common to the verge of illiteracy.'[4]

Mr Addison, QC, MP, a heavy-set, genial man, already beginning to suffer in the intense heat beneath his black silk gown and wig, stood to open the case for the prosecution. He began by cautioning the jury to disregard what they had read in the press: '. . . I know perfectly well that now you have ceased to be irresponsible members of the community, and are a jury who are sworn to decide the case according to law between the prisoner and the Crown, you will have no difficulty whatever in dismissing from your minds all that you have so heard and seen . . .'[5]

However, considering the huge amount of newspaper coverage over the last few months, it appears unlikely that the jury would suddenly be able to forget all the pre-trial publicity. It may also have been more to the point if Mr Addison had cautioned the jury to decide the case not by the law, but by the evidence.

He then read through the case, taking into consideration all that was already known from the evidence of the inquest and the magistrates' hearing, including the letters to and from Brierley. He concluded by submitting that James had been receiving arsenic in repeated doses, and then, looking at the jury, asked:

> *Gentlemen, who did it? I shall be compelled and am compelled, to submit there is very cogent and powerful evidence to show that it was his wife who administered it. Undoubtedly if she was the person who administered these repeated doses to him, then, gentlemen, she is guilty of the cruel offence of wilful murder, and it will be your painful but bounden and incumbent duty to say so.[6]*

With a flourish he returned to his seat, mopping the sweat from his brow and adjusting his wig. A Bootle surveyor was then brought in to show the plans of Battlecrease House, after which Michael Maybrick took the stand.

There was a rustle of enthusiasm from the gallery as the

ladies in the court raised their opera glasses and strained to have a closer view of the famous composer. Haughty and self-possessed, Michael appeared to be taking the proceedings in his stride.

When Sir Charles Russell rose to cross-examine, he soon established two important points: that nothing had been administered to James from the bottle of Valentine's Meat Juice, which had undoubtedly contained arsenic; and that no arsenic had been found in any of the other bottles that Michael had passed to the doctors for analysis.

Referring to the incident with Brierley, Russell asked: 'You are aware there were complaints on both sides?' Flushing uncomfortably, Michael barked: 'Yes.'[7] However, he did not elaborate, and nor did Russell pursue this line of questioning, probably in deference to his client's instructions. This was disappointing, as the motive put forward by the prosecution relied heavily on Florence's love affair with Brierley. The reply to this one question, however, had informed the court that James had been an adulterer and that Florence would have had grounds for a separation had she wished it. But how many of the jury had missed this important point?

'Have you come across the cash-box from Mrs Maybrick's wardrobe?' asked Russell next. 'Are you aware it has been asked for by the representatives of Mrs Maybrick?'[8] Michael denied all knowledge of the cash-box, and although it was only a small point, taken in conjunction with earlier evidence at the inquest it showed that Florence had to contend with suspicion and ill-feeling not only from her servants, but also from her in-laws, to the point that she was unable to retrieve her own property.

Further evidence admitted by Michael would be printed the following day by the *Liverpool Echo*, who reported it under the headline 'A Surprising Admission'.

> *The most startling part of the cross-examination, which aroused the first murmur of excitement in court, was when Sir Charles asked the witness if he had received a letter from Mrs Maybrick saying that her husband was ill 'physicing himself'.*
>
> *'Did she say,' asked the counsel, 'that she had seen him take a white powder frequently, and that if she talked about it he flew into a passion, and didn't like the subject talked about?' The witness admitted that that was the tenor of her letter.*
>
> *'Did she say that she had searched for this drug and could not find it?' The witness had no recollection.*
>
> *'Did she say that it was perhaps strychnine or some other drug? And did she ask you to speak to Dr Fuller about it?'*
>
> *The witness said it was very possible, and that the purport of her letter was that 'her husband was taking a powder', and she thought it was something he ought not to do. This extraordinary evidence was not adduced at the inquest or at the police court.*[9]

Michael left the courtroom somewhat bruised after admitting that he had destroyed the letter after receiving it. It was then Mrs Briggs's turn to enter the witness box. By the time she had completed her evidence, there was no doubt in the public's mind of the atmosphere of suspicion and unkindness which had prevailed against Florence, much of it orchestrated by Mrs Briggs herself.

When he stood up to cross-examine the witness, Russell questioned her about the letter to Brierley which Florence had written after James had died, and which Mrs Briggs had handed to the policeman: 'Is it not a fact that you suggested the writing of it?' he asked. 'I did, in sarcasm,' she replied.

'You were examined on this before the coroner's jury; did you say one word about making the suggestion in sarcasm then?' And Russell rolled the word 'sarcasm' around his mouth as if he had suddenly discovered a delicious morsel of food. 'No, I was too nervous,' Mrs Briggs replied, burning with embarrassment.

'At all events, whether you suggested it in sarcasm or not, you suggested it?'[10] Mrs Briggs looked at Russell, her face now ashen, and nodded her head in mortified agreement.

Further questioning elicited the fact that there had been discovered in the house more than a hundred medicine bottles. Mrs Briggs, however, confirmed that those containing arsenic found during the search undertaken on the Sunday morning had not been under lock and key or in any place exclusively used by Mrs Maybrick.

Under Russell's searching questions, the witness confirmed that on the morning of the day Florence had written to Brierley that James was 'sick unto death', Mrs Briggs herself had also believed him to be seriously ill. It appears that the Battlecrease House busybody was a much better diagnostician than the two attending doctors, both of whom, at this stage, had been confident of their patient's recovery. She also admitted that James had been 'dosing himself', something both Michael and Edwin had consistently denied.

Another ten witnesses gave their evidence on the first day, including Edwin Maybrick, who confirmed that Florence had not given his brother any medicine, food or drink without supervision from the Wednesday before his death. When asked if his brother took medicines, Edwin replied: 'From time to time he took ordinary liver medicine.'

'Any sort of arsenic?' asked Russell. 'No,'[11] replied Edwin firmly.

Four days later, however, Edwin would be recalled to the stand after handing over a pill box he had found at Battlecrease House almost eight weeks earlier. The pills, consisting of iron, quinine and arsenic, had been supplied to James when he had last been in Norfolk, Virginia. Edwin had undoubtedly lied about James taking arsenic, during both the trial and the magistrates' hearing.

'Where did you find this box?' asked Mr Addison. 'I found it in the drawer of the washhand stand in my brother's bedroom,' replied Edwin. 'I found it at the time the furniture was being removed from the house.'

Sir Charles Russell, with not a little sarcasm, asked: 'Did you know that Mr Cleaver, the president of the Law Society, was acting for this lady?' 'I did,' replied Edwin.

'Did you communicate it to him?' Edwin responded simply: 'No.'[12]

No further questions were asked and the matter was quickly forgotten. But how much more evidence favourable to Florence had been spirited away?

Witness after witness gave evidence, and the first long day drew to a close, Mr Justice Stephen adjourning the trial until the following day. The weary spectators left for home, the eager press ran with their copy to meet their deadlines, Florence rumbled back to Walton Prison in the Black Maria, and the jury retired to a nearby hotel.

The precautions for secluding the jury were shockingly lax, and it would later be discovered that some of them left the hotel in the evening and were seen playing billiards in a local bar, enjoying a glass of beer and discussing the case with anyone who was interested.

On Thursday, the second day of the trial, it was the turn of the servants to take the stand. Slowly a picture was coming together of James's illness, Florence's foolishness and the atmosphere of suspicion against her. The spectators were again finding the heat of the courtroom oppressive, while in the dock Florence was beginning to flag and had to be revived with a glass of water. However, when Alice Yapp took the stand, physical discomfort was disregarded as the packed courtroom tensed to hear the servant girl's vital evidence.

At the inquest and the magistrates' hearing, it had been noticed that Alice Yapp had been pert with her answers and appeared to be enjoying herself. Now, however, her demeanour had changed considerably and she presented a picture of a very quiet, shy and respectable young woman. Dressed in a well-cut coat and a saucy hat covered in pink flowers, her voice was so low during the examination that Mr Justice Stephen repeatedly had to ask her to speak up. Several times the Clerk of the Court wagged his quill pen at her in annoyance, as few people in the court could hear a word she was saying.

After Mr Addison had gently taken her step by step through the Grand National quarrel, her discovery of the fly-papers soaking in the basin and her opinion of her master's health, Sir Charles rose to cross-examine. It was some time before he arrived at the question of the letter to Brierley.

Pausing briefly, he quietly refreshed himself from his famous snuff box. His legal colleagues sat up with renewed interest. They alone had recognised the distinguished advocate's silent battle cry. His cross-examination of Piggot during the Parnell commission had opened in the same unconcerned way. Appearing more interested in the contents of his snuff box than in the witness, he began with almost complete disinterest: 'Why did you open the letter?' Alice replied innocently: 'Because Mrs Maybrick wished that it should go by that post.'

Raising his eyes, Russell glared at the servant and repeated: 'Why did you open the letter?' This time Alice said nothing, and after a pause the judge interrupted and asked: 'Did anything happen to the letter?' 'Yes,' she replied, relieved. 'It fell in the dirt.'

Annoyed with the judge's interruption of his famous cross-examination technique, Russell rudely ignored him and asked again: 'Why did you open the letter?' This time the question reverberated from the walls of the hushed courtroom, and although Alice blanched she replied with vigour: 'I have answered you.'

'Why did you open the letter?' shouted Sir Charles, emphasising every word. 'I opened the letter to put it in a clean envelope,'[13] replied the girl, ashen-faced.

With his eyes burning into Alice's face, Russell took the nursemaid through every painful step on her journey from the garden of Battlecrease House to her opening the letter on the post office step. With the envelope in his hand, he waved it at the witness and cried: 'Just take it in your hand. Is the direction clear enough? . . . did it never occur to you that you could get a clean envelope if you were particular about cleanliness and put it unopened into that?' Alice whispered: 'Oh I never thought of that.'

'On your oath, girl, did you not manufacture that stain as an excuse for opening your mistress's letter?' asked Russell. 'I did not,' exclaimed the servant.[14]

With a look of scorn, Russell sat down, and Alice Yapp tottered from the witness box, her face turning from white to crimson. Although she had stood up reasonably well and had been tougher than Russell had expected, there was not a woman amongst the spectators who would have employed her in their homes after that evidence.

The prosecution evidence continued on the third day, mainly examining the medical testimony. Dr Humphreys admitted that if he had not been told by Michael that arsenic poisoning was suspected he would have signed the death certificate. For his part, Dr Carter was now convinced that James had died from arsenic poisoning, but he had to acknowledge that he had never before treated anyone who had. Dr Barron, who had assisted in over five hundred post-mortems, including James Maybrick's, concluded that death was due to inflammation of the stomach, probably caused by some irritant poison. However, he testified that even with his experience he could not differentiate between the symptoms of food poisoning and those of arsenic poisoning.

The last of the thirty-two witnesses brought in by the prosecution was Dr Thomas Stevenson, a Home Office analyst. When he gave his evidence, on Saturday 3 August, the fourth day of the trial, he declared himself confident that death had been due to arsenical poisoning.

However, the medical evidence was not yet concluded. Sir Charles Russell would call on three more eminent medical men to speak for the defence: Dr Charles Meymott Tidy, who had been a Home Office analyst for twenty years and was examiner in forensic medicine at the London Hospital; Dr Rawden Macnamara, an expert on arsenic poisoning and Doctor of Medicine at the University of London; and a local expert, Dr Frank Thomas Paul, a pathologist and Professor of Medical Jurisprudence at University College, Liverpool. All three agreed that the amount of arsenic present in the victim's body was at the highest computation less than half a grain, and all were firm in their belief that James Maybrick had not died of arsenic poisoning.

The basic argument of all the medical men was that the cause of death had been ingestion of an irritant, which had then given the victim gastro-enteritis. What they appeared to disagree on was whether that irritant had been bad food or arsenic. They did not seem to have considered, however, the possibility that the irritant which had set up James Maybrick's gastro-enteritis was not arsenic but strychnine.[*]

When Sir Charles Russell opened the case for the defence on the Saturday afternoon, the courtroom was full to bursting

---

[*] Strychnine is not a mineral poison like arsenic and would have been tested differently.

A footnote on p.240 of *The Necessity for Criminal Appeal*, edited by J.H. Levy (1899), says: 'It has been stated, apparently on good authority, that Dr Tidy afterwards came to the conclusion that the irritant which caused death was strychnine; but the evidence given at the trial that Mr Maybrick had been dosing himself with strychnine, and ascribed his illness to it, was very defective.'

point, with spectators squashed at the back and in every place it was possible to stand. As he spoke his opening speech, Russell waved an elegant hand towards the prisoner and said: 'Gentlemen of the jury, with my learned friend Mr Pickford I share the very anxious duty of defending upon the most serious charge that can be preferred, the Friendless lady in the dock . . .'[15] All eyes turned to Florence, who burst into tears at the kindest words she had heard all week.

Russell went on to exhort the jury to remember two questions: was it death by arsenical poisoning, and if so, was that poisoning administered by Florence Maybrick? He continued:

> . . . *it is an extraordinary fact . . . that this lady was deposed from the position of mistress in her own house, deposed from the position of looking after her husband and pointed at as an object of suspicion — no adequate search or inquiry was made. For it does not seem that at any part of the case there was anyone manly enough, friendly enough, honest enough to go to her and name to her, in the form of words a statement of the charge against her, in order to see whether or not she had any explanation to offer.*[16]

Turning to the judge, Russell advised him that his client wished to make a voluntary statement to the court at the end of the defence testimony. Stephen snarled:

> *I wish you had mentioned this before, that she might have made her statement before you addressed the jury. However, I may allow it after you have addressed the jury. She can't unfortunately be sworn, nor can she be questioned about it, but I will allow her to make a*

statement; and the jury will take time to consider that it was a voluntary statement, a statement made, I am sorry for her sake that it is so – without the possibility of cross-examination, and without the sanction and weight attached to oath.[17]

In 1889, a person on the capital charge of murder was not allowed to give evidence in his or her own defence. Permitting the prisoner to make a statement to the court was completely at the discretion of the presiding judge, and Russell's timing, as Mr Justice Stephen had remarked, was very poor. If Florence made her statement at the end of the defence evidence, Russell would be left with the disadvantage of being unable to call on any witness to corroborate what she had said. Eventually, they agreed between them that she could prepare her statement over the weekend, but without the benefit of legal advice as to the content. Meanwhile Russell continued:

One concluding observation only remains. I refer to the dark cloud that passed over her life, and rests, and must for all time rest, upon her character as a woman and a wife. But I would earnestly entreat you not to allow any repugnance that you may find resting in your minds against a sin so abhorrent as that to lead you to the conclusion, unless the evidence drives you irresistibly there, that, because a wife has forgotten her duty and faithfulness to her husband, she is to be regarded as one who deliberately and wickedly will seek to destroy his life.[18]

As Sir Charles returned to his seat and the first defence witness was called, he was feeling quietly confident. He was aware of the altered attitudes of the crowd outside and the spectators in the court. They at least were moving towards the opinion that Mrs Maybrick was not guilty. On his recent journeys back and forth between the courtroom and the hotel, he had found himself mobbed by people cheering and clapping.

His line of defence would be that any arsenic found in the body of the deceased had undoubtedly been put there by the man himself. This would be supported by two old friends of the victim and a servant shipped over from America, who would all testify that James had been an arsenic-eater when he resided in the States.

Further evidence would be heard from city chemist Edwin Garnett Heaton, who had identified James from a photograph. He would testify that he recognised Mr Maybrick as a gentleman whom he had frequently supplied with a pick-me-up containing arsenic during the eighteen months prior to April 1888.

Unfortunately, there would be no corroboration that James had indeed been the man the chemist had been supplying. Russell had missed a vital mistake in the evidence. In the printed list of medicine bottles discovered at the offices of Maybrick & Co., the one marked 'Spirits of Sal Volatile' was wrongly attributed to Edwin G. Easton, instead of Edwin G. Heaton. This had been an error on the part of the police, and was later rectified by a memo from the Home Office, but not until 22 August 1889, after the trial had ended.

From her seat in the dock Florence too had noticed a change of attitude amongst the women in the court. Many of them now averted their eyes instead of rudely staring at her with condemnation, and her journeys in the prison omnibus were no longer subject to the frightening behaviour of angry crowds.

As Russell cross-examined his last witness for the day, Florence's thoughts drifted to the statement she was determined to read to the court on Monday afternoon. As events would show, it would turn out to be one of the biggest mistakes of her life.

CHAPTER ELEVEN

❧❧

Never be a pioneer. It's the early
Christian that gets the fattest lion.
Saki (H.H. Monro), 1870–1916

Monday dawned bright and sunny, as befitted a public holiday, and the population appeared determined to make the best of the continued good weather. Although shops and offices lay silent and deserted behind wooden shutters, the streets leading from the river and the railway station streamed with families carrying baskets of provisions. Since Saturday evening interest in the trial had reached boiling point, and many of the holiday-makers decided to stay in the vicinity of the assize courts, where it was business as usual as the Maybrick case entered its fifth day.

Bathed in a pool of sunshine, Florence Maybrick sat in the dock between two expressionless matrons who anticipated her every move. Looking slightly green from her recent journey in the prison omnibus, she fidgeted nervously, anxiously waiting for her chance to speak to the court. Kept in relative isolation over the weekend, the prisoner had spent the time pacing the floor of her cell, rehearsing the statement she was about to read with the aid of the blue foolscap paper clasped tightly in her hand.

With her mind focused on the ordeal to come, she was only vaguely aware of the vigorous voice of Sir James Poole, the last of the defence witnesses, who was disclosing to the court a conversation which had taken place at the entrance of the Palantine Club some weeks before James Maybrick's death:

> . . . *Mr Maybrick, who had an impetuous way, blurted out 'I take poisonous medicines.' I said, 'How horrid. Don't you know, my dear friend, that the more you take of these things the more you require, and you will go on till they carry you off.' I think he made some expression and shrugged his shoulders, and I went on my way . . .*[1]

As the one-time Mayor of Liverpool left the stand and the court fell silent, Sir Charles Russell had a whispered conversation with his client. Florence nervously refreshed herself with a glass of water, then stood up and stepped towards the front of the dock, clutching the precious notes in one hand and a white handkerchief in the other.

The court waited with interest as the defendant, after a moment's hesitation, took a hasty look at her notes. 'My Lord,' she whispered hoarsely, 'I wish to make a statement, as well as I can, to you, a few facts in connection with the dreadfully crushing charge that has been made against me – namely, the wilful and deliberate poisoning of my husband, the father of my dear children . . .'[2] Here her voice trailed off and she broke down and yielded to a violent fit of sobbing. In the gallery, more than one delicate handkerchief was hastily searched for.

'I wish principally to refer to the use of the fly-papers and to the bottle of meat essence.' With tears flowing freely down her face, she gasped and made a conscious effort to control herself. Grasping the rail tightly, she claimed:

The fly-papers were bought with the intention of using as a cosmetic. Before my marriage, and since, for many years, I have been in the habit of using a face-wash prescribed for me by Dr Greggs, of Brooklyn. It consisted principally of arsenic, tincture of Benzoin, Elderflower water and some other ingredients. This prescription I lost or mislaid last April, and as at that time I was suffering from slight eruption of the face, I thought I should like to try to make a substitute myself.

I was anxious to get rid of this eruption before I went to a ball on the 30th of that month. When I had been in Germany, many of my young friends there I had seen using a solution derived from fly-papers, Elder water, Lavender water and other things mixed, and then applied to the face with a handkerchief well soaked in the solution.

I used the fly-papers in the same manner. But to avoid the evaporation of the scent it was necessary to exclude the air as much as possible, and for that purpose I put a plate over the fly-papers and put a folded towel over that, and another towel over that. My mother has been aware for a great many years that I have used an arsenical cosmetic in solution.

My Lord, I now wish to refer to the bottle of meat essence. On Thursday night, the 9th of May, after Nurse Gore had given my husband beef tea, I went and sat on the bed beside him. He complained to me of being very sick and very depressed, and he implored me then to give him this powder which he had referred to early in the evening, and which I had declined to give him. I was overwrought, terribly anxious, miserably unhappy and his evident distress utterly unnerved me. He had told me that the powder would not harm him and that I could put it in his food. I then consented.

My Lord, I had not one true or honest friend in that house. I had no one to consult and no one to advise me. I was deposed from my position as mistress in my own house, and from the position of attending upon my husband, notwithstanding that he was so ill . . .³

Again the defendant burst into uncontrollable sobbing, and her evident distress was too much for some of the female spectators, who dabbed their eyes in sympathy. It was some minutes before Florence was able to continue:

Notwithstanding the evidence of the nurses and servants, I may say that he wished to have me with him. He missed me whenever I was not with him; whenever I went out of the room he asked for me, and for four days before he died, I was not allowed to give him a piece of ice without its being taken out of my hand. When I found the powder, I took it into the inner room, with the beef juice, *and in pushing through the door I upset the bottle and in order to make up the quantity of fluid spilled, I added a considerable quantity of water . . .⁴* [added emphasis].

The court gasped in amazement, the jury sat up, glancing at one another in surprise, and Mr Addison, who was rapidly making notes, nearly fell off his seat in delight at such an incriminating admission from the prisoner. Sir Charles Russell sat back in his chair, his arms folded and his head down, apparently unconcerned about his client's statement.

There was plainly no need for Florence to confess to interfering with the meat juice; she had already done so to the Cleaver brothers and her mother on the day of her arrest, and her defence counsel was well aware of it. Her statement was the complete responsibility of the defence, in the sense that it was made with their permission and would not have been made had they forbidden it, so they must have had a reasonable idea of what she was going to say. Had Florence simply ignored Russell's advice?

Nurse Gore had, after all, not actually witnessed Mrs Maybrick putting anything in the meat juice. She had merely suspected it, at a time when the prisoner's every action was being treated as potentially incriminating. Russell's defence had concentrated on the fact that James Maybrick had not received anything from the offending bottle afterwards. Had Florence simply not understood his strategy? Now, however, the damage was done and Florence had jeopardised the entire case, leaving the jury wondering what other opportunities she had had to tamper with her husband's food or medicine.

Meanwhile, completely unaware of having causing a sensation Florence was continuing blindly with her statement:

On returning to the room I found my husband asleep and I placed the bottle on the table by the window.

When he awoke he had a choking sensation in his throat, and vomited. After that he appeared a little better, and as he did not ask for the powder again, and as I was not anxious to give it to him, I removed the bottle from the small table where it would attract his attention to the top of the washstand, where he could not see it. There I left it, my lord, until, I believe, Mr Michael Maybrick took possession of it.

Until Tuesday, the 14th May, the Tuesday after my husband's death, and until a few minutes before Mr Bryning made this terrible charge against me, no one in the house had informed me of the fact that a death certificate had been refused, and that a post-mortem examination had taken place; or that there was any reason to suppose that my husband had died from other than natural causes. It was only when Mrs Briggs alluded to the presence of arsenic in the meat juice that I was made aware of the nature of the powder my husband had asked me to give him.

I then attempted to make an explanation to Mrs Briggs, such as I am stating to your lordship, when a policeman interrupted the conversation and put a stop to it.[5]

Florence's pleasant voice with its slight American accent had lowered considerably towards the end of the long speech, her face had turned deathly white and she appeared on the point of collapse. The silent, captive audience strained forward as she made one last effort and continued in little more than a faltering whisper: 'In conclusion, I have only to add that for the love of our children and for the sake of their future, a perfect reconciliation had taken place between us, and that on the day before his death I made a full and free confession to him and received his entire forgiveness for the fearful wrong I had done him.'[6]

In the ensuing silence, broken only by Florence's muffled sobbing and that of some of the women spectators, Sir

Charles Russell rose hastily to his feet. 'My Lord,' he said, 'I now desire to call two persons to whom that statement was made before the inquest to give evidence to that effect.'*[7]

On the bench, Mr Justice Stephen shook his bewigged head and replied: 'I wish to say it is very painful to me to have to refuse what I feel to be an essentially reasonable request, but I think I cannot allow it. I cannot go beyond what the law allows.'[8] Sir Charles responded with a courtly bow to the judge and answered: 'I do not for one moment make any complaint to what your lordship says.'[9]

Looking pale and visibly shaken by both his client's statement and Mr Justice Stephen's refusal to hear his two witnesses, Sir Charles shuffled some papers in a bid to gain time. After a brief pause and a few hearty sniffs from the contents of his famous snuff box, he launched into the closing speech for the defence.

He first attempted to curry favour with the jury by reminding them that Mrs Maybrick had not requested a change of venue, but had chosen to be tried before a local jury: 'She comes before you asking from you nothing but that you will willingly grant a careful, an attentive and a sympathetic hearing in her case,'[10] he asserted.

With little reference to his written notes, and in a voice unemotional, sincere and clear, he then undertook step by step to destroy the prosecution case. Concentrating on the controversial medical evidence and the prosecution's failure to fix with certainty the cause of death, he turned to the jury and said: 'The question I have therefore to ask you in this

---

* It was the Cleaver brothers – Florence's solicitors – Russell wanted to call.

connection in the case, touching the cause of death, can you say that you are satisfied as reasonable men, beyond reasonable doubt, that this was a case of arsenical poisoning at all. If you are not, there is an end of this matter . . .'[11]

Moving on to the motive, he suggested that if the letter to Brierley had not been intercepted by Nurse Yapp the charge would never have been made. However, he could not reject the overwhelming evidence of Florence's unfaithfulness, and he had little choice but to meet Victorian morality head on, declaiming gravely:

> *This lady fell. She forgot her self-respect. She forgot her duty to her husband . . .*
>
> *The sole suggested motive, as I understand, in this case is that she desired to conceal from her husband the grave error which she had committed, that she had conceived a feeling of estrangement towards her husband; and was tempted by wicked, deliberate, foul, criminal means to end his life. If there were not this act of infidelity on her part, there would be no motive assigned to this case.*[12]

He then briefly referred to James Maybrick, speaking of him as a man who seemed liked by his friends and was not without a kindly or generous nature. 'But certainly in some respects,' he added, 'and in respects that touch closely some questions which we have to consider in this case, his history is a peculiar one.'[13]

Alluding to the fly-papers which the prosecution had placed so much store by, he pointed out the fact that their use would have been superfluous when so much other arsenic had been available around the house. Arsenic which, he reminded the jury, the prosecution had not even attempted to prove had been acquired by the defendant. As for Florence's statement, Russell shrugged his shoulders and attempted to undervalue it by referring to it as:

> *At first sight a self-incriminating statement, although a statement which does not involve in any way the question of the direct cause of this man's death . . . I leave it to speak with such effect on your ears and hearts as the circumstances under which it was delivered, and the way in which it was delivered, and the tone in which it was delivered.*[14]

Finally, Sir Charles, his hands clenched tightly on the lapels of his silk robe, looked searchingly and sternly into the faces of the jury, saying:

> *And now I end as I began, by asking you each one of you in the perplexities, in the doubts, in the mystery, in the difficulties which surround this case, in view of the contrariety of things and opinions presented to you, upon some points more or less important, can you, can any one of you with satisfied judgment and with safe conscience, say that this woman is guilty . . .*[15]

The spectators drew in their breath in admiration as the gifted advocate finished his address. Relying more on argument than sentiment, he had manipulated the facts of the case with masterly skill and a remarkable memory. Although his performance had lacked the drama and flamboyance evident through the Parnell Commission, the consensus was that this had been Sir Charles Russell at his best. He, however, must have realised that he had blundered badly by allowing Florence to make that statement to the court.

As events would show, ill luck and bad judgement had dogged the defence during the whole of the case. In 1894 inventor Valentine Blake would claim in an affidavit that he had written to Mr Cleaver before the start of the trial but had never received a reply. It had been Blake who had given James Maybrick the packets of black and white arsenic, which Russell could have identified as being the sum of the arsenic discovered in the house. Disclosure of this evidence during the trial would have made all the difference to the defence case. However, Florence's solicitors had either never received the letter or dismissed it.

Finding people in Liverpool prepared to speak for the defence had also been a problem, as Mr Cleaver had discovered. On the last day of the defence evidence he asked Bessie Brierley, the housemaid, to testify that Mr Maybrick's clothes were wet on the day of the Wirral races. According to Mary Cadwallader, the waitress at Battlecrease House: 'Bessie tossed her head and refused to tell. She said she had given evidence on one side, and she was not going to give any on the other. Mr Cleaver remarked that at least she might give him a civil answer.'[16]

After the trial, both defence and prosecution would be criticised for not calling on more witnesses. Where was Mrs Samuelson, who had testified at the inquest that Florence had said she hated her husband? Why was John Baillie Knight not called? His letter to Florence, although not submitted during the trial, was read to the jury by the judge, who would subsequently suggest that Knight too had had an illicit relationship with Florence.

Why did the defence not call the Baroness to establish her daughter's use of fly-papers in Germany? And why was James Maybrick's most intimate friend, George Davidson, not asked to affirm his misuse of medicine? The two men were forever in each other's company, and Davidson had not only witnessed James's will, but was present in Battlecrease House the night he died.

It was half past three when Russell closed his speech for the defence and Mr Addison stood to deliver his address for the prosecution. He did not possess the power or personality of Russell, but he spoke with solid ability for two hours, one hour less than the defence. Unfortunately, his summing-up did not do him credit. He made a considerable number of errors, was vague with the facts and sometimes wild with the evidence. Sir Charles Russell found himself continually jumping up and down to correct him.

Addison suggested to the court that the servants at Battlecrease had shown only kindness to Florence, when in fact their loyalty had been divided, with Alice Yapp and Bessie Brierley on one side and Mary Cadwallader and Elizabeth Humphreys firmly on the other. He ignored the evidence of Sir James Poole, Mrs Briggs and every other witness who had testified that James 'dosed himself', and tried to insist that Maybrick only took medicine with intelligence and care.

Dealing briefly with the contradictory medical evidence, he concentrated on the theory that Mrs Maybrick had administered arsenic to her husband. In the dock Florence looked gloomy as she listened to Addison's speech. When he described her as a 'woman capable of duplicity, deceit and falsehood',[17] she shrank back into her chair in considerable embarrassment.

Moving on to Florence's statement, Addison remarked, with a sly dig at Sir Charles Russell: 'I can hardly help having a feeling of regret that the terrible statement which has been made to-day should have been made.' Describing it as 'inconsistent with the defence',[18] he proceeded to pull it to pieces while his opponents squirmed uncomfortably in their seats.

Some of Addison's interpretations of the evidence were certainly very imaginative and open to argument. For example, Nurse Wilson had testified that before James had died he had said to Florence: 'Oh Bunny, oh Bunny, how could you do it?' Russell had concluded that he had meant 'How could you be unfaithful?' Mr Addison, on the other hand, deduced that the patient had meant 'How could you poison me?' It occurred to more than one person in the court that if Addison's meaning was correct, it was curious that the sick man had not appealed to someone else in the house to protect him from any further administration of poison.

The prosecution counsel also emphasised Florence's 'adulterous intercourse' with Brierley, suggesting that she, 'by her own handwriting and her actual deeds, had so interwoven her adultery with her conduct that it was impossible to treat it as an ordinary case of adultery, and not treat it as having any actual connection with the alleged crime'.[19]

On concluding his speech, Mr Addison summarised the duties of the jury and left them in no doubt as to the prosecution opinion on the matter, saying solemnly:

If she be guilty, if these facts satisfy your minds, then, gentlemen, we have indeed, in this investigation, brought to light a very terrible deed of darkness, and proved a murder founded upon profligacy

*and adultery, and carried out with a hypocrisy and a cunning which
have been rarely equalled in the annals of crime.*[20]

By the time Addison regained his seat, it was too late for the
court to hear the judge's summing-up, and they retired for the
evening. The newspapers, whose verbatim reports of the trial
would be sold out almost before the ink was dry on the paper,
speculated that there would be a verdict the following day. As
it turned out, they were destined to be disappointed.

By Tuesday morning the fine weather had broken, and the
gusty wind and rain dispelled the gaping crowds, except for a
hardy few who huddled together under the smoke-blackened
colonnade of the law courts. As the sixth day of the drama
unfolded, dusky shadows invaded the courtroom as dim
daylight struggled in through the glass roof. The gas lights
fluttered to life with a gentle hiss, their subdued beam reflecting from the dark-grey granite columns.

When Mr Justice Stephen rose to commence his
summing-up of the mass of material, he appeared painfully
overanxious and his grasp of the evidence was not always
sure. He made many mistakes with dates and times, and
became waspish if corrected by the defence. All day he spoke
in a quiet, monotonous tone, and a feeling of extreme languor
crept over the courtroom. The reporters leaned exhausted
over the old jury box, scribbling constantly into their note-
books, and the eyes of the jury glazed over with fatigue as His
Honour droned on until late in the afternoon.

On the bench, the High Sheriff spent his time reading a
newspaper, while the judge's clerk wearily pasted clippings
into a book as Mr Justice Stephen spoke over his head to the

sleepy jury. Mr Addison had had a particularly heavy luncheon and fell fast asleep with his head on the desk. As none of his colleagues had either the nerve or the inclination to wake him, the judge continued with his mumbling address accompanied by the gentle snoring of the senior counsel for the prosecution. Sir Charles Russell was busy all day with another case in the civil court, and the only person who appeared to be listening to the soporific monologue was Florence.

Most of the judge's summing-up on this first day dealt with the conflict of medical testimony, which he repeated in all its tedious, incomprehensible detail, reminding the jaded jury that it was essential to the charge that the victim had died of arsenic poisoning.

On the second day, however, Mr Justice Stephen became much more animated and alert, enthusing about the defendant's infidelity and appearing to have forgotten that on the previous day his charge had indicated that there was doubt as to whether James Maybrick had actually died of arsenic. He advised the jury: 'I can hardly see how it could have been administered except by crime, and it had not been suggested that any one could well be the criminal except the prisoner in the dock.'[21]

As Florence flinched in her chair, the judge thundered poetically:

Recollect that while her husband lived, and according to her own account, while his life was trembling in the balance, even at that awful moment there arose in her heart and flowed from her pen various terms of endearment to the man with whom she had behaved so disgracefully. That was an awful thing to think of, and a thing you will have to consider in asking yourselves whether she is guilty or not guilty.[22]

Never had a court heard such a damaging and prejudicial speech from a judge. His Honour appeared to be doing a better job for the prosecution than the prosecution counsel had done before him. At one point he tried to suggest that Florence had slept with Brierley in London after the reconciliation with her husband. This was too much even for Mr Addison, who rose up sharply and corrected him about the date of the Flatman's affair.

There is little doubt that when Mr Justice Stephen tried the Maybrick case in the August of 1889, he had not completely recovered from his recent stroke. In 1891, questions were asked in the House of Commons as to his competence, and he was subsequently forced to retire from the bench. Less than five years after the trial he died in a private lunatic asylum in Ipswich.

Many years later, the *Daily Post* would publish a damning editorial about Stephen under the headline 'The Great Mad Judge':

Few who looked upon the strong, square head can have suspected that the light of reason was burning very low within. Yet as the days of the trial dragged by, days that must have been as terrible to the judge as to the prisoner, men began to nod at him, to wonder and to whisper.

Nothing more painful was ever seen in court than the proud old man's desperate struggle to control his failing faculties. But the struggle was unavailing. It was clear that the growing volume of facts was unassorted, undigested in his mind; that his judgment swayed backward and forward in the conflict of testimony; that his memory failed to grip the most salient features of the case for many minutes together. It was shocking to think that a human life depended upon the direction of the wreck of what was once a great judge.[23]

After twelve interminable hours of inaccurate summing-up and metaphysical speculation by the judge, the advocacy of Sir Charles Russell long forgotten, the spectators were left more confused than ever over the evidence and the jury retired to consider the case. As they were ushered out of the courtroom, Mr Justice Stephen's latest comments rang in their ears:

I could say a good many other things about the awful nature of the charge, but I do not think it necessary to say any one thing. Your own hearts must tell you what it is. For a person to go on deliberately administering poison to a poor, helpless sick man upon whom she has already inflicted a dreadful injury, an injury fatal to married life, the person who could do such a thing as that must indeed be destitute of the least trace of human feeling.

. . . There is no doubt that the propensities which lead persons to vices of that kind do kill all the more tender, all the more manly, or all the more womanly feelings of the human mind.[24]

It was eighteen minutes past three on the seventh day of the trial when the jury were eventually ushered into the room set aside for them to consider their verdict. In the courtroom, Mr Justice Stephen, mopping the perspiration from his brow after his marathon address, was approached by Mr Addison, who remarked casually: 'Oh, they can't convict her on that evidence.'[25]

As the court cleared, Florence was led down the dark passage to the chilly holding cell below. Settling on the hard wooden bench, she was surprised when the door opened and a wardress informed her that she had two visitors. Florence looked up in astonishment as her mother's American lawyer William Potter entered, followed by the US Consul. Potter approached her, stammering: 'Florence, I am very sorry for you, but I must insist on your signing these papers today.'

Stunned at his insensitivity, she replied hysterically: 'I cannot sign the papers today, I am not in a fit state to consider business, not in a mental condition. The court has adjourned, but it is expected to return in a few minutes. My life hangs in the balance and I cannot think of anything else.'

Potter, however, was adamant. 'You must sign them,' he argued. 'Because this money we want to get in the event of the trial going against you, to get a new trial at once.' When Florence asked him what the papers were for, he replied: 'They are deeds for the sale of the lands in Kentucky . . . for $10,000.'[26]

It had taken more than ten years, but at long last the Baroness had managed to sell the land she owned in America, a third of which belonged to Florence. Months of painstaking work by Potter to bring the sale to fruition had concluded with his hasty journey to Europe to complete the paperwork before Florence could be convicted. Nothing on earth was going to stop him from earning his commission and getting the Baroness off his back.

One of Potter's biggest problems had been discovering the whereabouts of the Baron von Roques, whose signature had also been required before completion. He had eventually tracked him down, with the assistance of the police, in a back street in Vienna. At first the Baron had refused to sign anything for fear he would be mixed up with the murder trial, but for a consideration of 1,500 marks he had relented on the condition that he should never have any other legal business with his estranged wife.

'I cannot sign any papers today,' Florence cried. 'Cannot you bring them to the prison tomorrow?' 'No,' insisted Potter. 'We must have your signature before the verdict, because if you are convicted it would be illegal.'

Florence hesitated. 'Are they alright?' she asked plaintively. Putting his hand on her shoulder, Potter said gently, 'Florence, they are alright, I would not ask you to do anything that was not in your own interest.'[27] In the dim light she signed the papers without reading a word of them, and the two men left the cell. Immediately the wardress reappeared to inform Florence that the jury was back and they had to return to the courtroom.

It was now thirty-eight minutes since the jury had retired. Florence, breathless with apprehension, stumbled back along the dark passage to return to the dock as the court reconvened to hear the verdict.

CHAPTER TWELVE

❧❧

No freeman shall be seized, or impris-
oned, or dispossessed, or outlawed, or
banished, or in any other way destroyed,
nor will we sit in judgment upon him,
nor will we pronounce sentence upon
him, except by the legal judgment of his
peers, and by the law of the land.
   39th Article of Magna Carta, 1215

The hammering in the old coach house had stopped. Whistling cheerfully, the foreman collected his tool bag and gave the wooden support of the gallows a last reassuring pat. Adjusting his worn-out cap to the back of his head, he looked with an expert eye over the heavy construction and quietly congratulated himself on a job well done. On Thursday 22 August, sixteen agonising days since receiving the death sentence, Florence Maybrick found the ensuing silence more eloquent than the noisy days of construction had ever been.

Endless time to consider her fate had taken its toll on the young American who had once been the toast of Liverpool society. Her eyes were dull and hollow, her cheeks and lips pallid, and wisps of limp hair escaped from beneath the simple prison cap, giving her a worn, unkempt appearance. She was mercifully unaware that her execution had been arranged for the following Monday morning.

Overcome with grief and crying bitterly, she would sit hour upon hour on a wooden chair, rocking back and forth, begging in vain to see her children. When the tears dried up, the dreadful hysterical sobbing would be replaced by a period of frightening calm. The prison routine, which had grated so badly on her nerves while on remand, now became her solace and she clung greedily to each fresh experience: the smell and texture of the unappetising meals sent from the prison hospital; her isolated afternoon walks in the high-walled yard, when she would stop to listen to the filtered sound of birdsong from the fields beyond; the days when the sun shone, warming her upturned face; the sensual feel of fresh rain on her skin, and the almost perverse delight as the droplets soaked through the thin prison cloak, making her teeth chatter and her body shiver. All served for a short time to distract her mind from the cruel thought of impending death.

During the night Florence would drift restlessly in and out of sleep, her dreams a confusion of memories, hope and horror. She became only vaguely aware of the muffled institutional sounds of the surrounding prison, and if the heavy iron door of the cell opened unexpectedly, she would jump up sharply, clenching her fists, the nails biting into the soft flesh of her hands and the blood draining from her terror-stricken face.

The two female attendants who sat with her day and night on the suicide watch would glance at each other, both with the same silent thought: was the poor creature going mad?

Like many a condemned prisoner before her, Florence embraced the religion of her youth and welcomed visits from the elderly prison chaplain, Mr Morris. Bent with age and a lifetime of comforting the inconsolable, the old man would shuffle painfully into the cell each morning, clutching a threadbare prayer book. He would sit and talk to Florence for long periods, doing his best to comfort her and rekindle some spark of hope. Before leaving, he would kneel and together they would pray fervently that the Home Secretary would consider a reprieve.

The Baroness would visit on alternate days and try to lift her daughter's spirits. She would tell her of the work being done on her behalf, of the endless petitions being sent to her solicitors by ordinary people from all over the country. Then she would ask Florence penetrating questions, making notes on the backs of envelopes or anything to hand, seeking to discover something positive that could be taken back to the lawyers.

But as the days advanced and the hoped-for clemency remained an unanswered prayer, Florence's grief overwhelmed her and the Baroness's energy began to fade. The longed-for visits turned into an emotional nightmare, with Florence sobbing constantly, impossible to communicate with.

The last day of the trial seemed a lifetime away. When the foreman of the jury had delivered the guilty verdict the stunned court had fallen into momentary silence. Cries of disbelief had quickly followed, and more than one woman who had sat through the seven days of testimony burst into tears. Competing newspaper reporters had literally fallen over each other in an attempt to leave the building and be first off the press with the result. With one enterprising journalist having managed to hire the only public telephone in St George's Hall, it had been left to the others to arrange more imaginative methods of communication.

The *Liverpool Echo* had set up a system whereby when the verdict was announced a reporter on the steps of the old jury box had been engaged to signal the result to a line of his colleagues, the last being situated within running distance of the editor. The system relied heavily on the first reporter holding up a red handkerchief for guilty and a white notebook for innocent. In the excitement of the moment, however, the man ran from the courtroom waving both handkerchief and notebook, which had somehow resulted in several hundred copies of the *Liverpool Echo* being circulated proclaiming Mrs Maybrick 'not guilty'.

When the growing multitude outside the court heard the true judgement there were loud groans and angry shouting from a section of the crowd. The police, although gathered in force, had difficulty controlling the mass of people and were forced to concentrate on protecting the witnesses as they left the building. Mrs Briggs, her hat askew, was carried through the crowd with the utmost difficulty, eventually finding refuge behind the locked doors of the North Western Hotel. As it was universally believed that Alfred Brierley would be lynched if the mob got their hands on him, the police advised the building manager of St George's Hall to smuggle him out of the side door.

At the north entrance of the law courts, the judge, accompanied by the High Sheriff, stepped hastily into a waiting carriage. Police and javelin men surrounded the heavy vehicle as it made its way through what had quickly turned into a howling mob. The driver nervously whipped up his frightened horses and the carriage picked up speed, leaving in its wake a long line of noisy, angry people.

In the days following the trial it appeared that people could talk of little else. In pubs and clubs the main subject of conversation was the Maybrick verdict. Countrywide, boisterous public meetings were convened where people signed endless appeals and fought over the verdict.

The offices of the Cleaver brothers opened late into the night and at weekends, preparing countless petitions. Eventually, unable to cope with the many requests, they suggested, via the press, that suitable forms published in the newspapers would be acceptable.

A petition from the *Strand* contained 6,000 signatures, measured thirty-seven yards and was accompanied by 15,000 postcards. The Ladies' Central Committee dispatched a petition which measured an impressive sixty-nine yards, containing 461 postcards and 1,048 signatures. In Birmingham, 10,000 signatures were collected on one petition alone and the promoters received an urgent telegram from a London solicitor warning: 'Be very urgent; worst is to be feared; Stephen dead against reprieve.'[1]

People from all walks of life joined the agitation: one Manchester petition included the names of eleven magistrates, thirty-three clergymen and 111 solicitors.

The Home Secretary, Henry Matthews, was dogged by the press, and much to his discomfort three petitions were dropped into his lap by fellow MPs as he sat on the Treasury bench. A simple petition asking that the death sentence be reprieved was introduced into the House of Commons and subsequently signed by eighty-eight Members of Parliament.

A cartoon of the Home Secretary appeared in one newspaper; by either coincidence or guesswork it was entitled 'Whitechapel at Whitehall' and showed Jack the Ripper at Matthews' right side with the caption reading: 'Attempted Murder of Florence Maybrick – save her Mr Matthews!'

In the United States, where the feeling about Florence's guilt or innocence was something of a mixture, the *New York Herald* stated: 'The prisoner may be guilty, probably she is, but no American jury would condemn a woman to the gallows on the evidence produced in this case.'[2]

Many of the American newspapers, however, were more concerned with Florence's moral standing, and the *New York Sun* wrote scathingly: 'The truth is that Mrs Maybrick has been a very bad woman. Letters that were not read at the trial show her to have carried on a number of intrigues with different men and that she was a depraved and conscienceless wanton.'[3]

Even with a negative press, Florence had a growing band of supporters in the United States, many of whom appealed to the government there. On her marriage to James, though, Florence had lost her American citizenship, and it was difficult to see how they could intervene. However, Robert Todd Lincoln, the son of Abraham Lincoln and Minister to the

Court of St James, held a watching brief and was in close communication with the American President.

Meanwhile, hundreds of petitions crossed the Atlantic, including one from 3,000 enthusiastic American women with a poetic bent who banded together to write a fervent entreaty to Queen Victoria. It referred to the Queen as: 'The possessor of a heart full of tender compassion and sympathy for the harrowing misfortunes and agonizing sorrows attendant on the lives of your sister women.' Cringingly it continued: 'This blessed, beautiful, and divine trait of character has endeared your name to all peoples throughout the world and such knowledge has inspired us with the courage to approach you with our humble petition . . .'[4]

John Aunspaugh, James Maybrick's American friend, also found himself caught up in the general excitement. While attending a meeting of his company, Inman Swan, to discuss the advisability of contributing towards funds for a possible retrial, he sprang to his feet, shouting theatrically: 'Gentlemen, I take the view that John Paul Jones did in revolutionary days, my country, right or wrong my country.'[5] During the ensuing cheers of approval, the director of the firm brought the meeting to order and pledged a cheque for $500.

Meanwhile, supporters in both England and America wrote to the Queen, the Prince and Princess of Wales and any politician or official who they thought had influence. The Home Office was slowly being buried beneath masses of paper as petitions from two continents rained down on it like confetti. Sir Charles Russell dispatched to the Home Secretary a seven-page memorandum asking two questions: was it proved beyond reasonable doubt that the deceased died from arsenical poisoning?; and if so, had the prisoner criminally administered that poison?

Within the memorandum he argued that the judge:

> *had honestly if mistakenly taken the view that the woman was clearly guilty — that there was practically little to be said for her, and that view he persistently and vehemently impressed upon the Jury in a summing up of 2 days, and in a manner which would justify the trial being described as a trial by Judge rather than jury.*
>
> *It is important to note that the verdict came as a surprise upon the trained minds of the Bar of the Northern Circuit and that to the very last moment (even after summing up) the leading Counsel for the Prosecution Mr Addison, QC, MP, persisted in saying that the Jury could not (especially in view of the medical evidence) find a verdict of guilty.*[6]

Inevitably there was a lighter side to the public's interest, and when the Sadler's Wells Theatre put on a three-act tragedy based on the court case there was standing room only. Madame Tussaud's cashed in a few days after the verdict by exhibiting a life-sized wax figure of Mrs Maybrick dressed exactly as she had been during her days in court. It drew immense crowds, the majority of whom were women and children. In deference to family feeling it was thought best not to place it in the 'Chamber of Horrors', and for some time it stood in splendid isolation at the entrance of the Napoleon Room.

Street hawkers on the sands of New Brighton, a holiday resort close to Liverpool, turned tragedy into farce during the height of the agitation, doing a roaring trade selling maudlin ballads to the summer holiday crowds. Questionable prose was illustrated by penny-dreadful woodcuts picturing a woman on her knees before a prison chaplain, overshadowed by a weeping willow.

The press continued to devote column after column to articles, letters to the editor and interviews. Mrs Briggs and the Baroness almost came to blows between the sheets of the *Liverpool Echo*, and the Baroness also managed a few uncharitable remarks about Michael Maybrick. This resulted in him granting an interview with the *Liverpool Echo*, from his holiday cottage on the Isle of Wight. With a nervous Edwin sitting silently by his side, Michael proclaimed pompously:

> *Nothing would please me more than to hear that the Home Secretary's decision is that Mrs Maybrick shall go free. I do not wish to exhibit any ill feeling against the Baroness or anyone else. I have however, felt the injustice to me of some of the statements and hints which she and others have made, and have at times thought of replying to them, but on second thoughts I concluded not to pay any attention to them and so have kept silent.[7]*

He did mention, however, that he intended to sue the *Manchester Courier* for libel after they hinted that he might have been implicated in the death of his brother.

In a letter addressed to the *Manchester Courier* and published under the name R. F. Muckley on 15 August, one man had penned a series of questions that many other interested parties had been asking:

> *Sir, There remain yet a few circumstances in this case that have*

*had very little airing, and which at least admit of some notice
from those who have a penchant for reflection and solution of
conundrums.*

1   *Who had a great antipathy to Mrs Maybrick?*
2   *Who had as much or more access to Mrs Maybrick about the
      period of his violent attacks than anybody else?*
3   *Who had as much chance as anyone else of adding extra
      'condiments' to Mr Maybrick's food or medicine?*
4   *Who, on one occasion, administered a pill to Mr Maybrick
      causing him illness?*
5   *Who made a mistake in stating that the pill administered was
      'written upon' by a doctor?*
6   *Who administered a pill that was not written upon by a doctor
      to Mr Maybrick, which pill caused illness?*
7   *Who takes charge of the bulk of the deceased's property?*
8   *Query: Why is Mrs Maybrick charged with murder any more
      than he whose name forms an answer to all the above questions
      – Why?*[8]

For all his bluster, Michael never did sue the newspaper in
question, or anybody else for that matter. Mr Muckley, though,
could have added to his list of questions:

Who almost certainly sent his brother a near-fatal dose of
strychnine two weeks before he died?
Who went out of his way to throw suspicion on his
brother's wife, by adding arsenic in solution to the meat
juice?
Who passed to the police only those letters which would

throw further suspicion on to Florence?

Who suppressed the letter from James which said 'Dr Fuller has poisoned me'?

Who discovered James Maybrick's store of arsenic and distributed it around the house, adding four handkerchiefs belonging to the innocent woman?

Who left for London the day after James had died and could have taken any evidence of his crime with him?

Who kept Florence prisoner without friends or family until the police came?

Who found James Maybrick a liability and would stand to lose his wealth, power and position if it was known that his brother was Jack the Ripper?

Edwin, who had been present at the interview with the *Liverpool Echo* but had contributed nothing more than the occasional nod of his head, had been with Michael almost continually since James Maybrick had died. Charles Ratcliffe, in a letter to John Aunspaugh written before the magistrates' hearing, reported that Edwin was 'in bed with "nervous prostration". Tom and Michael are seeing to it that he leaves England.'[9]

Edwin, however, had attended the trial, and there is ample evidence that he lied in parts of his testimony. At the eleventh hour he appears to have come suddenly to his senses and given Sir Charles Russell the pill box, found when the contents of Battlecrease House were being removed. These pills proved that James had been prescribed arsenic when he was in America and, had they been available earlier, may have made all the difference to the verdict of the magistrates' court.

Edwin was weak and completely under Michael's control; when he had eventually shaken himself free and tried to help the woman he had once loved, it had been too little, too late.

Another actor in the Maybrick tragedy had also been carefully guarding his back, but before his departure for the United States Alfred Brierley was eventually flushed out of hiding by a persistent reporter from the *New York Herald*, and agreed after much persuasion to give an interview, on the condition that

> . . . *it must not injure Mrs Maybrick. That is the sole reason why I have been silent hitherto. I have been maligned, persecuted and misjudged in every way. It has broken my business and will cause me to leave this city. But I am a man and I have made no complaint. I only desire that the terrible misfortunes of a woman whose treatment has been scarcely fair, may not be further increased through me.*[10]

Brierley claimed that the moment he heard Mrs Maybrick was in trouble he abandoned his proposed trip to the Mediterranean, losing his £25 deposit, and advised the Cleaver brothers that he was entirely in their hands. This, however, was far from accurate. On 6 July, more than seven weeks after Florence was arrested, Brierley's solicitor wrote a letter to the Treasury which began: 'Our client Mr Alfred Brierley has been subpoenaed in this matter . . .' The letter went on to argue that as Mr Brierley had no further letters or documents relevant to the court case:

> . . . *we shall be glad to hear from you that Mr Brierley need not attend upon his subpoena. It is inconvenient for him to do so as he*

had made arrangements to go away for his holiday and as you can well understand it is very unpleasant for him to have to attend Court in this case — particularly if his doing so can serve no useful purpose.[11]

So Brierley, far from putting himself into the hands of Florence's solicitor and cancelling his holiday, had gone to ground, eventually having to be subpoenaed to attend the trial.

His request was in turn placed before the prosecution, but not surprisingly the subpoena stood and Brierley was unable to wriggle out of attending court. Most people believed that he had been very lucky in not having been called to give evidence, and many were convinced that he should have been arrested initially with Mrs Maybrick and accused with her.

A special favourite of the American press was Alice Yapp, who was interviewed a number of times by the *New York Herald*, proclaiming a little late: 'I have always found Mrs Maybrick an exceedingly nice woman. I cannot say a word against her.' She denied categorically telling Mrs Briggs that 'the mistress is poisoning the master', and when asked about opening the fateful letter, she replied: 'I perhaps did wrong in reading it, but the loving words in it caught my eye at once, and I could not help reading it then. If I had only known that my doing so would have placed Mrs Maybrick where she is today, I would have torn it up, burned it, or done anything with it.'[12]

When the press eventually ran out of witnesses to interview, one newspaper wrote up a rather tasteless interview with the public executioner:

In consequence of the report which was current to the effect that Berry, the hangman, would refuse to hang Mrs Maybrick, a Bradford reporter has interviewed him at his house, which is of the sort occupied by the better-to-do working people, in Biltonplace, Bradford.

Berry was sitting reading the accounts of the Maybrick agitation in the evening papers before a cheerful fire. Asked if the rumour was true, Berry denied it without hesitation, and in the most positive manner he said that this was the first he had heard of the story.

'I have,' he added, 'made all my arrangements for the execution and unless Mrs Maybrick be reprieved I shall carry them out. I have no business with the guilt or innocence of a condemned prisoner. I have simply to carry out the sentence of the law and if the sentence is wrong the blame will not be with me.'

Berry seemed in no way intimidated by the strong feeling in favour of Mrs Maybrick, and made the remark, possibly with this feeling in mind that he would not think of shrinking from his duty, even if he believed he would be shot on the way to the place of execution.[13]

The days crawled by and the agitation continued. Mr Cleaver submitted further affidavits and was granted an interview with the Home Secretary in London, after which the rumour began that a reprieve was imminent. Mr Justice Stephen was joined by the scientific witnesses, Dr Stevenson, Dr Tidy and Dr Poole, for a conference with Mr Matthews, and shortly afterwards Mr Cuffe, the Treasury solicitor, was sent to Liverpool to re-interview some of the witnesses.

During his time in Liverpool, Mr Cuffe discovered that

James Maybrick had written to his brother Michael not long before his death. He demanded the letter, which was sent to the Home Office on 19 August. In neither his testimony to the Coroner and the magistrates, nor at the trial had Michael made any mention whatsoever about this letter, and the only information about it had been the edited version printed in the media. On receipt of the document at the Home Office, a puzzled civil servant wrote to Mr Matthews: 'Mr Maybrick's letter in no way implies his belief that he was being poisoned by his wife.'[14]

Four days before Florence's execution was due to take place, a meeting was held in the offices of the Treasury between the Home Secretary and Lord Salisbury, the Prime Minister. This resulted in the Home Secretary attending on Queen Victoria.

In the afternoon of the same day, a knot of eager newspaper journalists gathered in the pouring rain outside Walton Prison to hear the hoped-for news. When the giant gates opened with a metallic clank, it was the elderly prison chaplain who came out, to be surrounded immediately by the throng of reporters. 'There is no news,' he said, shaking his head. 'And I fear the result . . . No one could sit with her, as I do now, day after day and not feel something of her terrible burden.' As the old man walked on towards his house, which was a few yards to the left of the prison, he was overheard muttering: 'She is getting more nervous, the strain is telling on her.'[15]

The day wore on and the rain increased, and nothing further was heard. The reporters dejectedly seeking shelter against the tall prison walls left one by one, heading for home or the comfort of the nearest public house. At one o'clock in the morning the relative peace of Walton Prison was disturbed by a loud and persistent hammering on the gate. The sleepy turnkey on duty roused the Governor, who in turn sent word to awaken the prison chaplain while he verified the credentials of the unexpected visitor.

Florence sprang from her bed as she heard the shuffle of feet outside the cell door and the click of the key in the lock. The look of terror and expectation on her face hastened the Governor forward. 'It is well, it is good news,' he cried. 'I have just received a message from the Home Secretary which states that he advised the Queen to commute your sentence to imprisonment for life.'[16] It was all too much for Florence, and she dropped in a dead faint at the Governor's feet.

The following morning the Liverpool newspapers printed the communication from the Home Office:

We are given to understand that the Home Secretary, after the fullest consideration, and after taking the best medical and legal advice that could be obtained, has advised Her Majesty to respite the capital sentence on Florence Maybrick, and to commute the punishment to penal servitude for life; in as much as although the evidence leads clearly to the conclusion that the prisoner administered and attempted to administer arsenic to her husband with intent to murder, yet it does not wholly exclude a reasonable doubt whether his death was in fact caused by the administration of arsenic.

This decision is understood not to imply the slightest reflection on the able and experienced practitioners who gave evidence, or on the

*tribunal before which the prisoner was tried. We understand that
the course adopted has the concurrence of the learned judge.[17]*

On hearing the news, the Baroness, who had been staying with
friends in Blundellsands, seized her bonnet and cloak and
would have left immediately for the prison had she not been
reminded that it would be unlikely that they would admit her
without a visiting order. She was overcome with joy and told a
friend:

*Oh! The suspense has been something terrible. I thought I had the
strength to endure anything, but the fearful agony of the last few
days has been more than I thought it could be. If Florie had not
broken down I should. Only her misery and weakness has kept me
up. I have not slept a moment since the verdict. I could not sleep,
thinking that every moment brought her one step nearer to her
grave, and that I must use that minute in the way that would do
most good to her. I felt I know that the Queen could never depart
on her trip to Wales without doing this gracious act. She is a mother
herself and she knows what a mother feels.[18]*

After the initial euphoria of the reprieve, those engaged in
the law questioned why Florence had been given a life term
by the Home Secretary for 'administering and attempting to
administer arsenic to her husband with intent to murder',
when she had been tried by her peers for the very specific
charge that she had 'feloniously, wilfully and of her malice
aforethought, killed and murdered one James Maybrick'.

Had she been tried on the lesser charge, it would have been
necessary, according to law, to specify in detail the occasion

and date of the alleged act. Her defence counsel would have approached the case from a different direction, and had she been found guilty on this charge it would not have justified the extreme penalty of 'penal servitude for life'.

The Times the following day echoed what many people thought when it declared: 'The case against Mrs Maybrick was and remains a case of terribly strong suspicion, but suspicion which, after all is said, just misses moral certainty . . . it makes things comfortable all round for the experts.'[19]

Alexander MacDougall, the retired Scottish barrister who had become leader of the Maybrick Committee, formed initially to argue for Florence's reprieve, wrote an accurate but somewhat tangled legal response to the result:

> . . . *if the cause of death was not arsenic, James Maybrick was not murdered; and if he was not murdered, neither Mrs Maybrick nor anybody else could have been his murderer, and the verdict of the Jury which found that he had been murdered by Mrs Maybrick is, by the very fact that he was not murdered, a quashed verdict, and any sentence pronounced on that verdict so quashed is an invalid sentence, and the Crown cannot lawfully carry out an invalid sentence.*[20]

Florence had escaped an ignoble death, but now her greatest struggle would be with life, behind the cold grey walls of a brutal prison system, for a crime she had never been indicted on, or defended herself against, in any criminal court in England.

It was Queen Victoria who would have the final word, effectively destroying any hope that Florence would be released from prison in the near future. To the Home Secretary she wrote: 'The only regret she feels about the decision is that so wicked a woman should escape by a mere legal quibble! The law is not a moral profession she must say. But her sentence must never be further commuted.'[21]

CHAPTER THIRTEEN

*Call me guilty, I do but pay the tax
that's due to justice. But call me guilt-
less, then my punishment is shame to
those alone who do inflict it.*

Cited in A.W. MacDougall,
The Maybrick Case – A Treatise

The brick-walled cell measured seven feet by four, with nothing to sit upon but the cold stone floor. There was no heating and the only light filtered from a small barred window which had never been cleaned. A rolled-up hammock and bedding lay on the floor beneath a set of three shelves let into the wall. When the female warder opened the door, Florence stepped back in horror and cried: 'Oh, don't put me in there! I cannot bear it.'

The woman laughed coarsely, took her roughly by the shoulder and pushed her into the little room, locking the door loudly and firmly behind her. Beating wildly against the door, Florence screamed: 'For God's sake let me out, let me out,'[1] but her voice could not penetrate the massive barrier and she fell to her knees howling in despair.

On 29 August 1889, six days after the Home Office had issued the reprieve and five days before her twenty-eighth birthday, Florence Maybrick had been quietly transferred to the female prison at Woking. Her hasty departure from Liverpool's busy Lime Street Station had taken the newspapers by surprise, and there were few to witness the prisoner and her two companions board a third-class carriage en route to Woking.

The Home Office, determined to suppress the mounting criticism of the Home Secretary's decision, had sent instructions to Walton Prison to transfer her as soon as she was able to travel. 'The Governor of Woking Prison is a medical officer of experience and skill,' an official had written. 'And the present excitement of newspaper reporters and others would cease all the sooner for her removal from the scene of her crime.'[2]

Having come within days of death, Florence's initial response to the reprieve had been one of overwhelming relief. However, on reflection the thought of the alternative punishment filled her with a sense of hopelessness, and she was reported to have said to a warder: 'But for the disgrace of dying on the scaffold I would have preferred death to penal servitude.'[3]

Her destination, Woking Hospital Prison, had been built in 1859 to house 700 convicts. Thirty years later, half the cells stood empty. Only two per cent of female convicts were committed to prison for serious crimes, and it was more typical for women to be housed for short periods in local

gaols or houses of correction, the hard-core offenders returning on average forty or fifty times.

A vast construction of frowning masonry, the grim institution sat on a hill encircled by the flowers and trees of the
charming Surrey countryside. 'There are the elements of
innumerable tragedies in this pretty rural spot,' wrote the *Pall
Mall Gazette*. 'Giant prison houses, private and public lunatic
asylums, broad acreages of burial grounds and a neat crema-
torium . . . It is a colony of wasted lives and dead hopes.'[4]

After a tiring, dusty journey, Florence had been taken into
the reception office by two female officers and ordered to
strip. This would be the first of many strip-searches she would
have to endure over her term of imprisonment. Her clothing,
the property of Walton Prison, was taken away and returned
with her escort to Liverpool, and she was issued with a
well-worn brown serge dress and apron marked with the
broad arrow of the convict. A red star patched on the dress
revealed that she was a first offender, and her personal
identification number, LP 29, had also been stitched on to
black cloth and attached to each garment. 'L' identified her as
being under a life sentence, 'P' denoted the year of her
conviction, and '29' gave her the dubious distinction of being
the twenty-ninth prisoner admitted that year.

Once dressed, the prisoner was approached by a sour-faced
matron brandishing a large pair of scissors. She seized
Florence's hair roughly and with one deft action chopped it
off to the nape of her neck. 'This act seemed above all others
to bring me to a sense of my degradation,' Florence would
remember. 'My utter helplessness and the irony of the awful
tragedy of which I was the innocent victim, entered my soul.'[5]

Having suffered these indignities, she was taken to the infirmary and locked in a cell. 'At last I could be alone after the anguish and torture of the day, I prayed for sleep that I may lose consciousness of my intolerable anguish. But sleep that gentle nurse of the sad and suffering came not.'[6] In the adjoining cell, an insane woman raved and wept throughout the night, and by morning Florence wondered if in the years to come she would suffer the same fate.

The new prisoner would no doubt have been astonished to learn that she was occupying the most favoured and comfortable quarters in Woking Prison. Inmates would adopt any amount of deception in order to gain a few precious days in the infirmary, where the cells were larger and the meagre diet was supplemented with meat.

Some women would swallow soap, soda, ground glass or poisonous insects in order to make themselves ill. Others, in total despair after suffering for years the harsh conditions of penal life, would resort to self-mutilation. It was not unknown for convicts to wound themselves so severely that an amputation of a limb was required, ensuring a long period of hospitalisation. It was this constant battle between sceptical medical staff and the cunning malingerer which ensured that the truly ill were also treated with the utmost suspicion and most visits to the prison infirmary were not of long duration.

Within a week Florence was discharged and being conducted by a dour officer across a silent prison yard to the main section of the penal institution and her permanent quarters. For a brief, tantalising moment she felt the sun on her back before being led into a labyrinth of gloomy passages.

Passing through a series of gates, which were unlocked and

locked in rapid succession, she found herself in a cold central hall encircled by several landings of small cells. High above her head, like a gigantic spider's web suspended from the upper gallery, lay a net of iron meshing, placed there to thwart suicide attempts.

Every sound echoed from the cold grey walls as the two women climbed the iron stairway which led up to the landings. With a rattle of keys the warder opened a door no more than two feet across and thrust Florence into the confined space beyond. It was here she would complete the first cruel stage of her imprisonment: nine long months of solitary confinement.

Designed mainly with punishment in mind, this long and miserable internment had also been intended to give prisoners time to reflect and repent. Before 1848 the period of solitary confinement had been a gruelling eighteen months, but it had sent so many convicts to an early grave that it was subsequently reduced to nine. The Revd J. Kingsmill, of the Prison Discipline Society, suggested that this important period of punishment should be 'calculated to strike more terror into the minds of the lowest and vilest class of criminals than any other hitherto devised'.[7]

For the convict, this lengthy period of unnatural solitude tortured both mind and body. Perpetual silence dulled the intellect and blurred the memory, and the greatest fear of those confined was the onset of insanity. Of this, the darkest period of her prison life, Florence would write: 'It inflicts upon the prisoner at the commencement of her sentence, when most sensitive to the horrors which prison punishment entails, the voiceless solitude, the hopeless monotony, the long vista of tomorrow, tomorrow, tomorrow, stretching before her, all filled with desolation and despair.'[8]

Inmates had different methods of dealing with these lonely, silent months. Some would pace up and down in the confined space for hours at a time, counting or reciting prayers. Others would gain a degree of consolation by keeping as pets the insects and mice that invaded their cells. Women prisoners, however, were more disposed to vent their frustration on their surroundings, working themselves up into a frenzy, destroying their clothing or tearing bedding to shreds. This was known as 'breaking out'.

In the stillness of the night it was common for Florence to be awakened by shriek upon shriek from some tormented creature in a nearby cell: 'I lie in my darkened cell with palpitating heart. Like a savage beast, the woman of turmoil has torn her clothing and bedding into shreds, and now she is destroying all she can lay hands on . . . the bell rings summoning the warders and the woman, probably in a strait-jacket, is borne to the penal cells.'[9]

Discipline was strictly enforced, and the resulting punishments were harsh. They ranged from loss of remission to a diet of bread and water for three days, constrained in a straitjacket or hobbled. Hobbling, which caused great suffering, was reserved for women and consisted of binding the wrists and ankles, then strapping them together behind the prisoner's back. In violent cases an added torture was to shear and blister the convict's head, or confine her in the dreaded 'dark cell', an underground room with no light.

Shedding many useless angry tears, Florence had no choice but to conform to the isolated world of solitary confinement, regulated by the strident note of the prison bell. Although it was a silent world, this did not mean it was a quiet one. Her ears became sensitive to the sound of the spy-hole when it was raised by the warder, the sobbing of her fellow convicts, the coughing of the consumptive, the rattle of the dinner cans and the endless tramp of anonymous feet on the slate floor outside her cell.

Many years later she would remember with a shudder those first agonising months:

> *I felt that mortal death would have been more merciful than the living death to which I was condemned . . . never to feel the touch of anything soft or warm, never to see anything that is attractive — nothing but stone above, around and beneath. The deadly chill creeps into one's bones; the bitter days of winter and the still bitterer nights were torture . . .*[10]

With no light or candle allowed in the cell, fitting the hammock* and making it up in the evening became something of a struggle. In winter the task had to be achieved in complete darkness. As the straps supporting the hammock were prone to breaking, many times Florence found herself hurled out on to the cold slate floor in the early hours of the morning.

The first bell of the day sounded at 6 a.m., when the hammock would be taken down and folded neatly with the bedding. Slopping-out followed, and the foul air that rose in the central hall was enough to turn the hardiest stomach. Florence would return to her cell with two pails, one her

---

* A legacy of when the American War of Independence interrupted transportation to the American colonies and surplus prisoners were housed in converted warships moored on the River Thames, known as 'hulks'.

lavatory, the other filled with cold water with which she washed herself, rinsed her plate and jug and scrubbed the cell floor. By the following morning the water would be covered in a thick greasy scum.

A measure of hygiene was expected from the prisoners, but as the authorities only allowed each convict one ounce of soap and one change of clothing – including underclothes – every seven days, Florence fought a constant battle to keep herself clean.

Each morning the Governor would arrive with an escort to inspect the cells. When he asked each prisoner if she had any complaint, his tone would be terse and it was generally not recommended to voice any. Inmates, however, did complain on occasion, and when they did it was usually about the food, which was tasteless and disgusting.

The regulations which covered practically every act in the convicts' lives also instructed them how to complain about the food. The procedure was rather puzzling. The regulations relating to the treatment and conduct of convicted criminal prisoners read: 'If any prisoner has any complaint to make regarding the diet, it must be made immediately after a meal is served and before any portion of it is eaten.'[11] Which left the prisoner in something of a dilemma. How could you complain about food that you hadn't even tasted?

The same unappetising meal was served for both breakfast and supper to the prisoners undergoing solitary confinement. It consisted of a six-ounce brown wholemeal loaf and three-quarters of a pint of gruel universally known as 'stirabout' or 'skilly'. Prudent inmates found it wise to check the loaf for black beetles, as these were numerous in the kitchen and had an unfortunate habit of falling into the dough. The 'skilly', made from equal parts of oatmeal and Indian meal, was completely tasteless and thick enough to stand the spoon in.

After the prisoners had scrubbed the stone floor of their cells the bell would sound again and the cell doors would be unlocked. Florence would leave, falling in three paces behind her nearest fellow convict, and the long line of silent women would march to the chapel to attend divine service, which lasted twenty minutes. This short period beyond the confines of the gloomy cell walls became her one delight in a joyless day, and she would remember it as 'an oasis in a weary desert'.[12]

Her second outing of the day was for the morning exercise period, which all prisoners were obliged to do in every kind of weather. Through inches of snow or battling against bitter rain, a group of thirty-five inmates trudged each day around the prison yard, completing the 'devil's circle', a silent single file of miserable women walking in a never-ending circle around a forty-foot-square stone-flagged yard in the shadow of high dark walls.

If it rained and Florence came back to the cell soaked to the skin, there would be no change of clothing and she would have to carry on working in the same garments until she dried out. Due to this, many of the women developed painful chilblains or suffered with rheumatism.

Florence's assignment was to sew five shirts over a period of a week. It was hard work and offered nothing in reward. To fall below this quota would be to lose precious marks, which would ultimately lead to restrictions in receiving letters or loss of prison visits. Complaint led to a reduced diet of bread and water or total confinement in the cell for a twenty-four-hour period. Only if Florence was ill was she excused the full amount of work, and this had to be verified by the prison doctor.

As the months crept slowly by, late autumn turned to deep mid-winter. The days grew shorter and the little light which filtered through the tiny window dimmed. With no heating the cold became intense, and on frosty winter mornings Florence would find the water in her cell frozen solid after a miserable, shivering and sleepless night.

For prisoner LP 29 the day finished at 7 p.m. with the routine placing of the broom outside the door to indicate that she had been visited by the warder. Finally the cell door was firmly locked, heralding the start of the long night. For twenty-two hours out of every twenty-four, Florence was locked in the little cell, haunted by her memories and the ghostly spectres of the past, repeating day after day the monotonous soul-destroying routine.

CHAPTER FOURTEEN

❧❧

. . . She's the sort of woman who lives
for others — you can tell the others by
their hunted expression.
                    C.S. Lewis, 1898–1963

When the Home Office forecast the end of the Maybrick agitation with Florence's transfer to Woking, they had not anticipated the Baroness von Roques. Before the end of September 1889, she had closed her Paris flat and descended upon the unsuspecting town of Windsor, from where she embarked on a relentless campaign to gain her daughter's freedom. She petitioned anyone with influence, protested with bitterness, begged pathetically, lied continually and generally used every crooked trick in the book. In consequence she probably put more years on Florence's sentence than anyone could possibly have foreseen.

She wrote impassioned letters guaranteed to wring the heart

of the most cynical civil servant, and it was said that Henry Matthews, the Home Secretary, blanched whenever one of her tortured entreaties landed on his desk. One of her earliest letters began: 'I can no longer endure my terrible loneliness, anxiety and grief. I come to you a stranger in England, a helpless woman, an agonized mother – to entreat you to save my child from an evil and lingering death . . .'[1]

Within a week of returning to England, the Baroness had dispatched to the Home Secretary a long medical opinion as to the likely effect of prison life on her daughter's 'delicate constitution'. When she failed to convince the authorities that Florence was on the verge of consumption, she begged piteously to be allowed to visit her at Woking. 'Nothing has been sorted as to our family matters,' she wrote. 'Solicitors cannot act for us as we are strangers and Americans.'[2]

Although prison regulations forbade a family visit until six months had elapsed from the date of a prisoner's conviction, the Baroness won a half-hour visit on 'business matters' before Florence had served three months. Encouraged by this victory, she cunningly pressed to be made co-trustee with Arnold Cleaver, who had applied for a warrant to administer Florence's estate and recover some of his expenses.

However, by this time Home Office officials had realised that they were dealing with a tricky character, and she was outmanoeuvred, one civil servant cautioning:

I think it well to point out that the convict is not likely to refuse her consent to an arrangement which will enable her mother to pay her a visit on every occasion of business. And as the Baroness von Roques has already stated her intent of residing in the neighbourhood of the prison, she will in all probability, if appointed co-trustee, make such appointment grounds for the frequent access to her daughter.[3]

Ultimately it was Florence, however, who with little confidence in her mother's business ability rudely demolished the proposed scheme by refusing point blank to allow the Baroness access to her business interests. But for once in her mother's life, money was not a pressing problem. She had recently received the considerable sum of $6,000 for the sale of the American land, the remaining $4,000 of the sale price going to William Potter, her long-suffering financial manager.

In a letter at the beginning of September Potter had advised her to pay $5,000 on the mortgage of her 14th Street property and cautioned her: 'Now my dear Carrie, I want you to be prudent with this little sum. It may be all you will have hereafter. I have worked hard to save, or get it for you and I feel that I have a right to ask you to be prudent.'[4]

Perhaps the Baroness intended to take Potter's well-meant advice, but towards the end of the month she may have been presented with a large unlooked-for expense.

It was reported in a number of newspapers that an unknown man, claiming to be a relative of the Maybrick family, had approached a Ludgate Circus publisher with three hand-written volumes which he alleged to be Mrs Maybrick's diaries. The *Liverpool Echo* reported:

The gentleman was seen by the manager of the firm ... The manager was unable to decide what offer to make in the absence of the head of the firm, so he told the gentleman to call again at the same time advising him that it might be worth his while to offer the books . . . to the Baroness von Roques who might probably purchase them to prevent their publication.[5]

The man never returned and the diaries were never published. What happened to them? Did the Baroness purchase them? Could one of the volumes have been the journal that James Maybrick had allegedly been writing before his death? If she had purchased them it would certainly have been in the Baroness's interests to suppress the contents. She was intelligent enough to realise that if, in fact, James Maybrick had been Jack the Ripper, and it could be proved that Florence had suspected this, it would have given her a remarkably strong motive for the crime of which she had been accused.

In the mean time the Baroness continued with her paper war. As Florence came towards the end of her first nine months of imprisonment, her mother petitioned Queen Victoria, who was at that time residing at her beloved Balmoral. The almost illegible ten-page document was laid before Her Majesty on 6 June 1890. It contained a fervent plea to the Queen asking her to pardon Florence for the crime of murder and have her retried for attempted murder.

In this astonishing and ill-judged document, the Baroness admonished the judge, the Home Secretary and the British legal system, and revealed:

There are circumstances known to me which would have rendered it very easy for her to have obtained a divorce. I do not desire to say one unnecessary word against her husband, nor did she instruct her counsel to do so, hence strong evidence in her favour was suppressed, but which can now be produced if required . . .

She then went on to describe Florence as: 'a good religious woman, dedicated quiet and dignified, a good daughter, a devoted mother and a patient wife. She was educated with the greatest care . . .'[6]

The Baroness had made two fatal mistakes with this petition. The first was that she began with a brief record of her own history and family background, claiming that she had been widowed at the age of nineteen – losing with one stroke of the pen approximately five years of her life – then widowed for a second time and married to the Baron von Roques. It was well known in court circles that Queen Victoria had nothing but contempt for a widow who embarked on a second marriage, let alone a third.

Her second mistake was that the appeal was far too lengthy and barely readable. It was unlikely the Queen wrestled for long with the handwriting, if in fact she read it at all, and it was returned to the Home Office on 14 June with a note: 'Laid before the Queen, but the Secretary of State was unable to recommend Her Majesty to comply with the prayer of the petition.'[7]

Undeterred by the battery of negative responses being received from the Home Office, the Baroness continued pressing for unofficial visits. When permission was refused, she changed tactics and asked Sir Charles Russell to plead on her behalf, which he did several times without success.

The Baroness also wrote letter after letter to influential Americans, imploring them to exert pressure on the American government to intervene with the British government. She had too developed a working relationship with the English Maybrick Committee, who were still agitating for

Florence's release. During 1890 they sent her a pamphlet produced by Dr Charles Meymott Tidy and Dr Rawdon Macnamara, two of the scientific witnesses who had been brought in by the defence. They argued that there was no evidence to show that James Maybrick had died from the effects of arsenic, and 'that the quantity so found is perfectly consistent with its medicinal ingestion'.[8]

After living for a short period in 1891 in London's Forest Gate, the Baroness tired of England and moved her headquarters to an isolated cottage in Rouen, France, from where she continued to harass the Home Office. Not long after her arrival in Rouen, her maid, Marie Salome Meyer, was unpacking a box belonging to Florence which had been given to the Baroness by Arnold Cleaver before she left England. When the woman passed her Florence's Bible, a small piece of paper fluttered to the floor.

On picking it up, the Baroness recognised it as a prescription for a face-wash containing arsenic, written for Florence by a Dr Bay of New York. Stamped on it was the name 'Brouant', a well-known Paris chemist who had filled the prescription in 1878, three years before Florence was married. Exalted with her find, the Baroness took the next boat back to England.

During her last residence in London, she had met Alexander MacDougall, the retired barrister who was continually in mortal combat with the Home Office pressing for Florence's release. He was currently writing a 600-page treatise on the case. She took the prescription to him, and he immediately contacted the French chemist and received a certified copy of the entry from their books. He then arranged for a number of facsimiles to be made, and for the Baroness and her maid to sign affidavits. The evidence was safely tucked away to be used when the continuing agitation had gained a fresh trial.

Meanwhile, on the other side of the Atlantic, an influential group of women had thrown themselves into the debate with energy, gusto and good old American know-how. Helen Densmore, an American doctor living in London, had taken a great interest in the case from the beginning and had corresponded with emancipated women friends in Europe and America suggesting they form the International Maybrick Association, to be dedicated to agitating for Florence's release.

One of Dr Densmore's contacts was the author and academic Miss Mary Dodge, who wrote under the pen name Gail Hamilton. By a happy chance, she was also the cousin of Mrs James Blaine, wife of the Secretary of State, who in turn was a great friend of Mrs Harrison, the First Lady of America and wife to Benjamin Harrison, the President of the United States. In 1968 Trevor Christie wrote of this enthusiastic group:

> *No mountain of opposition was too high for these feminine Zolas to scale, no pit of apathy too deep for them to scour in their zeal for their heroine. No Crusader ever set out to rescue the Holy Sepulchre from the accursed infidel with more courage, fewer facts, and such a penchant for purple prose.*[9]

However, these intrepid daughters of the revolution had thrown themselves honestly into the battle to save their fellow American. They were fired by an emotive letter from the Baroness von Roques to Mrs Harrison in April 1891: 'At present my child is slowly dying... Your American blood would boil at the injustice, the cruelty which has been done to this delicate, innocent girl.'[10]

In August 1891 they sent an uncompromising petition directly to Queen Victoria. Since it was passed through official channels via Robert Todd Lincoln at the American Embassy, one assumes it must have had the tacit approval of President Harrison. It was signed by all the wives of the American Cabinet and ran:

> ... *There seems to be the very highest medical and scientific authority in support of the proposition that Mr Maybrick's symptoms were not compatible with arsenical poisoning. There was, it is understood, an entire absence of proof that Mrs Maybrick administered or attempted to administer arsenic to her husband with intent to kill; while evidence that Mr Maybrick had been in the habit of taking arsenic as a medicine was present in the case.*
>
> *In view of all these facts we earnestly, respectfully and trustfully entreat of your Most Gracious Majesty a pardon and release for Mrs Maybrick.*[11]

Although their argument was embarrassingly legitimate, the Queen and the Home Office were furious. The Government resented the fact that the United States was criticising the internal justice of a friendly power, and the petition almost sparked off an international incident.

The Home Secretary, being slowly buried beneath a constant stream of correspondence from the Baroness, Helen Densmore, MacDougall and the Maybrick Committee, contacted Lincoln at the American Embassy in London. He advised him to inform the President that he would not

THE MAYBRICK MURDER TRIAL.

Contemporary sketch of the major characters in the Maybrick trial.

Drawing of James used at the time of the trial.

Drawing of Florence in the dock.

The Valentine's meat juice at the centre of James Maybrick's murder trial. Florence admitted adding a white powder to it, but was it arsenic? (*Richard Whittington-Egan*)

St George's Hall in Liverpool, where the murder trial took place in 1889. (*Richard Whittington-Egan*)

The opium-smoking, misogynistic judge, Mr Justice Stephen. Was he fit to preside over Florence's trial?

Sir Charles Russell, the flamboyant Irish counsel who led Florence's defence.

Mr Addison, QC, MP, the senior counsel for the prosecution, who himself remarked: 'Oh, they can't convict her on that evidence.'

Aylesbury Prison, where Florence was to spend eight of her fifteen years behind bars, suffering a nervous breakdown in the process. (*Richard Whittington-Egan*)

The Home Secretary Sir Henry Matthews considering a pardon for Florence. (*Stewart Evans*)

Photograph of Florence taken shortly after her release from prison in 1904. (*Richard Whittington-Egan*)

Florence Maybrick in her late forties, as shown on the cover of her autobiograph (*Richard Whittington-Egan*)

'Bobo' - Florence's son, James Chandler Maybrick, who died in mysterious circumstances in 1911.

Waxwork effigy of Florence. (*Richard Whittington-Egan*)

Florence aged 77, two years before her death.

The shack in Connecticut, in which she died in 1941.
(*Richard Whittington-Egan*)

James Maybrick's grave in Anfield Cemetery, Liverpool, both before (*left*) and after (*above*) it was smashed in two and defaced by vandals. (*Richard Whittington-Egan, Carol Emmas*)

Florence's simple grave, the Episcopal church, South Ken, Connecticut. (*Stephen P. Rya*)

be recommending further clemency by the Queen in the Maybrick case, and left him with the distinct impression that he regretted having commuted the sentence in the first place.

While all this excitement was boiling in the corridors of Whitehall, Florence had been moved out of the tiny cell in solitary confinement to her new residence in Hall A to start the next stage of her imprisonment: nine months of probation.

Her new cell was double the size of the one she had just vacated, with the luxury of a camp bed as opposed to the perilous hammock. The mattress was a sack stuffed with coconut fibre and also provided were two rough sheets, two blankets and a red counterpane. An upturned log fastened to the floor served as a seat from where she could be seen by the warder, and there was a piece of board attached to the wall which acted as a table. The only decoration in the cell was a fitting of three iron shelves holding a Bible, a prayer book, a hymnal and a library book. These new quarters were still bleak and freezing, but after her previous accommodation, where she had to work all day sitting on the floor and eat standing up, it must have seemed like pure luxury.

The daily routine was exactly the same as that of solitary confinement, and she was still confined to the cell for twenty-two hours a day. However, the door was left open, with a locked gate covering the entrance, and she gained a little comfort by sensing her fellow convicts and watching the comings and goings of the staff.

From their post in the hall, the warders on duty could view the prisoners in their cells and enforce the regime of silence.

Sometimes the women managed to whisper to each other, but if caught the punishment was three days of bread and water or the loss of seven days' remission. 'The silence rule gives supreme gratification to the tyrannous officer,' Florence would complain. 'For on the slightest pretext she can report a woman for talking, a turn of the head, a movement of the lips is enough of an offence for a report.'[12]

As she was now in the second stage of her imprisonment, Florence could look forward to an official thirty-minute visit from her mother every two months. Neither hail, rain nor snow deterred the Baroness, and she would make the fatiguing journey from Rouen to Woking for a visit over almost before it had begun.

Escorted into a room by a warder, the Baroness would sit behind a large grilled screen almost in the centre of the floor. A yard or two away, behind an identical screen, would be the hazy figure of her daughter. A warder sat in the no-man's-land between the two divisions, listening to the conversation. 'No kiss, not even a clasp of the hand, no privacy sacred to mother and daughter, not a whisper could pass between us. Was this not the very depth of humiliation?'[13] Florence would remember.

In the short time available, the Baroness would tell her daughter of the efforts being made on the outside, of the continued work of Dr Densmore, MacDougall and the many other interested parties working so tirelessly for her release. They would speak of the children, now living with Dr Fuller and his family, and perhaps on one occasion, towards the end of 1892, the Baroness informed her of the marriage of Edwin Maybrick, in the registry office at Marylebone.

These visits were bittersweet for both parties, but while the Baroness would leave the prison fired up and ready to do further battle, Florence would return to her cell feeling utterly depressed:

> *Goodbye we would say with a lingering look and then turn our backs on each other, she to go one way I another, one leading out into the broad open day, the other into the stoney gloom of the prison. Do you wonder that when I went back into my lonely cell the day had become darker . . . for these visits always created a passionate longing for freedom, with their vivid recollections of passed joys that at times were almost unbearable.*[14]

After eighteen months of prison routine, conducted in perpetual silence, Florence began the third stage of her imprisonment: hard labour. Now she wore a green uniform and was allowed to leave the cell and assist in carrying meals from the kitchen. With the help of another prisoner, she would struggle up and down three flights of stairs with a fourteen-quart can of tea, then return to fetch bread baskets weighing a total of thirty pounds or more. Florence recalled: 'The physical strain was far beyond our strength and left us utterly exhausted after the task.'[15]

Hard labour, however, had its compensations for Florence, one of which was being allowed to sit at the door of her cell and converse with her neighbour for two hours daily, though always in the presence of an officer, who controlled and limited the conversation. The food had also improved a little, and for breakfast the 'skilly' had been replaced by three-quarters of a pint of cocoa made from a half-ounce of cocoa, two ounces of milk and a half-ounce of molasses.

Six months on, Florence was sent to work in the hot and steamy kitchen for eleven hours a day. She washed endless dishes, scoured sticky pans, peeled mountains of potatoes, assisted in serving dinners in the officers' mess and scrubbed mile upon mile of stone floor:

> *The combined heat of the coppers, the stove and the steamers was overpowering, especially on hot summer days; but I struggled on doing this work preferably to some other, because the kitchen was the only place where the monotony of prison life was broken. It was the show place and all visitors looked in to see the food.*[16]

During the four years Florence worked in the kitchen, she saw many of the personalities of the day being escorted on a tour of the prison: magistrates, authors, philanthropists, and on one occasion Queen Victoria's third son Prince Arthur, the Duke of Connaught. One wonders how many of them would have attempted to taste the soup had they known that the most famous poisoner in England was being employed in the kitchen.

All the visitors had differing opinions of Britain's penal system. Florence would recall how one elderly member of a visiting party was scandalised at the sight of a juicy mutton chop and a milk pudding being prepared for a sick prisoner. The Governor hastened to explain that it was not part of the ordinary prison diet: 'Even then the old gentleman was not satisfied,' Florence remembered. 'And he stalked out, audibly grumbling about people living off the fat of the land and getting a better dinner than he did.'[17]

During 1892, the Baroness retained the law firm Lumley & Lumley to draw up a brief for the basis of a new trial. In America, Gail Hamilton (the pen name of Mary Abigail Dodge) launched a public fund-raising appeal to pay the bill. In a letter to the *New York World*, she pleaded colourfully: 'What I want you to do is immediately, tomorrow, this minute open a subscription fund and keep it open – blow upon the coals and kindle pity into life.'[18]

Mrs Blaine and Dr Densmore kick-started the fund with generous donations of $100 each, and the money soon began to trickle in from kind-hearted supporters from all over the States. Some sent substantial donations; others donated nickels and dimes. The popular actress Clara Morris swelled the fund by giving a benefit performance of *Odette* at the Grand Opera House on 28 October 1892, and the following month the *New York World* was able to send the Baroness a cheque for $1,641.55.

Florence was delighted, and wrote lyrically to Miss Dodge: 'I feel that I owe you such a debt of gratitude for the truly noble, beautiful and womanly manner in which you have used that glorious gift of God – your genius – in the cause of a helpless and sorely afflicted sister . . .'[19]

Unfortunately, all the hard work and effort turned out to be nothing but an expensive waste of time. While the brief was being prepared, a new Liberal government under Gladstone had been returned to power. Matthews had been replaced by Herbert Asquith, and it was some time before the new Home Secretary was able to reply to the appeal. On 26 August Asquith noted in his diary that he had attended a meeting with Queen Victoria and talked about Mrs Maybrick and two other prisoners. What was said at the meeting was not recorded, but early in September he announced that he could take no action in the case.

When Sir Charles Russell and his committee completed an analysis of the brief they reported depressingly: 'There is no mode by which a new trial can be obtained, nor can the prisoner be brought up on a habeas corpus.'*[20] They did, however, add that if a court of criminal appeal existed, there would be matters in the case which could be given grave consideration.

The Baroness fell into a fury and completely lost her temper with the Home Secretary, sending him a long, detailed letter taking the case to pieces. Fortunately, this time it was readable, as she had invested in a typewriting machine.

> *I confess I am amazed you should demand not only that there should be a doubt of guilt, but that before release we must prove someone else guilty of crime or of conspiracy. I have never so understood British law or British equity. Doubt of guilt I thought means at least legally innocence, my daughter has never been proven guilty.*[21]

Florence may not have been guilty of murder, but while this continuing warfare was being waged across the Channel, she was certainly guilty of foolishness. After accepting a gift of wool from a fellow prisoner in order to knit herself some

---

* Habeas corpus is prerogative writ used to test the legality of any form of detention, commanding a person detaining another to produce that other before a court and show why he is being detained, and to do whatever the court shall direct (*The Reader's Digest Great Encyclopaedic Dictionary*, 1964).

warm stockings, she soon discovered that it had been stolen from the tailor's shop. The wool was discovered in her cell and she was hauled to the penal wards and subsequently degraded to a lower stage for one month, with a loss of twenty-six marks and six days added to her sentence. This punishment also carried with it the loss of working in the kitchens for twelve months.

According to Florence, when she asked her fellow inmate afterwards why she had done it, the woman replied weakly that she did not think Florence would get into trouble. Her own sentence was under consideration by the Home Office and she could not take the risk of the prospect of marks against her record. She had obviously off-loaded her booty on to Florence as soon as she realised the theft had been noted. Florence had learned to her cost the harsh realities of prison survival.

Not long after this incident, and the rejection of the Lumley & Lumley brief, Florence became even more downhearted and discouraged. She had now been in prison for three years, and for all the continuing agitation she was no closer to the possibility of release than she had been on the day of her sentence. At this point she decided to do something to help herself, and on 28 November 1892 she petitioned the Home Office to review her case on the grounds of injury to her health. She was not aware that the prison doctor had also written to the Home Office on the very same day.

. . . her health has recently shown a tendency to deteriorate. She daily shows a quantity of blood which she alleges she has 'spit up', but I am not able by physical examination to find any evidence to

corroborate her statement and am inclined to believe the blood spitting to be fictitious. Under these circumstances I think it is desirable to have another medical opinion on the case . . . [22]

A month later, the *Liverpool Echo* picked up the following story:

The St James Gazette *has authority for stating that the recent alleged illness of Mrs Maybrick is definitely ascertained to have been caused by her own actions. The facts the journal believes are that the prisoner contrived to secrete some needles and by either pricking herself with these or swallowing them managed to produce an effusion of blood and other apparent symptoms of a most serious disease of the lungs.* [23]

Although in January the needle story was denied vigorously in the press by the Baroness, there was certainly truth in the statement that Florence had become ill through a self-inflicted injury. In fact she had come very close to death, and it had all happened in a much more dramatic manner than that reported in the newspapers.

CHAPTER FIFTEEN

❧

Children begin by loving their parents;
after a time they judge them; rarely, if
ever, do they forgive them.
　　　　　Oscar Wilde, 1854–1900

In November 1892, Florence Maybrick, driven by despair almost killed herself in an effort to have her case reopened. It did little to improve her chances of release. Some time later a series of confidential cables flew back and forth across the Atlantic, and the American government was informed of her attempt to deceive the authorities.

The full dramatic story was told to the Home Office by Dr Glover, the Medical Inspector of Woking Prison:

Last Monday, November 28th, at about 10 a.m. when the other
patients in the hospital ward had gone out to exercise, the Principal
Infirmary Matron looked through the inspection aperture and saw

Maybrick, who was not aware that she was being watched, get out of bed. She stealthily placed the spitting cup in the chamber on the floor, then reached down for her dinner knife from the shelf, introduced this knife as far as the Matron could see, into the vagina and withdrew it covered with blood. She then appeared to kneel over the chamber.

The woman's object was no doubt to incise the mucous membrane of the vagina just so far as to give rise to slight bleeding, and then to catch the blood in the spittoon placed in the chamber. The medical officer, being desirous of more evidence, very properly ordered her to be watched closely every day, but she was not observed to repeat this proceeding until this morning at the same hour as before (10 a.m.) when the other patients were out of the ward. Having done as she did before, she got into bed again and nothing happened until about 12.40, when there was a sudden haemorrhage from the vagina . . .[1]

Evidently Florence, undertaking a plan worthy of the Baroness in an attempt to convince the doctor that she was spitting blood, had unintentionally divided the vaginal artery, resulting in a haemorrhage. 'That would have been fatal,' Dr Glover claimed, 'if it had not been quickly arrested . . .'

Two medical officers who happened to be visiting the ward at the time of Florence's collapse immediately administered a mixture of ether and brandy *per rectum* and applied further remedies. The senior medical officer concluded: 'She is alarmed about her condition, and is not likely to repeat her attempt to simulate spitting of blood.'[2] Perhaps under the circumstances she was equally alarmed about the cure.

Florence continued to be very ill for some days, and her

condition deteriorated further when she refused food. She was reported as depressed and sullen, and on 6 January 1893 the prison doctor had her fed artificially. 'Should complications arise her life would be in danger,'[3] the medical officer warned the Home Office.

Florence soon started eating, but ten days later she again apparently spat up blood, and it was believed that this time she had obtained it by sucking her gums. The previous day it had been reported that she had asked the hospital cleaner to procure her a needle. Over the following few weeks, Florence's mental and physical condition slowly improved as she came to the realisation that her efforts to deceive the hospital staff were not working, but it would be more than four months before she recovered completely.

At the United States Legation in London, First Secretary Henry White had been briefed on the whole affair, but was most uneasy. Nine months earlier, when James G. Blaine had been the American Secretary of State, Blaine had written in confidence to Robert Lincoln at the Court of St James:

. . . The fact that she was never indicted or tried by a jury of her peers on a specific count of felonious attempt to administer arsenic, yet is condemned to penal servitude for life on the Home Secretary's statement that she evidently made such an attempt, can never be reconciled to the English principle that an accused person shall be tried by a jury of his peers. Lawyers here are among the strongest believers in the illegality of her imprisonment. Indeed, the sense of injustice is developing and deepening into horror . . .[4]

With this in mind, and still being unable to interfere officially,

White made a compromise move and did what most married men do when they are in a fix: he turned to his wife. Mrs White dutifully departed to Woking Prison to visit the prisoner and found Florence sitting up in bed in the infirmary. On her return to London she reported her findings to her husband, who immediately wrote to the new American Secretary of State, John W. Foster:

> *She said she was perfectly comfortable and could not possibly be better cared for . . . but she thought they had rendered her a doubtful service in bringing her back to life . . . The Governor hinted that they do not seem to be able to make Maybrick out — her views or feeling on any subject.*
>
> *She is very reticent and has never portrayed emotion or feelings of any kind, save a great depression at times. He says she had no very profound confidence in her mother . . .* [5]

The Baroness, who had been informed of her daughter's illness by a telegram sent direct from Woking, had rushed from Rouen and taken up quarters close to the prison. She had implored the Home Office to allow her own physician, Sir Spencer Wells, to examine Florence, but the authorities had refused, claiming that it was contrary to prison practice. However, they had allowed the Baroness to see her daughter while she was ill.

Once Florence was fully recovered, she lost her visiting rights due to the incident, and the Baroness returned dejectedly to France. Her enthusiasm for a good fight, however, had not been dampened, and having recently discovered that the land she had sold in 1889 for $10,000 had been resold for a staggering $131,000, she wrote to William Potter accusing him of double-dealing and enclosing a nineteen-point demand to explain the deal with the original buyer, David W. Armstrong. Potter replied stingingly:

> *... it may be possible that your domestic troubles have placed the veil of hallucination over your memory ... So far as I know, Mr Armstrong has fully performed his part of the contract made with you before I knew him or you. If you have further claims upon him, please address him upon the subject and not me. My patience has a limit and so has my time. Do not I beg of you encroach with too much freedom upon either.*[6]

The Baroness immediately set sail for America and commenced proceedings at Richmond Chancery Court, Virginia, in the August of 1893, to recover her interests in two and a half million acres of land in Virginia, West Virginia and Kentucky. She claimed that when Florence was undergoing her trial, both she and her daughter had signed papers for what they thought was the Kentucky property only, and that neither of them had realised they covered the sale of all her lands.

Armstrong fiercely defended the action, swearing that the Baroness 'had victimised and defrauded all who dealt with her'.[7] William Potter wholeheartedly agreed with him, and a series of letters shot back and forth between the two men. Potter fumed: 'What possible claim she can have on you even if you sold the land for ten times the amount she names, I cannot imagine.'[8] Armstrong replied, requesting that Potter release copies of some of the Baroness's correspondence to him concerning the sale, to which the lawyer responded: 'I have one or two thousand other letters from her which you could have if you desired, but fear they might upset your Christian patience and destroy your respect for the "ten commandments". They taught me long ago how to swear. I am just now about to enter on a course of reform by removing the cause of my relapse.'[9]

While the Baroness was fighting this rearguard action across the Atlantic, she had not forgotten Florence, and had employed an English solicitor, Jonathan Edward Harris of Leadenhall Street, to investigate the entire case and look for fresh evidence. After advertising in a newspaper for potential witnesses, he was approached by Valentine Blake, who confirmed in an affidavit that he had given Maybrick three packets of arsenic in February 1889. '. . . I handed him all the arsenic I had at my command, amounting to about 150 grains, some of the "white" and some of the two kinds of "black" arsenic, in three separate paper packets,'[10] he attested. The substance of his affidavit was confirmed by his employer.

Blake also took pains to explain that after he had received no reply from his letter to Cleaver, and during the time Florence was undergoing her trial, he had heard that his son had perished at sea when his ship had foundered en route to Valparaiso. Overwhelmed with grief, he had taken little interest in anything else.

After his undoubted success with Blake, Harris moved to contact Alice Yapp. He employed a private detective, who discovered that the nursemaid had since married and was living in Rosebery Avenue, London, as Mrs Murrin. The detective contacted her and interviewed her on the pretext that she had come into a legacy. Then, according to Alice, he accused her of 'having worked up the case against Mrs Maybrick'. Her husband was very much annoyed and complained to Scotland Yard, who soon discovered that both Mr Harris and the detective were in the employ of the Baroness von Roques: 'Mr Harris can hardly have any evidence of importance to produce if he descends to this method of working up a case for the convict,'[11] a Home Office official noted scathingly.

Meanwhile, Harris sent the authorities affidavits from Blake, the Baroness, her maid and a Captain Fleming; the latter confirming that James Maybrick had frequently put arsenic in his food when he resided in America. 'They only show that James Maybrick had been in the habit of taking arsenic with his food and that Mrs Maybrick was accustomed to use cosmetics containing arsenic,'[12] replied a weary Home Office official, failing, however, to comment on the remarkable evidence of Valentine Blake.

In his covering letter, Harris threatened: 'I have other evidence in my possession and power which (on the grounds of public policy and respect for our legal system) I am anxious to suppress if my present application is successful.'[13] The Home Office though took little more interest in Mr Harris, his evidence or his warning, and the new material was left to gather dust in the Home Office files, while Jonathan Harris never did disclose what the evidence was that he was so 'anxious to suppress'.

In May 1894 Sir Charles Russell, who had taken every available opportunity to protest on Florence's behalf, accepted a life peerage and became Lord Russell of Killowen. The following June he succeeded Lord Coleridge as Lord Chief Justice of England, thus achieving the highest judicial office in the country. That same month he wrote to Florence:

> . . . *I beg to assure you that I have never relaxed my efforts where any suitable opportunity offered to urge that your release ought to be granted. I feel as strongly as I have felt from the first that you ought never to have been convicted, and this opinion I have very clearly expressed to Mr Asquith, but I am sorry to say hitherto without effect.*
>
> *Rest assured that I shall renew my representations to the incoming Home Secretary, whoever he may be, as soon as the Government is formed and the Home Secretary is in a position to deal with such matters.*[14]

When the government changed and the Conservatives regained power, Lord Russell, true to his promise, wrote to the new Home Secretary, Sir Matthew White-Ridley, with his strong opinion that Florence should never have been convicted:

> *That in fact there was no murder . . .*
>
> *I know that it requires some strength of judgment to order the release of Florence Maybrick when Mr Matthews and Mr Asquith have not done so. It is the resource of weak men to shelter themselves behind the action or inaction of others. I do not for an instant harbour the idea that you are one of those men.*
>
> *I do not deny that my feelings are engaged in this case. It is impossible they should not be. But I have honestly tried to Judge this case and I now say that if called upon to advise you; in my*

*character of Head of the Criminal Judicature of this country, I
should advise you that Florence Maybrick ought to be allowed to
go free.*[15]

White-Ridley's uncompromising reply was: 'I can only express
my regret that sense of my public duty prevents me recommending any further extension of the clemency of the Crown
in Mrs Maybrick's behalf.'[16]

Russell then requested that his opinion on the case be made
public, but when the House of Commons asked the Home
Secretary to lay the document on the table in order that it
might be accessible to the members, White-Ridley declined to
do so. Troubled by his attitude, the *Daily Mail* suggested:

*The only conceivable reasons for declining to give publicity to the
letter, which was actually intended for publication, are apparently
official red tape and the fear of giving new life to the agitation in
favour of Mrs Maybrick's release. This result will be almost as
effectually achieved by surrounding the case with further mystery
and leaving upon the public mind the grave suspicion that justice
may not have been done.*[17]

The newspaper had made a very valid point, and once the
opinion of the Lord Chief Justice was widely known, agitation
from both home and abroad for Florence's release did
increase considerably.

In England the Maybrick Committee had never ceased their
campaigning, but they were now without the hot-tempered
leadership of the elderly barrister Alexander MacDougall. At
some point he had broken with the other members and fallen

foul of the Baroness. He was, however, continuing to work independently on the case; in fact, he was practically making a career out of it and had recently reissued his entire thesis. Hardly a week passed without a long-suffering postman staggering into the Home Office under the weight of the next episode, which was politely read and quickly filed away.

In 1896 the Baroness was so confident that Florence would shortly be freed that she wrote to the Home Office asking that her daughter be granted a free pardon after release. As this would be tantamount to an admission by the government that Florence had been imprisoned illegally, it was an irresponsible move on her part at such a delicate time, and it is possible that it effectively closed the door on any future clemency.

Questions about Florence's continuing imprisonment were asked in the House of Commons and in the American House of Representatives, but again the Home Secretary proved intractable and refused to advise any extension of the clemency beyond that already exercised.

In the spring of 1896, after seven long, uncomfortable years in Woking Prison, Florence was transferred to the new women's prison at Aylesbury. Wearing a dark cloak covered with broad arrows, she was marched out of the prison gates weighted down with clanking chains, attached in a chain-gang to nine other 'star class' convicts. A special train waited for the prisoners at Woking Station, and the platform was lined with crowds, who laughed and jeered as the women were ushered into the carriages. When Florence arrived at the new prison, after a five-hour journey, her wrists were bruised and sore from the pressure and weight of the shackles.

Some weeks before her move, Florence had again made

headline news, this time in an American newspaper, the *Chicago Tribune*, who reported that she had given birth to a child fathered by a high prison official. The Baroness was outraged by the story, and demanded that Sir Matthew White-Ridley allow Florence to bring an action of libel against the press. 'I have always declared to exist, an organised system of conspiracy against Mrs Maybrick,' she thundered, 'and cause you an Englishman loving fair play and honest dealings, to wonder if all which has been sent you against her is true and worthy of credence.'[18]

The Home Office declared that there was no substance to the report, but duly investigated if there was any way in which a libel case could be brought by a felon, and reported back: 'The Secretary of State does not propose to take any steps as he is advised that the imputation complained of cannot give rise to either civil or criminal proceedings.'[19] The Baroness, however, was far from satisfied and tracked down the original reporter who had sold the tale to the *Chicago Tribune*.

He confessed that the story had been told him late one Saturday evening by a Member of Parliament who had come to his club especially to see him and pass on what he thought was a factual story. 'I may add,' he replied to the Baroness, 'that my friend is also a physician . . . and merely repeated in entire good faith a statement which was current among his fellow physicians at his hospital.'[20] He added: 'Before your letter reached me I had, however, consulted the Revd W. D. Morrison, Chaplain of Wandsworth Prison, and obtained his promise to investigate the matter. He did so and reported to me that there was nothing in it, and moreover that the story seemed merely a revival of one which had been heard several times before.'[21] The Baroness received retractions from several newspapers who had picked up the story, and was grudgingly forced to let the matter rest.

Florence soon settled into the new routine of Aylesbury Prison, which had a far more relaxed regime than that at Woking, being intent more on rehabilitation than punishment. Whereas at Woking the prisoners slept in their clothes, at Aylesbury they were provided with nightdresses; instead of sitting with their feet on the cold stone floor, they now had the luxury of a small mat, and much to Florence's delight they had also been provided with toothbrushes.

Despite these changes, it was still an uncomfortable and unnatural way of life. There was no heating in the cells, and in winter Florence rose and ate in the dark, as the authorities, determined to save money, refused to light the gas jets. Her daily life was controlled by the clangour of bells and the jangle of keys, and most mornings she would head for the scullery in the officers' mess, where she washed dirty dishes from morning until night.

Aylesbury Prison, as well as being the training ground for female warders from all over the country, also actively encouraged the Lady Visitors' Association, assigned by the Women's Suffrage Society and headed by Adeline Mary, Duchess of Bedford. 'I can talk to them alone,' Florence happily told a visitor. 'And say to them a great many things I could not say to anyone else, and you do not know what it is to be for a little while alone in the presence of cultured, refined women.'[22]

Prison rules now allowed the convict the luxury of keeping

three family photographs in her cell, without them having to be returned to the Governor after a twenty-four-hour period, as had been the case at Woking. Florence waited impatiently for her long-overdue annual photograph of the children from Thomas Maybrick, who, over the years, had written to her keeping her abreast of their progress.

During the time Florence suffered her imprisonment there is no doubt that she endured great physical and mental anguish, but none so cruel as that which came towards the end of 1895. Many years later she would write:

When I could endure the silence no longer, I instructed Mr R. S. Cleaver to write to Mr Thomas Maybrick to forward fresh photographs of my boy and girl. To this request Mr Thomas Maybrick replied that Mr Michael Maybrick refused to permit it.
... Mr Michael Maybrick himself wrote to the Governor to inform me that my son, who had been made acquainted with the history of the case, did not wish either his own or his sister's photograph to be sent me.[23]

Not long afterwards, Florence suffered a mental breakdown and was in the prison hospital for many months. During that time the Baroness wrote to the American Secretary of State: 'I have given up all hope of her recovery. She is weak, emaciated, grey in colour, like a dead person...'[24]

The hospital authorities, however, had their own opinion of Florence's condition, and it would appear from the records that prisoner LP 29 had been up to her old tricks again. In September 1896 the Governor Medical Officer wrote a detailed report to the Home Office about her condition:

. . . *we have failed to discover any evidence of any organic disease. Her heart and lungs are sound, her appetite is fairly good, and she has not lost weight to any great extent, her present weight being 102 lbs, or 10 lbs lighter than she was on first reception into a Convict Prison.*

In spite of this she has, during the past four months, exhibited symptoms of great nervous depression. She sits listlessly in her chair all day, appears to take no interest in her surroundings, and makes no effort to arouse herself either by reading, or employing herself at needlework, or in any other way. I have urged her to try and rouse herself, but she says she has nothing to live for, that she has lost all hope, and that her only wish is that she may die speedily.

In consequence of her depressed condition, and knowing full well her antecedents, I have thought it unadvisable that she should remain in a cell, and I consequently had her removed on the 7th July to a Hospital Ward with other prisoners, where she remains at the present time, but much against her will.

She is reported to sleep badly at night, but this I believe to be at all events partly voluntary on her part, as she has been found, on more than one occasion, fast asleep in her chair.

She has lately had several fits, epileptiform in character, but of a very doubtful nature. These fits have sometimes been accompanied by a peculiar dark colour about her lips and mouth. She had one of these fits on Saturday night last, accompanied by the peculiar colour of the lips and mouth.

Assistant Matron Green, who was present, applied a damp handkerchief to her lips and noticed that the dark colour came off upon the handkerchief, leaving her lips and mouth of their natural colour. The same thing was noticed by the Assistant Surgeon when she had a similar attack about a month ago.

I have thought it my duty to bring these facts to your notice in order that you may be better able to form a correct opinion upon the accompanying letter of the Baroness de Roques.

With regard to the statement contained in that letter, as to the condition in which she found her daughter on the occasion of her last visit, I can only characterise them as gross exaggerations. I certainly do not consider that the prisoner is 'very ill', nor is she 'almost unrecognisable from a few months ago'. I see very little difference now in her appearance from what it was when she first came under my observation in April last. From enquiries I have made, it would appear that she is naturally pallid, but she certainly has not, at the present time, a grey skin. Nor is she emaciated. With regard to the 'fainting fits', I have myself seen the prisoner in one of these fits, and it bore no resemblance to a fainting fit . . .[25]

The 'peculiar dark colour' on Florence's lips was soon discovered to be black lead used to clean the grate. Throughout her sentence, the Baroness and her supporters always portrayed Florence as an exemplary prisoner, a martyr bravely accepting imprisonment and ill-health with saint-like resolution. The reality, however, was far more mundane: for a considerable part of her imprisonment, Florence remained miserable, sullen and at times overwhelmed with self-pity, which was not unnatural considering her character and the circumstances behind her incarceration. Years later, the prison doctor confirmed: 'Imprisonment has no injurious effect on her general health, but makes her at times morose and bad tempered.'[26]

By October 1896 her mental condition was much improved

and it was reported: 'She sleeps better, is less despondent . . . she no longer says she has no wish to live and from my own observation am of the opinion she is endeavouring to free herself from the mental depression from which she has suffered.'[27]

The following year was Queen Victoria's diamond jubilee, and it was generally expected that a number of pardons would be granted as part of the celebrations. On 19 June 1897, the American Embassy in London received a cipher telegram from John Sherman, the American Secretary of State, addressed to John Hay, the Ambassador: '. . . the President suggests that, if brought to the attention of her Majesty she might welcome the present as a most fitting opportunity to extend mercy . . .'[28]

However, Mr Hay was briskly informed that Sir Matthew White-Ridley, the Home Secretary, 'felt quite unable in view of the opinions which had been formed by himself and his predecessor as to Mrs Maybrick's guilt to recommend to the Queen that any exceptional treatment should be accorded the prisoner'.[29] In Aylesbury Prison on Jubilee Day, when it seemed that the whole world was celebrating sixty glorious years of Queen Victoria's reign, Florence learned that there would be no mitigation of her prison sentence; instead she was given an extra helping of meat and plum pudding.

Florence was now receiving visitors once a month. In 1897 Mary H. Krout, a reporter from the *Chicago Inter-Ocean*, accompanied the Baroness to Aylesbury for an hour-long interview. Krout was very much in favour of Florence's release, and had been one of the first to sign a petition on her behalf from American newspaperwomen in 1894. She was also very probably a member of the American Maybrick Committee. It is unlikely that the prison authorities or the Home Office realised that Florence's visitor was a newspaper journalist; just to be on the safe side, she introduced herself to Florence as a friend of Gail Hamilton.

Krout described Florence as:

> *A slight fragile woman, she still retained marked traces of her beauty, her features were regular and fine, but the large melancholy eyes were dimmed and faded . . . her expression fixed and staring. Her manner however, throughout the interview was that of a refined well bred woman.*[30]

Although the doctors had reported that Florence had recovered from her mental breakdown, she was still deeply depressed and on occasion acted rather strangely. 'She persists in sleeping either in a chair or on the floor,' the medical officer had recently reported. 'But she makes herself very comfortable with pillows and blankets and the night officers report that as a rule she sleeps soundly.'[31]

Mary Krout was also made aware of the prisoner's low spirits. 'I have ceased to hope,' Florence said wearily during the interview. 'I no longer hope for anything. If this were an American prison there might be some chance for me; but there is none here. I once used to like the English, but I like them no longer. They are hard, hard as stone.' The journalist was very much affected by Florence's condition and concluded her article:

> *I have witnessed harrowing scenes, but nothing that even*

*approached the anguish of that meeting between a broken-hearted
mother and a daughter who for eight long years had been walled up
alive, cut off from the companionship of kindred friends and who
at last has sunk into the hopelessness and apathy of despair.*[32]

Florence was soon cheered, however, by a letter she received
in the August of that year from Florence Aunspaugh, the
young daughter of John Aunspaugh, who had stayed at
Battlecrease House the year before the trial. She wrote in
reply:

My Dear Florence,

*I received the invitation to your graduation exercises, with your
letter enclosed.*

*It was so sweet, and thoughtful of you to remember me in my
pitiful, sorrowful condition.*

*You ask if I remember you? Indeed I do remember the
vivacious, pert little miss, with big brown eyes and long brown curls,
who kept the entire household in an uproar of laughter.*

*For months after you left, when Mr Maybrick was eating with
the children, he would often remark, 'I feel like little miss should be
here eating with us, I wonder who she is speeling off to this
morning. Those little pert answers of hers made life spicy.'*

*Those were happy days, never to come back to me again in this
life. Now I am a miserable deserted, lonely woman, with nothing to
look forward to in the future. I labour hard all through the day;
and at night I lay awake, thinking, until physical exhaustion
carries me to unconsciousness. It is hard and cruel to be imprisoned
for a crime of which I am not guilty. I have never seen my children
since I kissed them good-bye, the day the officers carried me to jail.*

My boy is now almost fifteen years old. Oh, what would I give to gaze on his face once more.

All the cotton men of Liverpool and London and their wives have been so kind and thoughtful of me. Especially Mr and Mrs Ratcliffe. If it were not for them, I feel it would not be possible for me to exist. They never come to see me without bringing me some remembrance. When Mr Ratcliffe leaves he always says, 'Cheer up Mrs Maybrick, and don't lose heart, you will yet be outside the prison bars.'

Mr Ratcliffe told me your father tried to get permission to see me when he was in England last summer, but the papers came after his boat sailed for the US. Tell him when he comes to England again, he must make another effort to see me.

Mr Maybrick often remarked 'friend John is a good man'. If you ever come to England again you must be sure to come and see me. I have shown the invitation of your graduation to all your father's friends who have come to see me; and they all say they remember you. When I showed it to Mr Ratcliffe, I asked him if he remembered the little girl who visited us the summer before Mr Maybrick died, and he said 'sure you never could down that little American, she was a regular George Washington'. He then told me he saw you when he visited the US in 1894.

I suppose those beautiful curls are now tucked high on your head, and the dresses are below the ankles, but I hope those big brown eyes that were always so expressive, remain the same. If the old happy days were still in existence, I would most assuredly have you visit me this summer and would give you the largest ball Battlecrease ever witnessed. You should have a number of state dinings; and this time you would not have to retire when dinner was announced, as you and Sonny had to do when you were here before.

It is growing too dark for me to see any longer to write, and as prisoners are not allowed lights, I must now bid you farewell, with a most loving God bless you.[33]

Confined to her cell with a feverish cold one February morning in 1900, Florence looked up and to her surprise found Charles Russell smiling at her from the doorway. They spoke together for half an hour, and as he left he held her hand and said: 'Be brave, be strong, I believe you to be an innocent woman. I have done and will continue to do all I can for you.'[34]

Some months earlier Russell had written enraged to the Home Secretary:

I consider the history of this case reflects discredit on the administration of the criminal law . . . I think my protest ought to be attended to at last. The prisoner has already undergone imprisonment for a period four times as long as the minimum punishment fixed by law for the commission of the crime of which she has never been convicted . . .[35]

On his return from Aylesbury Prison he continued his protest, beginning: 'I saw the wretched woman last week at Aylesbury, looking wretched, although I believe she is not ill in the ordinary sense.'[36]

Six months later, in August 1900, Lord Russell of Killowen died after a brief illness. For eleven long years he had persistently and repeatedly protested against Florence's continued imprisonment, perhaps carrying with him the troubling suspicion that he was partially responsible for her fate.

After thousands of words and endless gifted argument, with the power of the British judiciary firmly behind him and mounting new evidence before him, with the confirmation of the mental instability of the presiding judge and the uncertainty of the verdict, Russell in the end had been powerless to achieve the release of his 'friendless lady'.

CHAPTER SIXTEEN

> *My country 'tis of thee,*
> *Sweet land of liberty,*
> *Of thee I sing.*
> *Land where my fathers died,*
> *Land of the pilgrim's pride,*
> *From every mountain-side*
> *Let freedom ring.*
>> *Samuel Francis Smith,*
>> *1808–95*

On Christmas Eve 1903, as a thick, silent blanket of snow settled over the Berkshire hills, prisoner LP 29 gaily helped to decorate the cold prison chapel with evergreens. There would be no special dinner of goose and plum pudding the following day, no brightly wrapped gifts under decorated trees, and no further celebration of the festive season, but

Florence Maybrick had never felt so happy. In July 1901 she had been promised by the Home Secretary that after more than fourteen years behind bars, this would be her last Christmas in prison.

On 22 January 1901, the old Queen had died at Osborne House on the Isle of Wight, and the crown had passed to Albert, the ageing Prince of Wales, who now reigned as Edward VII. At Aylesbury Prison, news from the outside world was kept to a minimum, and the inmates had only learnt of the great event from the whispered conversation of the warders and the lowering of the prison flag.

In the summer following the Queen's death, a period of fifteen years had been fixed as Florence's total term of imprisonment. However, the Home Office had cautioned: 'That decision is not irrevocable, but will depend on her conduct and the difficulty of acting on it will be increased if agitation against the justice of her conviction is renewed.'[1]

Fortunately the agitation had quietened considerably since the death of Lord Russell. The Maybrick Committee no longer bombarded the Home Office with their appeals, Alexander MacDougall's hot-headed advocacy had ceased and many of Florence's American supporters had drifted away to take up other causes. The Baroness had been reluctantly forced to rest after developing a heart condition, due to the strain and tension of the last decade, and was currently being nursed back to health by her dearest friend, the Countess de Natemme, at the Hotel du Fores in Paris.

Even the US government had ceased debating the Maybrick case, recognising that they had reached a royal impasse: 'It is understood that the Queen is inflexibly convinced of Mrs

Maybrick's guilt,' the American Under Secretary of State had written confidentially to John Sherman in 1897. 'And will permit no appeal on her behalf. The successive Home Secretaries who have refused to reopen the case are understood to have acted on the Queen's peremptory orders. A direct request to the Crown is useless. I am ... satisfied that there is not the slightest chance of Mrs Maybrick being released during the Queen's lifetime.'[2] In 1899 the American government had reluctantly informed the Home Office that official representation on behalf of Mrs Maybrick would now cease.

During the late 1890s, once recovered from her mental breakdown, Florence had appeared to settle down. She blotted out all thoughts of her past life and the outside world and consoled herself by taking a healthy interest in her fellow prisoners' welfare. Slowly prisoner LP 29 matured and became the model inmate she would later claim she always had been. Years afterwards, reflecting on those long, bitter, angry years and the foolish actions of times past, Florence would admit: 'During the long years of my imprisonment I learned many lessons I needed, perhaps, to have learned during my earlier life.'[3]

Following her long illness the prison doctor had suggested that she be given lighter duties, and Florence had been sent to work in the library. There she assisted the schoolmistress, changed the library books in the inmates' cells twice a week and lovingly nursed the books, repairing them when they threatened to fall apart. In the association hour, inmates would ask her to read their letters from home, and she would help the semi-illiterate to painstakingly form their replies.

By the opening of the new century, Florence Maybrick had

the questionable distinction of being the longest-serving inmate in Aylesbury Prison and the only one who had lived through the harsh regime of Woking. In fact, within the enclosed community she had grown into something of a celebrity and was being treated with the greatest respect by convicts and prison staff alike.

At Woking Prison, first offenders had been strictly segregated from their more hardened sisters in crime. At Aylesbury, however, 'star class' prisoners were sandwiched between two wards of habitual criminals and continually came into contact with them. Their offensive language and violence continually shocked Florence, even after she had served more than a decade behind bars, but even some of the most degraded characters had developed a soft spot for the little American.

One morning while distributing her library books, Florence crossed the prison hall and turned a corner to find herself caught up between two groups of fighting women. As fists, blood and hair flew in all directions, one of the main combatants, a huge, rough-looking woman covered in blood, gathered Florence in her arms and threw her out of harm's way into an empty cell. When Florence thanked her the following day for her timely rescue, the woman, now nursing a black eye, replied: 'Why bless your heart, Mrs Maybrick, did you think I would let them hurt a hair on your head?'[4]

On another occasion, a young woman with whom Florence had worked closely in the prison kitchen had been admitted into the infirmary in a very depressed condition. Desperately in need of someone to talk to, she asked if she could see Florence. The chaplain intervened when the initial request was refused, and Florence was allowed to speak to the girl for a short time. For about seven days her condition was seen to improve and she asked again if she could talk to Mrs Maybrick, but there was nobody available to give permission. At five o'clock in the evening the infirmary matron found the poor soul dead in her cell, having hanged herself from the window bars.

The following morning, as the prisoners came out of their cells, news of the suicide spread like wildfire and the women surged enraged into the prison hall. One of the ringleaders, catching sight of Florence on another level, shouted: 'Mrs Maybrick, is it true that she was driven to it?'[5] In an attempt to calm what was developing into a noisy and potentially dangerous situation, the chief matron allowed Florence to enter the wing and speak to the prisoners. She emerged triumphant some half-hour later, her head held high, gliding silently through a corridor of nervous prison officers, leaving in her wake a large group of hardened criminals calmly returning to their cells.

When three male visitors entered Florence's cell one day in July 1901, she assumed they were from the Prison Department on a tour of inspection. The taller of the three conversed pleasantly with her for several minutes about her work in the library before the trio continued on their way. Florence later discovered that the man she had spoken to had been none other than Sir Matthew White-Ridley, the Home Secretary.

A week later Florence was summoned to the Governor's office and informed that a period of fifteen years had been decided on for her term of imprisonment, and that she would be due for release in three years' time. Overwhelmed by the news, she returned to her cell completely dazed. At last she could allow herself the indulgence of looking into the future, to a time when she would no longer have to live within the rigorous confines of a penal institution.

During the last year of her imprisonment she applied to the Home Office for permission to complete the final six months of her sentence at a religious retreat on a conditional licence. The authorities seemed to consider this a reasonable request, as it was known that on her release she was wanted in America to give evidence to the Richmond Chancery Court, where the case brought by the Baroness for the return of her lands was pending.

The prison doctor supported Florence's application and wrote on her behalf:

> ... *owing to her long confinement in prison with the necessary monotony and routine she feared the sudden change with the unaccustomed excitement might be prejudicial to her health and mental condition, at a time when she more particularly wished to be calm and clear headed.*[6]

The Duchess of Bedford was approached to find a suitable institution and make the necessary arrangements. However, finding a religious retreat which would accept a convicted murderer and a notorious adulteress proved a problem even for the redoubtable Duchess; the Mother Superior at a convent in Wantage had blanched at the suggestion and refused her point-blank.

Fortunately, Mother Julian, the superior of the Sisters of the Epiphany, was made of sterner stuff and accepted on the condition she meet with the prisoner first. Florence, with her impeccable manners and well-bred air, came as a great relief to the nun, and there and then she offered her a temporary home at their convent in Truro, Cornwall.

On a cold, crisp morning in the early hours of 20 January 1904, Florence Maybrick put aside the hideous clothes marked with the broad arrow and dressed herself in a smart new costume sent by her mother from Paris. There were no tearful farewells from her fellow inmates or the staff who had shared her life for so many years, and very few people knew of her release. At 6.30 a.m., in the company of Miss Stewart, the principal matron, she passed for the last time through the tall iron gates of Aylesbury Prison.

Truro lies a few miles inland from Falmouth Bay in Cornwall, amid a peaceful hollow surrounded by a string of wooded hills. Viewed from the surrounding ridges, the city was a perfect picture of repose, the small white houses clustering around a new cathedral, which rose majestically from their centre. The convent of the Sisters of the Epiphany was of Tudor style and was situated in large and beautifully kept grounds. Adjacent to the main building was a rescue home for fallen girls, and a laundry.

Florence had found the journey across London exciting but frightening and clung pathetically to Miss Stewart's arm in bewilderment at the noise and bustle of the capital. They caught the train from Paddington Station, arriving at the Cornish retreat the same evening. The Mother Superior received Florence tenderly, introduced her to the small community as 'Mrs Graham' and conducted her to the room she would occupy during her stay. Florence would remember:

How the restful quiet soothed my jarred and weakened nerves, and above all what a comforting balm the dear Mother Superior and the sweet sisters poured into the wounds of my riven soul. I look back upon the six months spent within those sacred walls as the most peaceful and the happiest in the true sense of my life. The life there is so calm, so holy and yet so cheerful that one becomes infected, so that the sad thoughts flee away.[7]

'Mrs Graham' occupied her hours sewing and walking between the hedgerows with the sisters or other visitors. With the freshness of the air and the breezes blowing across the Cornish moorland, she soon regained her vitality, weight and the colour in her cheeks.

Florence's secret release to the home had been engineered to avoid the prying eyes and ears of curious journalists, but inevitably the press soon discovered her destination. One editor wrote with respect:

The Mother Superior has guarded Mrs Maybrick with the vigilance worthy of a militant abbess in centuries gone by. So far all enquiries have been imaginatively warded off by the reply that Mrs Maybrick was not in the home, by which the sisters meant the rescue home for fallen girls. This pious little prevarication has so far been successful.[8]

As her release date approached, so did her popularity with the press. With tenacity and cunning, the Edwardian paparazzi lay in wait among the hedgerows of the quiet rural community. Eventually the local vicar was forced to protest angrily to the police.

Aware that Florence was about to attract unwanted publicity, the American Embassy contacted the Baroness, advising her that they had arranged with the Home Office to bring the release date forward by five days. On 20 July 1904, the infamous Mrs Maybrick, dressed in a grey costume with a white feather boa scarf, became a free woman. Standing before the arched doorway of the white convent, Florence bade a sad farewell to the sisters who had guarded her so tenderly during the past six months, and they in turn whispered their blessings and good wishes for the future.

Florence travelled first to the home of the Hon. Miss Dalrymple, a close associate of the Duchess of Bedford, and together they journeyed to London, where she was met by Home Office officials who issued her with her longed-for release papers. These stipulated that she must not appear on the public stage, write a book, talk to newspapers or attract public attention in any way.

At the American Embassy Florence was greeted by her mother, and the two women hugged and kissed each other for the first time in almost fifteen years. After a tearful farewell to Miss Dalrymple, mother and daughter, accompanied by an official from the American Embassy, crossed the Channel to the Baroness's little cottage in Rouen.

The newspapermen of two continents were soon hot on her trail, and within days of arriving at their secluded retreat, where her mother was known as 'Mme de Moremont', Florence's curiosity got the better of her and she gave her first newspaper interview, contrary to the terms of her release. Perhaps it was intended as a deliberate snub to the British authorities, as there was very little they could do to her now she was resident in another country.

The chosen journalist was invited into the cottage with the playful comment: 'You are the first unofficial gentleman I have spoken to for over fifteen years.'[9] He found Florence 'clear-witted, outspoken and mildly robust, perfectly calm and pleasing looking . . . true'. He added: 'The face was drawn . . . and the eyes were listless, but there was a confidence of demeanour and entire absence of nervousness or embarrassment.' On being asked about the trial, she became visibly upset, her eyes filled with tears and she refused to talk about it, saying she wanted to forget it all.

With regard to her future she said:

I want a change of scene. I want to forget and I want to forgive. I have many kind hearted friends and I should like to spend some time with them. Then I shall travel . . . let me die out a memory. I have suffered enough. God knows. Make the rest of my days as easy as you can.[10]

Just three weeks later, Florence embarked on her journey to America to testify at the hearing in Richmond. Her mother did not accompany her; the Baroness was too ill to travel and was forced to remain in Rouen. Before her departure, Florence was delighted to receive a telegram from the Bureau of Immigration confirming her position as an American citizen: 'The Commissioner of Immigration for the Port of New York, has been instructed by the Commissioner General to facilitate the landing of Mrs Maybrick upon her arrival in this country, as she is regarded as an American citizen, with every right as such.'[11]

It was agreed that Florence should travel initially to Antwerp to meet up with her relatively new American solicitor, Mr Samuel V. Hayden, and his wife, who had been touring Europe. They had volunteered to escort her to America on the *Vaderland*. As the name of Maybrick was too well known, Florence had elected to travel under the name of Mrs Rose Ingraham, but within a few days aboard ship her identity became common knowledge.

Most of her fellow passengers, though curious, remained courteous, except for two women who had been placed next to her at the dining table. When her true identity was disclosed to them, they immediately asked to be seated as far away as possible.

On 23 August the *Vaderland* entered New York Harbour and Florence, for the first time, saw Bartholdi's Statue of Liberty, looming out of the mist. 'This is the happiest moment of my life!'[12] she cried delightedly to Mrs Hayden. Later she would record: 'When I first caught sight of the Statue of Liberty, I perhaps more than anyone on board, realised the full meaning of what it typifies, and I felt my heart stirred to its depths at the memory of what all my countrymen and countrywomen had done for me during the dark days of my past.'[13]

Leaning on Mrs Hayden's arm, Florence stepped on to the gangplank with her head held high, and a rousing cheer went up from the mass of people waiting below as the band broke into 'Home Sweet Home'. Laughing and sobbing, she walked triumphantly to the crowd, once more on the beloved soil of her native land, a free woman.

A time will come when the world will acknowledge that the verdict which was passed upon me is absolutely untenable. But what then? Who shall give back the years I have spent within prison walls; the friends of whom I am forgotten; the children to whom I am dead; the sunshine; the winds of heaven; my woman's life and all I have lost by this terrible injustice?

Florence Elizabeth Maybrick, *My 15 Lost Years*

CHAPTER SEVENTEEN

❧❧

*This is not the end. It is not even the
beginning of the end. But it is, perhaps,
the end of the beginning.*
    Winston Churchill, 1874–1965

On a golden October morning in 1941, six fresh-faced
schoolboys self-consciously hoisted to their shoulders a
small oak coffin and walked with slow, measured steps from
the Episcopal chapel in South Kent, Connecticut, to a freshly
dug grave in the centre of the local churchyard. As the
mourners emerged from the dimness of the picturesque
church, they discovered, to their surprise, that the state police
had closed the grounds and were holding at bay a pack of
excited newspaper reporters.

Once the prayers for the dead had been read over the open
grave by the Revd Austin Wood, and the funeral party had
broken up to go their separate ways, Samuel Bartlett, Head-

master of the South Kent School for Boys, found himself in the company of John O'Connell, the editor of the *New York Times*. With a brief nod towards the grave, the newsman said: 'You know, at the time of the trial she was considered the most beautiful woman in Liverpool.'[1]

The headmaster shook his head, puzzled, and vaguely wondered if the journalist had made a mistake. For the life of him he could not reconcile the woman he had known as old Mrs Chandler with the notorious adulteress who had been condemned for the murder of her husband almost fifty years earlier.

There were, however, others in the small farming community nestling in the foothills of the Berkshires who had learned the story of Florence Chandler's past soon after her arrival, and had nursed their secret for more than two decades.

Inside the tiny church, Mrs Genevieve Austin collected the hymn books and stacked them neatly in the cupboard. She smiled to herself as she remembered how, almost twenty years before, she had by chance discovered Mrs Chandler's scandalous background. A cleaner's card on the hanger of a Spanish lace dress that Florence had given her had disclosed that the garment was the property of 'Mrs Florence E. Maybrick, The Moraine, Highland Park III'. The name had struck a chord with Mrs Austin, her husband and her sister-in-law Alvie, and they had written to a niece who was a librarian in New York, asking her to investigate the name.

'My, but we were greatly thrilled,' Mrs Austin would recall to writer and journalist Trevor Christie, some months after Florence's death. She related to him how they had passed the news to Miss Banwell, a mutual friend, and of how the four conspirators had taken an oath never to confront Florence or to tell anyone of her secret past while she still lived. 'We felt she had burned her bridges behind her, she had come here to bury her past, we felt sorry for her and thought what's the use of betraying her secret?'[2]

Before her arrival in the small Connecticut farming community, Florence had spent thirteen years drifting around the States. In 1906 the American Embassy had tried unsuccessfully to gain her a free pardon, and her mother had petitioned King Edward VII. All attempts had, however, met with the usual well-worn response: 'The Secretary of State regrets that he is unable to advise his Majesty to take any action thereon.'[3]

With or without a free pardon, Florence was determined to return to England, even though she had broken the conditions of her release by speaking to the press, and could therefore have been subject to arrest. In the summer of that year she sailed once more to Europe, travelling under the name of Madam F. Chaney. She toured Europe for almost three months and returned to New York on the French liner *La Gascogne*.

When entering the port, Florence was recognised by an immigration officer, who alerted a newspaper reporter. 'How can I be interviewed dressed like this?' she teased the journalist, after he had followed her home and caught her wearing a housecoat. 'While abroad did you visit England?' he asked. 'It stands to reason,' Florence replied with an impish grin, 'that I did not stay in the same place all the time.'[4]

Three years later, in February 1909, the lawsuit which had been pending for so long at Richmond Chancery Court eventually came to fruition after a ninety-day hearing. The

Baroness, by some miracle, won the complicated case and a portion of the land sold to David Armstrong under an early contract was returned to her.

Judge Daniel Grinnan, who presided over the case, also ruled that although Armstrong had entered into the later contract in good faith and with no intention of defrauding the Baroness, he should have disclosed to her the settlement he proposed. He then awarded Florence and her mother $52,912.50, plus interest at six per cent accruing since 1889. This represented one half of the proceeds of the subsequent sale, less expenses. However, Armstrong refused to pay, and the Baroness never saw a penny of the money. 'This suit has made me take a vow never again to accept a woman as a client,'[5] Armstrong was reported to have thundered at a local journalist.

In April 1910, fourteen months after the judicial decision, the Baroness, who had been ill for some time in a Stamford sanatorium, was sent by Florence to stay with friends in the South. Unknown to Florence, her mother diverted to New York and boarded a ship, returning like a homing pigeon to her beloved Paris. Ten days later, at an Anglican retreat run by English nuns on the Avenue de Ternes, Caroline von Roques, under the name Mrs Morehouse, fought and lost her last battle. She was buried next to her only son in Passy Cemetery.

Just over a year later tragedy struck yet again, when Florence learned from a journalist of the death of James Chandler Maybrick, the son who had rejected her so cruelly when she had been in prison. On receiving the shocking news at the entrance of the Moraine Hotel in Chicago, Florence was reported to have collapsed into a chair. After a little hesitation she cried: 'The past is dead . . . this boy has been dead to me for more than twenty years.'[6]

While Florence had been enjoying her first taste of freedom in America, young James, then twenty-two, had secured a job as chief engineer in the Le Roi gold mine at Rossland, British Columbia, just seven miles across the Canadian border. He had been working in the small mining community for seven years, was well respected and had been due to marry a Vancouver girl in the June of 1911.

James and Gladys Maybrick had been adopted after the trial by Charles Fuller, the London doctor James had gone to see at Michael's insistence in the April before his death. The children had changed their name and lived happily with the Fullers until 1899. Michael Maybrick, much to the Fullers' regret, had then demanded their return, and they had gone to live on the Isle of Wight with their uncle and Michael's new wife, the woman who had for years been his housekeeper. Gladys eventually married a naval officer, whose family had promptly disowned him when his bride's background had been disclosed to them.

In April 1911, two months before his wedding, James was working alone in his laboratory at the mine. He was apparently eating lunch while he worked, and accidentally drank from a beaker of potassium cyanide* instead of from the glass of water which was also on the bench in front of him. The mine manager claimed that he received an internal telephone call from James and, sensing that something was very wrong, ran

---

* Cyanide salts are used in metal cleaning and in the recovery of gold from ore.

to the laboratory, where he found the chief engineer on the floor outside the building. In one hand he was clutching a sandwich; on the other he wore an asbestos glove. A pair of tongs he had seemingly been using had been dropped and lay close to the body.

The verdict of the coroner's court was accidental death, but it had been a very odd scenario. Assuming that he would have had to put down the sandwich, or the tongs, or both, after drinking the quick-acting poison, in order to ring the manager on the internal telephone, why would he have picked them up again before staggering out of the laboratory, dying in agony?

Many of the newspapers hinted at suicide. It is certainly possible that James had been following his mother's well-documented career since her release and was suffering from depression. Was there a well-intentioned cover-up by his friends at the mine for the sake of the young lady he was soon to marry?

On her return to America in 1904, Florence had violated her prison parole for a second time and written a book. *Mrs Maybrick's Own Story: My 15 Lost Years* turned out to be a flowery, sentimental version of her prison life, very badly written and with little apparent help or editorial input from her publisher. She had promised to 'tell all', but hardly mentioned anything of the least interest to anyone whose reading taste was not for the English prison system. One critic wrote: 'Such a tale cannot help being morbid, but in the main it rings true. To those who have an interest in prison life it will not fail to be of value. Yet for the ordinary reader it would be a book worthwhile avoiding.'[7] The majority of prospective readers obviously took his advice and avoided it like the plague, and Florence failed to make much money from her first effort at authorship, but it had enabled her to launch herself on to the lucrative lecture circuit, and she was taken on by the Slayton Lyceum Bureau to travel America speaking on prison reform.

It seemed that everyone wanted to see the wicked Mrs Maybrick in the flesh, and her name filled halls from coast to coast. It was reported by William T. Houston, who appeared with Florence on the stage, that she was a quiet, refined and cultured woman who spoke quite well and was never at a loss for answers to the questions she was asked. Florence was greatly amused at the surprise which people displayed on seeing her, and said to Houston once: 'I wonder what sort of an individual they expect to see?'[8]

Perhaps after having lived such a restricted existence for so many years, Florence enjoyed the comparative freedom of living out of a suitcase, in a series of anonymous hotel bedrooms. She also appeared at last to have found a purpose in life.

From the lecture platform she set forth to aid forgotten prisoners all over America, arguing on their behalf for the common decencies of life and advocating the building of special penitentiaries for boys under sixteen. She told a friend in Chicago: 'I believe I have a mission and fifteen years of one's life in prison on a false charge entitles one to speak don't you think?'[9]

By 1907, apart from countless lectures, she had also visited twenty-seven prisons, voting Joliet, Illinois, as the best and Philadelphia and Sing-Sing the worst. In 1909, she went to Washington and spoke to Congress, petitioning for improved sanitation facilities and more humane conditions for federal prisoners:

> *I hope that many Statesmen who have honoured my case with their interest, sympathy and support will use their influence in furthering the interests of the prisoners whose cases, unlike mine, have not become the focus of two continents and whose dumb cries I am now voicing.*[10]

During her first year on tour with the lecture bureau, the *Sunday Magazine* had asked her to cover the New York murder trial of a young woman called Nan Paterson, who had been accused of killing her English-born lover and was subsequently acquitted. Florence met Paterson in prison and wrote an article contrasting the American justice system with its British counterpart.

She praised the impartiality of the presiding American judge and was outspoken, if not downright rude, about both the judge and jury who had heard her own case. She also took the opportunity to advocate the need for a British court of criminal appeal* arguing: 'With an authentic record of over thirty flagrant miscarriages of Justice within fifty years surely there must be some justification in such a request.'[11]

Five years into her lecture programme, stories about Florence's private life began to circulate in the mischief-making press. She was reported to have been having an affair with, and to have subsequently become engaged to,

---

* The creation of the Court of Criminal Appeal in England eventually took place in 1907, after more than half a century of Parliamentary argument and a long series of defeats in the House of Commons.

Charles Wagner, the manager of the lecture bureau, who was ten years her junior. 'Mrs Maybrick is a charming woman whom I know, however, in a purely business way,' he protested. 'The report that we are to marry is an injustice to both of us.'[12]

Some years later, in his book *Seeing Stars*, Wagner gave his own frank and less than complimentary impression of Florence:

> *Her face was the stillest I have ever gazed upon. It was as isolated from the real meaning of life as a white sheet of paper before it receives the printed impression. It had no cry, no need, no desire, no hunger ... It stood for what fifteen years of life in an English prison can do to sterilise a human countenance.*

He admitted that she was sincere in the work she had undertaken, but called her a 'freak attraction' and complained that she was 'constantly overdressed and overdid her appearance'.[13]

The newspaper reports forced Florence to sever her ties with Wagner and the Slayton Lyceum Bureau. She continued privately with her lectures, but the pressure of speaking as well as arranging her own venues became too much for her to handle. Her health suffered and she was forced to take time off from her lectures. Over the years she had made a good income, but due to bad advice over her investments soon found herself in financial difficulties.

By 1910 she was living in rooms in the Moraine Hotel, Highland Park. She resided there for about five years. The hotel owner, Frederick Cushing, took an interest in her finances and tried to get some money for her from the land which had been returned to the Baroness with the Richmond judgement. He soon discovered that as neither women had ever paid taxes on the claim, and settlers and a coal company had been holding possession of the land for the last twenty years, there was little he could do.

The next few years of Florence's life are something of a mystery. At one point she was employed by the publisher Shuman and Company, travelling the state of Virginia selling books, but her health broke down and it was rumoured that she returned to Chicago destitute and was forced to sell everything she possessed.

In 1913, while Florence was desperately trying to get her life together in America, Michael Maybrick, now aged seventy-two, was staying at a hotel in Buxton, England, for the benefit of his health. On the morning of 26 August, he failed to come down for breakfast and was later discovered dead in bed.

After Florence's trial in 1889, Michael's career as a popular music hall artist went into decline. However, he continued with his musical compositions and was extremely successful. In 1893 he left London and retired to his holiday home on the Isle of Wight. He married Laura Withers, the daughter of a butcher, with whom he had been co-habiting for the last fifteen years.

In the October of 1899, while Florence was still in prison, she had been informed that her teenage daughter Gladys had been removed from the home of Dr Fuller and was living with Michael and Laura Maybrick in their home on the Isle of Wight. She had been furious, and, in an attempt to have his guardianship of the children removed, claimed that Michael had been living a dissolute life and that Gladys was in moral danger. To the Home Office she fumed:

> ... *the wife of the testamentary guardian, is neither by birth,*
> *education, previous life or associations, a suitable person to be*
> *entrusted with the training of a young gentlewoman!*

Much to Michael's discomfort an investigation was undertaken and Dr Fuller was interviewed: 'He could not say that the child was in any moral danger,' the investigator reported. 'Mrs Maybrick may not be well educated, but she is getting on in years and is, so far as he knows, leading a quiet respectable life.'[14]

In fact, Michael's life had become so respectable, that during the twenty years he was resident on the island, he was elected to the office of Mayor of Ryde five times. He became president of the Isle of Wight Conservative Association and Chairman of the County Hospital. He also represented the island at the coronation of George V in 1911.

His impact on Ryde over the years had been remarkable and his funeral some two years later in the August of 1913 reflected his standing in the community. It was the largest the little town had ever seen. However, it would be interesting to discover who it was who designed the epitaph on his tombstone which reads: 'There shall be no more death'.

By 1917 Florence's finances had made a recovery, and she took the opportunity to start a new life by returning to her maiden name and leaving the notoriety of the past firmly behind her. Florence Elizabeth Maybrick disappeared, and Mrs Florence Chandler emerged in the small farming community of South Kent, Connecticut, applying for the post of housekeeper to a Miss Henrietta Banwell, who ran a local chicken farm.

Florence and the chickens took an instant dislike to each other, however, and Miss Banwell very soon discovered that her new housekeeper was even less well informed about house-keeping than she was about the birds. The two women soon parted, although on amicable terms, and Mrs Chandler, who had fallen in love with the beautiful valley and the Connecticut countryside, decided to make her home in the area.

After about a year in rented rooms belonging to Mr and Mrs Austin, she bought a plot of land off the road that wound through the pretty valley connecting South Kent with the neighbouring town of Gaylordsville. She had a small three-roomed cottage erected on the site, with a six-foot porch built on the outside, commanding a magnificent view of the Housantonic Valley. It was the simplest of homes, with a pot-bellied boiler heating the living room and kerosene lamps serving for lighting. The cottage had no running water and she collected what she wanted from a nearby spring.

The newcomer appeared to have little love of people, although she made some friends in the district and among the staff of the South Kent School for Boys, a private Episcopal preparatory institution which accepted young boys intent on studying for university entrance.

For companionship Florence turned to cats, and it was the talk of the district when her neighbours learned that she had stolen Miss Banwell's. The lady made a number of attempts to retrieve the poor creature, and the bewildered animal under-took several journeys back and forth until Miss Banwell gave up the fight and Florence held on to it. It was the first of many feline friends she would give a home to over the years.

When Florence had arrived in South Kent she had had capital of $2,000, which had enabled her to purchase the land and build the cottage. From then on, her income came from various benefactors, including a cousin who was vice-president of the Florida East Coast Railway. Another was Alden Freeman, a political reformer, who sent money through a lawyer every month for more than twenty years. Miss Clara Dulon, housemother at the school, had also taken a shine to Florence and was giving her five dollars a month.

Suffering from an agonising insecurity and a tendency to think the world owed her a living, 'Mrs Chandler' took the help of strangers for granted. In fact, she developed quite a business out of other people's philanthropy and rapidly gained financial support from friends and strangers alike. After her death it was discovered that during her South Kent period she had at least twelve people contributing to her upkeep at one time, with each one thinking they were her only means of support.

It was over money that she fell out with the Austins. In 1926 she asked them if they would endorse a note for $400 in order to get electricity brought into her little cottage. Dubious about her financial position, Mr Austin wrote to Julian Gregory, an attorney who had been relaying money to Florence from a benefactor in New Jersey. Florence found out and refused to speak to them again in public. Although she would talk to them on the telephone, if she happened to meet them on the road, she would rudely snub them and walk the other way. Mrs Austin, who obviously had the kindest of hearts, would often leave a basket of food by the front door of the cottage, but Florence still refused to speak to her.

Although her Connecticut neighbours believed her to be completely poverty-stricken, Florence managed to scrape up enough money to return to England for one last time in May 1927.* She travelled to Liverpool and attended the annual Grand National meeting, claiming in an English newspaper that she had returned to Europe in order to be reconciled with her children. James, however, had been dead for sixteen years, and only Gladys remained. The possibility is that she had also been trying to make contact with the son she was reported to have given birth to before her marriage to James. While Florence was visiting Liverpool, he was living less than three miles away from the famous Aintree racecourse.

During this last trip to England, one Liverpool newspaper reported: 'Sad faced, gentle-voiced, with hair turned to silver, the Mrs Maybrick of to-day is but a shadow of the striking-looking woman who made a lasting impression on those who saw her in the dock at Liverpool thirty-eight years ago.'[15]

Florence soon returned to her cottage in South Kent and continued with her reclusive life, becoming widely known in the district as the 'cat woman'. She established cat stations all over the countryside and would daily walk miles with food, feeding any and every stray animal on the way.

When the Depression hit the States in the 1930s, many of Florence's benefactors stopped sending money and her income dropped considerably. Out of kindness more than necessity, Miss Clara Dulon found her work twice a week with

* In January 1927 Sarah Ann Robertson, James Maybrick's long-term mistress, had died at the age of seventy-two at Tooting Bec Hospital. She was still calling herself Sarah Ann Maybrick.

Mrs Robertson, whose husband came to South Kent in 1931 as chaplain at the school. Mrs Robertson would remember:

> *I encouraged her to linger with me many times when her work was done and I enjoyed her. She seemed to me a very unusual personality, the finest example I had almost ever seen of buoyant courage in the utmost adversity. I soon discovered she was telling me some incredible things to dramatise herself, but this seemed to me a natural and excusable psychological development for one in her situation as I understood it.[16]*

When the Robertsons returned to their home in Cambridge, USA, in 1934, they continued to contribute to Florence's upkeep for almost two years, and Mrs Robertson even wrote to other people asking them to help Mrs Chandler financially.

Over the years Florence had become very close to the staff at the South Kent School, and when Miss Dulon died she was heartbroken. However, she soon transferred her loyalty to Amy Lyon, who was employed as school nurse.

> *After Miss Clara Dulon's death Mrs Chandler came to the school infirmary to see me almost every day . . . she loved to talk to the boys, always remembering their names and asking for them afterwards. They thought her very interesting and often asked who she was, living alone in her little shack in the woods. They thought she was a lady . . . She often cried and tears rolled down her cheeks. I sat down beside her and asked her why she cried. She would say 'it makes me feel better'.[17]*

As the years passed and Florence grew into old age, her

mental health began to deteriorate and she told more and more bizarre stories. She once informed Samuel Woodward, the history master at the school, that men on the mountain had left a sick baby with her. The school sent blankets and food and Mrs Lyon called at the cottage, armed with formula milk and demanding to see the baby. Florence told her bemused friend it had been sent to hospital in Didsbury.

In 1932, when the newspapers were full of the kidnapping of the Lindbergh baby, she reported to the authorities that men on the mountain had picked up a carrier pigeon with a note saying that the baby was on a ship off the Atlantic coast. The note was turned over to Princeton University, who declared it a forgery.

Florence Chandler's bent and huddled figure was a familiar sight on the road to Gaylordsville. Each day, in all kinds of weather, she would tramp the two miles to the general store for a newspaper, feeding stray cats and dogs on the way. She always refused lifts from her neighbours, claiming her legs were too stiff to get into the car, and if an unfamiliar car passed she would hide herself in the bushes.

Florence took to wearing a woollen hat permanently, hardly ever washed or changed her clothing and wore several layers at a time, held together by safety pins or string. The little wooden cottage, so picturesque in its early years, had turned into a filthy, untidy den, with cats of every size and description occupying the three small rooms. In the evenings, old Mrs Chandler developed an alarming habit of flitting around the countryside, spying on people, suddenly bursting into a neighbour's house without knocking or watching the occupants through the window.

Florence might never have indicated that she appreciated her neighbours' many good turns, but there is no doubt that she had been very lucky to have made her home with the kind-hearted people of South Kent. As the years passed, the staff at the school became more and more concerned for her welfare, and everyone in the district took turns keeping watch on the old lady in the cottage.

Mrs Conkrite, the milkman's wife, took a hot meal to her every afternoon, the boys from the school would stop by and collect wood for the stove, and others would fetch her water from the stream. Sam Bartlett arranged for her to apply for an old-age pension, and his wife, worried at the old lady's isolation, arranged and paid for a telephone to be installed.

In October 1941, when she had just turned seventy-nine (or eighty if she was born in 1861), Florence was found by a delivery man in her garden after having suffered a mild stroke. She refused to be taken to hospital and insisted on staying in the little wooden cottage. The following day, Mrs Conkrite and her eleven-year-old granddaughter, Doris Chase, came with a hot meal and had to help Florence to sit up to enable her to eat it. Early the following morning, 23 October, Mrs Conkrite's husband, Howard, called at the shack with the daily delivery of milk and found Florence lying dead on the sofa. Close to her lay her last few miserable possessions: two rosaries, the Bible which had held the face-wash prescription and a faded address book with all the Gs torn out.

Howard Conkrite sent for Amy Lyon, who on arrival almost fainted at the smell which permeated throughout the three small rooms. On discovering that the mattress in the bedroom was crawling with bugs, she laid Florence out in the main room.

Tenderly washing the frail old body, Amy dressed her in a plain white gown and prepared her for the undertaker.

They buried Florence a few days later next to the grave of her old friend and benefactor, Miss Clara Dulon. A simple wooden cross marking the grave recorded: 'F.E.C.M. 1862–1941'.

Born into a world of affluence where she had once been the envy of the plain and the dull, Florence Elizabeth Chandler Maybrick died with her unspoken secrets; a frail old lady in filthy rags, her two front teeth fastened together by a piece of string.

REFERENCES

Chapter One

1   H.B. Irving (ed.), *Trial of Mrs Maybrick*, 1912.

2   *Liverpool Post*, 19 January 1925.

3   Irving, op. cit.

4   *Recollections of Sir Henry Dickens*, 1934.

5   Cited in Trevor L. Christie, *Etched in Arsenic*, p.148.

6   *Review of Reviews*, 30 August 1892.

7   Alexander William MacDougall, *The Maybrick Case – A Treatise*, 1891.

8   *Liverpool Post*, 4 November 1928.

9   *Liverpool Citizen*, 21 August 1889.

10   *Liverpool Echo*, 22 August 1889.

11   *Weekly Times*, 18 August 1889.

12   *Liverpool Echo*, 9 August 1889.

13   HO 144/1639 19990.

14   Letters of Florence Aunspaugh to Trevor Christie, 1941–3.

15   Irving, op. cit.
16   Ibid.
17   Florence Elizabeth Maybrick, *My 15 Lost Years*.

Chapter Two

1   Cited in Trevor L. Christie, *Etched in Arsenic*, p.26.
2   Letters of Florence Aunspaugh to Trevor Christie, 1941–3.
3   Headstone at Magnolia Cemetery, courtesy of Carol Cain.
4   Florence Elizabeth Maybrick, *My 15 Lost Years*.
5   Letter from the Baroness von Roques to William Potter, Richmond Chancery Court.
6   Maybrick, op. cit.
7   Letters of Florence Aunspaugh, op. cit.
8   Inscription on Sarah Maybrick's Bible, courtesy of Barbara Bills.
9   Cited in Bernard Ryan, *The Poisoned Life of Mrs Maybrick*, pp.217–18.
10   J.H. Levy, *The Necessity of Criminal Appeal*.
11   Letters of Florence Aunspaugh, op. cit.
12   Ibid.

Chapter Three

1   Letter to the Baroness von Roques from James Maybrick, 1886.

2   Letter to David W. Armstrong from Florence Maybrick, 1 November 1881.

3   Letter to David W. Armstrong from the Baroness von Roques, 1885.

4   Letters of Florence Aunspaugh to Trevor Christie, 1941–3.

5   Ibid.

6   Ibid.

7   Letter to the Baroness von Roques from Florence Maybrick, 1887.

8   Letters of Florence Aunspaugh, op. cit.

9   *Liverpool Echo*, 22 August 1889.

10 Shirley Harrison, *The Diary of Jack the Ripper*.

11 Letters of Florence Aunspaugh, op. cit.

12 Ibid.

13 *Liverpool Review*, 6 July 1889.

14 Letters of Florence Aunspaugh, op. cit.

15 Shirley Harrison, *The Diary of Jack the Ripper*.

16 Letter to the Baroness von Roques from Florence Maybrick, October 1887.

17 Letters of Florence Aunspaugh, op. cit.

18 Ibid.

19 Ibid.

20 Harrison, op. cit.

Chapter Four

1   *Liverpool Echo*, September 1888.

2   Shirley Harrison, *The Diary of Jack the Ripper*.

3 Ibid.
4 Ibid.
5 Ibid.
6 Begg, Fido and Skinner, *The Jack the Ripper A to Z.*
7 Ibid.
8 Harrison, op. cit.
9 Ibid.
10 *Liverpool Daily Post*, 11 October 1888.
11 Harrison, op. cit.
12 HO 144/1638 A50678D/6.
13 Harrison, op. cit.
14 Begg et al., op. cit.
15 Harrison, op. cit.

Chapter Five

1 Letter to the Baroness von Roques from Florence Maybrick, December 1888.
2 Letter from Charles Ratcliffe to John Aunspaugh, 22 November 1888.
3 Shirley Harrison, *The Diary of Jack the Ripper.*
4 J.H. Levy, *The Necessity of Criminal Appeal.*
5 Ibid.
6 HO 144, statement of Richard Humphreys, no record number.
7 Alexander William MacDougall, *The Maybrick Case – A Treatise*, 1891.
8 HO144/1640/A50678D/272.

9   Sir Charles Russell's brief, from the papers of Trevor L. Christie.

10 *Liverpool Echo*, 29 May 1889.

11 H.B. Irving (ed.), *Trial of Mrs Maybrick*, 1912.

12 MacDougall, op. cit.

13 Ibid.

14 Irving, op. cit.

15 MacDougall, op. cit.

16 HO 144/1639 19990.

17 MacDougall, op. cit.

18 Ibid.

19 Ibid.

20 Ibid.

21 HO 144/1639 19990.

22 Letter to Florence Maybrick from Margaret Baillie Knight, 13 April 1889.

23 HO 144/1639 A50678D/29.

24 Harrison, op. cit.

25 Last will and testament of James Maybrick.

Chapter Six

1   HO 144/1639 19990.

2   H.B. Irving (ed.), *Trial of Mrs Maybrick*, 1912.

3   Ibid.

4   HO 144/1639 A50678/442.

5   Irving, op. cit.

6   Shirley Harrison, *The Diary of Jack the Ripper*.

7   HO 144/1639 A50678/442.

8   Alexander William MacDougall, *The Maybrick Case – A Treatise*, 1891.

9   Irving, op. cit.

10   *Liverpool Daily Post*, 9 September 1889.

11   Harrison, op. cit.

12   Ibid.

13   Letter to Alfred Brierley from Florence Maybrick, 8 May 1889.

14   Letter to Florence Maybrick from Alfred Brierley, received on 6 May 1889.

15   HO/144 1638 A50678D/13.

16   HO/144/1638 A50678D/13.

17   Irving, op. cit.

18   *Lancet*, 21 September 1889.

19   *Liverpool Echo*, 13 August 1889.

20   *Liverpool Echo*, 14 August 1889.

21   *Liverpool Echo*, 22 August 1889.

22   *Liverpool Echo*, 22 August 1889.

23   MacDougall, op. cit.

Chapter Seven

1   Letters of Florence Aunspaugh to Trevor Christie, 1941–3.

2   *Liverpool Echo*, 15 August 1889.

3   H.B. Irving (ed.), *Trial of Mrs Maybrick*, 1912.

4   *Liverpool Medical Chirurgical Journal*, 1890.

5   Ibid.

6   Ibid.

7   Ibid.
8   Irving, op. cit.
9   Ibid.
10   Alexander William MacDougall, *The Maybrick Case – A Treatise*, 1891.
11   HO 144 A50678D/331.
12   *Liverpool Medical Chirurgical Journal*, 1890.

Chapter Eight

1   Florence Elizabeth Maybrick, *My 15 Lost Years*.
2   Letter from Charles Ratcliffe to John Aunspaugh, 7 June 1889.
3   Alexander William MacDougall, *The Maybrick Case – A Treatise*, 1891.
4   Letter from Charles Ratcliffe to John Aunspaugh, 7 June 1889.
5   Maybrick, op. cit.
6   MacDougall, op. cit.
7   Ibid.
8   H.B. Irving (ed.), *Trial of Mrs Maybrick*, 1912.
9   HO 144/1638 A50678D/24.
10   HO 144/1638 A50678D/24.
11   Maybrick, op. cit.
12   *Liverpool Echo*, 14 August 1889.
13   *Liverpool Echo*, 14 August 1889.
14   *Liverpool Echo*, 14 August 1889.
15   MacDougall, op. cit.
16   Ibid.

17   Ibid.
18   Ibid.
19   Ibid.
20   Ibid.
21   Ibid.
22   *Liverpool Daily Post*, 18 May 1889.
23   MacDougall, op. cit.
24   Letter from Charles Ratcliffe to John Aunspaugh, 7 June 1889.
25   *Liverpool Daily Post*, 28 May 1889.
26   MacDougall, op. cit.

Chapter Nine

1   *Liverpool Daily Post*, 1 June 1889.
2   *Liverpool Courier*, 3 June 1889.
3   *Liverpool Courier*, 31 May 1889.
4   HO 144/1640 A50678D/279.
5   *Liverpool Echo*, 6 June 1889.
6   Florence Elizabeth Maybrick, *My 15 Lost Years*.
7   Alexander William MacDougall, *The Maybrick Case – A Treatise*, 1891.
8   Ibid.
9   Maybrick, op. cit.
10   *Liverpool Daily Post*, 6 June 1889.
11   MacDougall, op. cit.
12   Ibid.
13   *Liverpool Review*, 22 June 1889.

14   Letter to the Baroness von Roques from Florence
      Maybrick, 21 July 1889.

15   Cited in *Justice of the Peace*, 18 September 1993.

16   Cited in John Hostettler, *Politics and Law in the Life of Sir
      James Fitzjames Stephen*, 1995.

17   MacDougall, op. cit.

18   Maybrick, op. cit.

19   MacDougall, op. cit.

20   *Review of Reviews*, Vol. XXII (1900).

21   Maybrick, op. cit.

22   Ibid.

Chapter Ten

1   Philip Priestley, *Victorian Prison Lives: English Prison Biog-
      raphy 1830–1914*, 1985.

2   Florence Elizabeth Maybrick, *My 15 Lost Years*.

3   Alexander William MacDougall, *The Maybrick Case – A
      Treatise*, 1891.

4   *Sunday Magazine*, 22 January 1905.

5   H.B. Irving (ed.), *Trial of Mrs Maybrick*, 1912.

6   Ibid.

7   Ibid.

8   Ibid.

9   *Liverpool Echo*, 31 July 1889.

10   Irving, op. cit.

11   Ibid.

12   Ibid.

13   Ibid.

14   Ibid.
15   Ibid.
16   Ibid.
17   Ibid.
18   Ibid.

Chapter Eleven

1   H.B. Irving (ed.), *Trial of Mrs Maybrick*, 1912.
2   Ibid.
3   Ibid.
4   Ibid.
5   Ibid.
6   Ibid.
7   Ibid.
8   Ibid.
9   Ibid.
10   Ibid.
11   Ibid.
12   Ibid.
13   Ibid.
14   Ibid.
15   Ibid.
16   Alexander William MacDougall, *The Maybrick Case – A Treatise*, 1891.
17   Irving, op. cit.
18   Ibid.
19   Ibid.
20   Ibid.

21 Ibid.
22 Ibid.
23 Cited in Trevor L. Christie, *Etched in Arsenic.*
24 Irving, op. cit.
25 Cited in Christie, op. cit.
26 Deposition of Florence Elizabeth Maybrick held at Richmond Chancery Court, Richmond, Virginia.
27 Ibid.

Chapter Twelve

1   *Manchester Courier*, 20 August 1889.
2   Cited in Trevor L. Christie, *Etched in Arsenic.*
3   Cited in Christie, op. cit.
4   Cited in Christie, op. cit.
5   Letters from Florence Aunspaugh to Trevor Christie, 1941–3.
6   HO 144/1638 A50678D/12.
7   *Liverpool Echo*, 21 August 1889.
8   *Manchester Courier*, 15 August 1889.
9   Letter from Charles Ratcliffe to John Aunspaugh, 7 June 1889.
10 *Liverpool Echo*, 18 August 1889.
11 HO 144/1639 A50678D.
12 *New York Herald* (London), 21 August 1889.
13 *Liverpool Echo*, 15 August 1889.
14 HO 144/1639 A50678D/29.
15 *Liverpool Echo*, 22 August 1889.
16 Florence Elizabeth Maybrick, *My 15 Lost Years.*

17   *Liverpool Echo*, 23 August 1889.

18   *Liverpool Echo*, 23 August 1889.

19   *The Times*, 23 August 1889.

20   Alexander William MacDougall, *The Maybrick Case – A Treatise*, 1891.

21   George Earle Buckle (ed.), *The Letters of Queen Victoria*.

Chapter Thirteen

1   Florence Elizabeth Maybrick, *My 15 Lost Years*.

2   HO 144/1639 A50678D/41.

3   *Liverpool Echo*, 23 August 1889.

4   *Pall Mall Gazette*, 5 September 1889.

5   Maybrick, op. cit.

6   Ibid.

7   Cited in Philip Priestley, *Victorian Prison Lives*.

8   Maybrick, op. cit.

9   Ibid.

10   Ibid.

11   Cited in Priestley, op. cit.

12   Maybrick, op. cit.

Chapter Fourteen

1   HO 144/1639 A50678D/45.

2   HO 144/1639 A50678D/45.

3   HO 144/539 A50678E/7.

4   Letter to the Baroness von Roques from William Potter, 2 September 1889.

5   *Liverpool Echo*, 16 September 1889.
6   HO 144/1639 A50678D/57.
7   HO 144/1639 A50678D/57.
8   C.M. Tidy and R. Macnamara, *The Maybrick Trial – A Toxicological Study*.
9   Trevor L. Christie, *Etched in Arsenic*.
10 Cited in Christie, op. cit., p.195.
11 Cited in Christie, op. cit., p.195.
12 Florence Elizabeth Maybrick, *My 15 Lost Years*.
13 Ibid.
14 Ibid.
15 Ibid.
16 Ibid.
17 Ibid.
18 Cited in Bernard Ryan, *The Poisoned Life of Mrs Maybrick*.
19 Maybrick, op. cit.
20 Cited in Ryan, op. cit.
21 HO 144 1639 A50678D/99.
22 HO 144 1639 A50678D/133.
23 *Liverpool Echo*, 31 December 1892.

Chapter Fifteen

1   HO 144/1639 A50678D/133.
2   HO 144/1639 A50678D/133.
3   HO 144/1639 A50678D/169.
4   Cited in Florence Elizabeth Maybrick, *My 15 Lost Years*.
5   Cited in Trevor L. Christie, *Etched in Arsenic*.

6   Letter to the Baroness von Roques from William Potter, 18 July 1893.

7   Cited in Christie, op. cit.

8   Letter to David W. Armstrong from William Potter, 26 May 1893.

9   Letter to David W. Armstrong from William Potter, 29 May 1893.

10 J.H. Levy (ed.), *The Necessity for Criminal Appeal*.

11 HO 144/1639 A50678D/192.

12 HO 144/1639 A50678D/202.

13 HO 144/1639 A50678D/202.

14 Cited in Maybrick, op. cit.

15 HO 144/1640 A50678D/267.

16 HO 144/1640 A50678D/267.

17 Cited in Maybrick, op. cit.

18 HO 144/1640 A50678D/301.

19 HO 144/1640 A50678D/305.

20 HO 144/1640 A50678D/305.

21 HO 144/1640 A50678D/305.

22 *Chicago Inter-Ocean*, October 1897.

23 Maybrick, op. cit.

24 HO 144, no record number.

25 HO 144/1640 A50678D/312.

26 HO 144/1640 A50678D/320.

27 HO 144/1640 A50678D/315.

28 HO 144/1640 A50678D/323.

29 HO 144/1640 A50678D/323.

30 *Chicago Inter-Ocean*, October 1897.

31 HO 144/1640 A50678D/319.

32 *Chicago Inter-Ocean*, October 1897.

33   Letter from Florence Maybrick to Florence Aunspaugh, 10 August 1897.

34   Maybrick, op. cit.

35   R. Barry O'Brien, *Life of Lord Russell of Killowen*, 1901.

36   Ibid.

Chapter Sixteen

1   HO 144/1640 A50678D/343.

2   Cited in Trevor L. Christie, *Etched in Arsenic*.

3   Florence Elizabeth Maybrick, *My 15 Lost Years*.

4   Ibid.

5   Ibid.

6   HO 144/1640 A50678D/350.

7   Maybrick, op. cit.

8   *Daily Illustrated Mirror*, 15 February 1904.

9   Maybrick, op. cit.

10   *Daily Chronicle*, 1904.

11   *Daily Chronicle*, 1904.

12   Maybrick, op. cit.

13   Ibid.

Chapter Seventeen

1   Cited in Bernard Ryan, *The Poisoned Life of Mrs Maybrick*.

2   Interview notes of Trevor Christie.

3   HO 1654/7 A50678D/861.

4   *New York Times*, 6 August 1906.

5   Interview notes of Trevor Christie.

6   *Chicago Daily Tribune*, 10 May 1911.

7   Cited in Trevor L. Christie, *Etched in Arsenic*.

8   Interview notes of Trevor Christie.

9   *Chicago Tribune*, 3 April 1907.

10   *New York Times*, 17 January 1909.

11   *Sunday Magazine*, 22 January 1905.

12   Cited in Christie, op. cit.

13   Ibid.

14   HO 144 1640 A50678D/331.

15   *Liverpool Post*, 2 May 1927.

16   Interview notes of Trevor Christie.

17   Interview notes of Trevor Christie.

BIBLIOGRAPHY

❧

Books

Begg, Paul, Fido, Martin, and Skinner, Keith, *The Jack the Ripper A–Z*, revised edition, Headline Publishing, London, 1996.

Boxer, Arabella, and Back, Philippa, *The Herb Book*, Mandarin, London, 1983.

Buckle, George Earle (ed.), *The Letters of Queen Victoria*, Vol. 1, John Murray Publishers, 1930.

Christie, Trevor L., *Etched in Arsenic*, George G. Harrap & Co., 1968.

Densmore, Helen, *The Maybrick Case*, Swan Sorrenschein, 1892.

Dickens, Sir Henry, *Recollections of Sir Henry Dickens*, Heinemann, 1934.

Dreisbach, Robert H., *Handbook of Poisoning*, Blackwell Scientific Publications, Oxford, 1969.

Feldman, Paul, *Jack the Ripper: The Final Chapter*, Virgin Publishing, London, 1997.

Harries, W. Tyndale, *Landmarks in Liverpool History*, Philip Son and Nephew Ltd, 1946.

Harrison, Shirley, *The Diary of Jack the Ripper*, Smith Gryphon Ltd, London, 1994.

Hostettler, John, *Politics and Law in the Life of Sir James Fitzjames Stephen*, Barry Rose Law Publishers, 1995.

Irving, H.B. (ed.), *Trial of Mrs Maybrick*, Notable British Trials edition, William Hodge & Co. Ltd, 1927.

Levy, J.H. (ed.), *The Necessity of Criminal Appeal*, P.S. King and Son, 1889.

MacDougall, Alexander William, *The Maybrick Case: A Treatise*, Bailliere Tyndall and Cox, 1891.

Marriner, Sheila, *The Economic and Social Development of Merseyside*, Croom Helm, London and Canberra, 1982.

Maybrick, Florence Elizabeth, *My 15 Lost Years*, Funk & Wagralls, 1909.

Moreland, Nigel, *This Friendless Lady*, Frederick Muller Ltd, London, 1957.

O'Brien, R. Barry, *The Life of Lord Russell of Killowen*, Smith Elder & Co., 1901.

O'Donnell, Bernard, *Should Women Hang?*, W. H. Allen, 1956.

Priestley, Philip, *Victorian Prison Lives: English Prison Biography 1830–1914*, Methuen, London and New York, 1985.

Ryan, Bernard, *The Poisoned Life of Mrs Maybrick*, Penguin, London, 1977.

Tidy, Charles Meymott, and Macnamara, Rawdon, *The Maybrick Trial: A Toxicological Study*, Balliere, Tindall & Cox, 1891.

Wilson, Patrick, *Murderess*, Michael Joseph, 1971.

Zedner, Lucia, *Women, Crime and Custody in Victorian England*, Oxford Historical Monographs, Clarendon Press, 1991.

The Concise Oxford Dictionary of Quotations, Oxford University Press, Oxford, 1981.

Everyman's Encyclopaedia, J.M. Dent and Sons Ltd, London, 1978.

Newspapers and Periodicals

Liverpool Citizen
Liverpool Courier
Liverpool Daily Post
Liverpool Echo
Liverpool Medical Chirurgical Journal
Liverpool Post
Liverpool Post & Mercury
Liverpool Review

Daily Chronicle
Daily Illustrated Mirror
Echo (London)
Manchester Courier & Lancashire Advertiser
Oldham Standard
The Times

Chicago Daily Tribune
Chicago Inter-Ocean 1897
Justice of the Peace
The Lancet 1889
New York Herald
New York Times
The Pall Mall Budget 1889
Review of Reviews
Sunday Magazine 1905
Weekly Times 1889
The World

Home Office Files

HO 144/1638 A50678D/6 A50678D/13-I A50678D/13
A50678D/331 A50678D/24 A50678D/2

HO 144/1639 A50678D/29 A50678D/45 A50678D/442
A50678D/202 A50678D/41 A50678D/57 A50678D/99
A50678D/133 A50678D/69 19990

HO 144/1640 A50678D/272 A50678D/279 A50678D/267
A50678D/301 A50678D/305 A50678D/312 A50678D/320
A50678D/315 A50678D/323 A50678D/319 A50678D/343
A50678D/350

HO 144/539 A50678E/7 HO 144 1654/7 A50678D/861

INDEX

❧

More True Crime from Headline

Jack the Ripper
The Simple Truth

BRUCE PALEY

The identity of the most notorious murderer of all time has long remained a mystery – *until now*. After twelve years of research, true crime expert and former private detective Bruce Paley has finally uncovered the real face behind the chilling murders of Jack the Ripper.

Paley shows that his suspect:

- was skilled with knives and knowledgeable about anatomy

- was a familiar local figure, who had lived near all the victims and murder sites

- changed his story regarding his relationship with the last victim, his lover

- fits contemporary eyewitness descriptions exactly

- had an avowed hatred of prostitutes

- matches precisely the model of the archetypal serial killer, as formulated by the FBI's top psychological criminal profilers

Jack the Ripper is revealed at last to be a man so overcome by sexual obsession and jealousy he believed murder was his only recourse . . .

'If I had to recommend a single book on Jack the Ripper to someone who knew nothing about the subject, I would unhesitatingly choose this one' Colin Wilson

'Apart from convincingly identifying the Riper, Paley's book paints an extraordinarily vivid picture of late 19th-century London' *Daily Mail*

NON-FICTION / TRUE CRIME 0 7472 5218 1

Lock, Stock and Two Smoking Barrels

GUY RITCHIE

Streetwise charmer Eddy walks into the biggest card
game of his life with £100,000 of his own – and his
mates' – money. But the game is fixed and Eddy ends
up owing half a million to porn king and general bad
guy Hatchet Harry. Eddy has a week to come up with
the money before he starts losing his fingers to Harry's
sinister debt collector, Big Chris – unless he can
persuade his dad to hand over his beloved bar instead.
Or maybe Eddy and his mates can come up with a
better plan . . .

'a hilariously twisted, razor-sharp, comedy gangster
thriller . . . *The Long Good Friday* for the
Trainspotting generation' FHM

'Mixes the authenticity of *The Long Good Friday* with
the jet-black humour of *Reservoir Dogs* and the
intricately plotted wit of *The Italian Job* . . . one of the
funniest films I have seen in years' Neil Norman
Evening Standard

NON-FICTION / CINEMA 0 7472 6205 5